CUTTING EDGE

NEW EDITION

ADVANCED

STUDENTS' BOOK
WITH DVD-ROM

SARAH CUNNINGHAM PETER MOOR
JONATHAN BYGRAVE AND DAMIAN WILLIAMS

CONTENTS

Pronunciation	Task	World culture/ Language live	Language summary and practice
Varieties of English	Give tips on learning a language well **Preparation**: Listening and reading **Task**: Speaking	**Language live** **Writing**: A report **Listening**: Varieties of English	Language summary 01, page 112 Grammar practice 01, page 114 Vocabulary practice 01, page 152
Word stress	Describe a story that provokes strong emotions **Preparation**: Listening and speaking **Task**: Speaking **Follow up**: Writing	**World culture**: Luxury superbrands	Language summary 02, page 116 Grammar practice 02, page 119 Vocabulary practice 02, page 153
	Decide which project to back **Preparation**: Reading and vocabulary **Task**: Speaking **Follow up**: Writing	**Language live** **Speaking**: Describing quantities **Writing**: Summarising statistics	Language summary 03, page 120 Grammar practice 03, page 122 Vocabulary practice 03, page 154
Accuracy	Decide who wins the award **Preparation**: Listening **Task**: Speaking **Follow up**: Writing	**World culture**: Three minutes of exercise	Language summary 04, page 124 Grammar practice 04, page 126 Vocabulary practice 04, page 155
Intonation of phrases for getting people to do something	Deal with a problem tactfully **Preparation**: Reading and vocabulary **Task**: Speaking **Follow up**: Writing	**Language live** **Writing**: Asking people to do things by email **Speaking**: Getting people to do things	Language summary 05, page 128 Grammar practice 05, page 130 Vocabulary practice 05, page 156

CONTENTS

Pronunciation	Task	World culture/ Language live	Study, Practice & Remember
Stress on particles	Teach a practical skill **Preparation**: Vocabulary and listening **Task**: Speaking **Follow up**: Writing	**World culture**: Teaching happiness	Language summary 06, page 132 Grammar practice 06, page 134 Vocabulary practice 06, page 157
Emphasis with auxiliaries and inversion	Rant or rave **Preparation**: Listening **Task**: Speaking **Follow up**: Writing	**Language live** **Writing**: An online review **Speaking**: Comment adverbials	Language summary 07, page 136 Grammar practice 07, page 138 Vocabulary practice 07, page 158
Stress in compound phrases	Choose celebrities for a charity trek **Preparation**: Reading **Task**: Speaking **Follow up**: Writing	**World culture**: Running a large family	Language summary 08, page 140 Grammar practice 08, page 142 Vocabulary practice 08, page 159
	Present a fantasy invention **Preparation**: Listening and speaking **Task**: Speaking **Follow up**: Writing	**Language live** **Speaking**: Explaining technical problems **Writing**: Demanding urgent action	Language summary 09, page 144 Grammar practice 09, page 146 Vocabulary practice 09, page 160
	Detect the lies **Preparation**: Listening **Task**: Speaking	**World culture**: Cyber crime	Language summary 10, page 148 Grammar practice 10, page 150 Vocabulary practice 10, page 161

01

GLOBAL LIVING

Vocabulary and speaking

Globalisation

1a Work in pairs. Spend one minute thinking of five ways in which globalisation affects your everyday life.

I eat a lot of food from American chains.

b Compare your answers with the class.

2 Work in groups. Which of the things below have you experienced personally? Describe what happened and what you found interesting about the experience.

- visiting another country to go shopping, for a sporting event, to visit a theme park, etc.
- making **online contact** with someone from another country
- using English as a **lingua franca** to communicate with other non-native speakers
- working/studying with someone from another country
- travelling abroad to work or study
- following an international celebrity on Twitter, etc.
- participating in **international conference calls**, **webinars**, etc.

4 Add the words/phrases in bold from exercises 2 and 3 to the word web below. Some can go in more than one category.

travel

culture/society

food

globalisation

business/ money

shopping

communication/language
online contact

3 Work in groups. In your opinion, which of the following have happened in your country as a result of globalisation? Compare your ideas and give reasons.

- There's more **immigration/emigration**.
- There is greater tolerance of **cultural and religious diversity**.
- People mix more with people of other **races** and cultures.
- Our **way of life** has changed considerably.
- There is **a clash of cultures** within our society.
- We have become **a multi-ethnic society**.
- Our culture has become very **Americanised**.
- There's more freedom and choice.
- There are more **multinational corporations** and fewer local businesses.
- **Mass tourism** from abroad has really changed some parts of the country.
- People eat more **imported** food rather than **local produce**.
- People have **a higher standard of living**.
- There has been a '**brain drain**' of talented people going to work abroad.
- Many of the goods we buy are made in **sweatshops** in other parts of the world.
- We are more vulnerable to **global financial crises**.
- People have become obsessed with **global brands**.

5 List five advantages and five disadvantages of globalisation. Use vocabulary from exercise 3 and your own ideas. Then work in pairs and compare your answers.

6a 🎧 **1.1** Listen to six people talking about globalisation and make notes on the questions below.

  1 What aspect of globalisation do they discuss and what examples/pros and cons do they mention?
  2 Are they for or against globalisation? Or do they have mixed opinions?

b Work in pairs and compare notes. Listen again if necessary to complete your answers. Do you agree with the speakers? Why?/Why not?

c Look at audio script 1.1 on page 162. Add any useful words and phrases to the word web in exercise 4b.

7 Work in pairs and take turns to describe the difference between each pair of words/phrases.

  1 emigration, immigration
  2 multinational, multi-ethnic
  3 cultural diversity, a clash of cultures
  4 a business, a corporation
  5 your standard of living, your way of life

Reading and vocabulary
Urbanisation

1 Work in pairs and discuss. How has your town or local area changed since you were born? What problems, if any, have the changes caused?

2a Look at the words/phrases in the box. Tick the ones you know, write a question mark next to the ones you can guess, and cross the ones you need to check.

reclaimed land	availability of housing
green-belt land	infrastructure
overcrowding	demolition of old buildings
residential areas	high-rise buildings
shanty towns	no-go areas
sky-high property prices	slums
urban sprawl	congestion
squalor	

b Work in pairs and compare your answers. Check the meaning of any words/phrases you don't know. How many can you use to describe your town/city or a place you know well?

The capital of my country doesn't have the infrastructure to support the millions of people who live there.

3a You are going to read an article about urbanisation which mentions the cities of Washington DC, Dhaka, Songdo and Medellin. Which countries are these cities in?

b Read the article and answer the questions.

1 What has recently changed about humans?
2 Why is there so much slum housing in the world?
3 What was Le Corbusier's solution to the problems of urbanisation in Paris?

URBANISATION: is there a solution?

Humans are good at building cities – after all we've been doing it for nine millennia – but a few years ago, for the first time in history, we officially became an urban species. More of us now live in cities than in the countryside. That's over three and a half billion people and this global trend is heading ever upwards. Experts believe that by 2050, seven billion of us will be living in an urban environment, and the numbers just keep rising. The speed and scale of this change is unprecedented; just to keep up with demand, we are currently building a new city the size of Washington DC every three days. Building more of the same, however, is just a temporary solution, as fast-growing cities bring with them numerous issues such as overcrowding, slum housing, congestion, crime, pollution and more.

Part of the problem is that despite the number of people they house, cities only occupy three percent of the earth's land surface. That's an awful lot of people to fit into such a small space and most cities just weren't designed to cope. São Paulo, for example, suffers traffic jams of up to 180 kilometres on a bad day and everywhere from Abu Dhabi to Zurich, limited availability and unlimited demand are driving property prices sky-high. In turn, this is leading to a massive global growth in slum housing. In Dhaka, for example, the capital of Bangladesh and a city which will soon be bigger than Beijing or Mexico City, 60 percent of residents live in shanty towns. So what, if anything, can be done about urbanisation?

Perhaps the solution is to knock down our old cities and start again. City planners are always coming up with hare-brained schemes like this, and the famous French architect and designer Le Corbusier was no exception. He devised a plan in the 1920s to demolish the centre of Paris to make space for a series of high-rise buildings. To Le Corbusier, this was just a sensible solution to the dirt and squalor of Paris at the time, but had he succeeded, it is doubtful that Paris would be attracting nearly 30 million tourists a year, as it is today.

Demolishing and rebuilding cities to meet modern needs is clearly impractical, so what are the alternatives? The brand new city of Songdo in South Korea and the more historic city of Medellin in Colombia offer two exciting but contrasting visions of how to cope with the problems of urbanisation.

4 Find phrases in the article that mean the following.

1 Across the world, urbanisation is happening faster and faster.
2 Urbanisation of this size and speed has never happened before.
3 Cities that grow quickly have a lot of problems.
4 Cities weren't planned to house so many people.
5 Too many people chasing too few homes is causing very high house prices.
6 What can we do about people moving to the cities?
7 Le Corbusier suggested doing this.
8 He made a plan to knock down the centre of Paris.
9 Knocking down and rebuilding cities is not going to work.

5 Work in pairs. Student A: Turn to page 106 and read about Songdo. Student B: Turn to page 109 and read about Medellin.

Songdo, South Korea

Medellin, Colombia

6a Take turns to tell your partner about the city you have read about. Your partner listens and asks questions to find out more information.

b Work in pairs and discuss the questions.

- Which city, Songdo or Medellin, do you find most impressive? Why?
- Which model offers the best hope for the future?
- What solutions can you think of for the problems of the major cities in your country?

Grammar review
Continuous verb forms

1a Read the sentences. In which sentence is the writer more interested in the action in progress? In the result?

1 Since 2004, the city has invested over $600 million in cable cars.
2 Since 2004, the city has been investing money in cable cars.

b Does the writer use a simple or a continuous form when the focus is on the action?

2 Look at the verbs in bold in the sentences and find examples of the verb forms in the box.

a simple form	the Present continuous (x2)
the Future continuous	the Present perfect continuous
a continuous passive	

1 Humans **have been building** cities for nine millennia.
2 Experts **believe** that by 2050, seven billion of us **will be living** in an urban environment.
3 … we **are** currently **building** a new city the size of Washington DC every three days.
4 This global trend **is heading** ever upwards.
5 … plans **are** in the process of **being drawn up** for 20 more cities like Songdo.

3a The continuous aspect is commonly used to express the ideas below. Which sentence(s) in exercise 2 reflect each idea?

a to show that a situation is temporary
   3: we are currently building a new city …
b to show an action happening around a point of time
c to describe changes and developments
d to show duration
e to show that an action is incomplete

b Why can't *believe* in exercise 2, sentence 2 be used in the continuous form? Do you know any other verbs like this?

4 Complete the sentences to make them true for you. Use an appropriate continuous form. Then work in pairs and compare your answers.

1 People from my country are currently …
2 In 2020, I hope I …
3 I've … for ages.
4 Recently, I've been …
5 At the moment, I …
6 This time tomorrow, I …

> **Grammar extension bank, pages 112–115**

English around the globe: the facts

1.4 bn non-native speakers

375 m native speakers

official language in **55** countries

over **175** dialects

over **1 m** words

125 m speakers in India

Did you know?

- There are far more non-native speakers of English in the world than native speakers. It's hard to calculate, but it is believed that there are around 375 million native speakers and over 1.125 billion non-native speakers – a total of about 1.5 billion.

- English is an official language in 55 countries. The USA has the largest number of English speakers (250 million), followed in second place by India (125 million), then Pakistan (89 million), Nigeria (79 million) and the UK (59 million).

- Most linguists agree that English has the largest vocabulary of any language in the world. It is almost impossible to say how many words there are, but some people say there are over a million. It is said that a new word enters the language every 98 minutes, on average.

- More English words begin with 't' than any other letter – about 25 percent of all words.

- There are estimated to be about 175 dialects of English around the world.

- Special, simplified versions of English exist to help various professionals to communicate internationally, for example, 'air-speak' for pilots and air-traffic controllers, 'police-speak' to help deal with international crime and 'doctor-speak' to simplify communication between doctors.

- Modern British people probably wouldn't have been able to understand the English spoken in Shakespeare's time. Pronunciation and grammar were different and many words had different meanings. For example, 'nice' meant 'foolish' in the 16th century.

- The relationship between spelling and pronunciation in English is notoriously irregular: the combination 'ough' can be pronounced in nine different ways! The following sentence contains them all: *A rough-coated, dough-faced, thoughtful ploughman strode through the streets of Scarborough; after falling into a slough, he coughed and hiccoughed.* Turn to page 106 to see how this is pronounced.

Listening and speaking
English in a changing world

1 Work in groups and discuss. In what circumstances and with whom do you think you will use English in the future? Think about work, travel, social situations, the internet, etc.

2a Read the facts above about the English language. Then work in pairs and guess which two pieces of information are false. Turn to page 106 to check your answers.

b Work in pairs and discuss. Do any of the facts surprise you? Why?

3 Read the statements below. Tick the ones you agree with and cross the ones you disagree with. Then work in groups to compare your answers.

1 I am more likely to use English to speak to native speakers (e.g. British or Australian people) than I am to use it to speak to non-native speakers.

2 Learners of English should try to pronounce the language as closely as possible to the way that native speakers do.

3 It is very important for learners of English to have a good command of British and American idioms.

4 People can't understand you when you speak a foreign language unless you use grammar correctly.

5 English doesn't just belong to native speakers; it belongs to everyone in the world who uses it.

6 When I speak English, I don't want to imitate a British or American person. I want to keep my own identity.

4 🎧 1.2 Listen to Doctor Jennifer Jenkins talking about English as an international language. Which ideas from exercise 3 does she agree/disagree with? Why?

5a Doctor Jenkins mentions the following language areas in relation to international English. Have you had problems with any of them?

- the pronunciation of *th-*
- British and American idioms
- uncountable nouns like *information*
- the third-person *-s* in the Present simple

b Listen again. What does Doctor Jenkins think may happen to the language areas in exercise 5a as international English develops?

6a Work in pairs and discuss. Do you agree with Doctor Jenkins? Why?/Why not? Has she made you change your mind about any of your answers in exercise 3?

b Work in groups and interview your teacher about this issue. First think of at least three questions to find out what he/she thinks. Then take turns to ask your questions.

PATTERNS TO NOTICE

Introducing points in an argument

1 🎧 1.3 Listen to the way points are introduced in the interview and complete the sentences. How do the introductory phrases help the listener?

1 Well, _____ . _____ they're intelligible to each other.
2 _____ nobody owns English any more.
3 _____ learners have less to do.

2 Here are some similar ways of introducing points. Decide which are useful for introducing points for and against an argument. Which could be either?

One (important)	point to consider	is that ...
Another (strong)	reason (for) ...	would be that ...
The most (obvious)	drawback/advantage (of) ...	might be that ...
The second	problem/concern/ issue (with) ...	
A further	consideration ...	
The main	explanation ...	

One important issue is that *many people use English online.*

Another problem is that *there are so many varieties of English.*

7 Put the words in brackets in the correct order to introduce the rest of the sentence.

1 (point / the / that / main / consider / be / would / to) it's important to give learners a choice.
2 (Global English / advantage / a / of / that / is / further) it makes using the internet easier.
3 (problem / one / possible / be / British English or American English / that / with / might) it isn't what learners need.
4 (reason / pronunciation problems / most / the / for / that / is / obvious) learners don't have the sound in their first language.

8 Decide whether the points below are for or against globalisation, or neutral. Then introduce each one using an appropriate phrase.

1 _____ people are more aware of other cultures and ways of life.
2 _____ a lot of small local businesses cannot compete with big multinationals.
3 _____ there is a lot more choice available in shops than there used to be.
4 _____ there are a lot more opportunities for people to travel and work abroad.
5 _____ big multinational companies have a lot of power.
6 _____ a lot of local skills and customs are disappearing.
7 _____ we all recognise the same music, celebrities and brands.

9a You are going to answer one of the questions below. You will have 30 seconds to give your answer. Spend a few minutes preparing what to say. Use introductory phrases to make your points.

1 Will English remain the global language of the future? Why?/Why not?
2 Should each country or region try to preserve its customs and identity? How?
3 Should people be free to live in whichever country they like or do we need immigration controls?
4 What are the advantages and disadvantages of increasing urbanisation?
5 How do you see your city/country changing in the future? What would you like to happen?
6 Is a more globalised world a good thing? Why?/Why not?
7 Is it a good thing to have so many large, multinational corporations in the world?
8 Should richer countries do more to help poorer countries? If so, what?

b Work in groups. Take turns to give your answer and respond to other students' questions.

Task

Give tips on learning a language well

Preparation Listening and reading

1 🎧 1.4 Listen to seven high-level language speakers talking about learning strategies that helped them or someone they know. Make notes about the questions below for speakers.

- Which languages were learnt?
- What strategy does ... describe?
- In what ways did it he...

2 Read the profiles. Then wor... summarise the needs of each language l... h, if any, of the strategies in exerci... ant to each person?

Task Speaking

1 Work in groups. Think of your own useful tips or suggestions for the five language learners in the pictures. Ask your teacher for any words/phrases you need.

> Useful language a

2 Compare your answers with the class and compile a list of useful tips for more advanced language learners.

3a Work in pairs and discuss the questions below.

- Which learner(s) in the profiles do you have most in common with? Think about:
  - your motivation.
  - your job/study needs.
  - the skills you want to develop most.
  - your strengths and weaknesses.
- Which tips and suggestions that you have discussed might help you?
- Do you have any other plans for improving your English?

> Useful language b

b Choose two tips from your list to actively follow. After a few weeks, report back to the class on how you are progressing.

Language around

Adriana from Buenos Aires studied English for nine years at school, but has never had the opportunity to use the language in real life. She has just been offered a job with an international company and has been told that she will be using English on a daily basis; to answer the phone, to communicate with English-speaking colleagues and to attend meetings in English. She is very anxious as she doesn't feel that the English she learnt at school prepared her for this aspect of her new job. She has two months before the new job starts and plenty of time, but not much money!

David is 26 years old and qualified as a chef, but cannot find a job in his own country. His girlfriend has found a job in Germany. David has joined her there and they are staying with some cousins for a few months while he finds a job. He learnt German for several years at school, but has forgotten a lot of it and needs to improve his communication skills quickly before he can get the kind of job he would like. He does not have much money to spend on language lessons.

learners
the world

Kareem from Jordan is planning to do a Master's degree in Business Studies at an Australian university in a couple of years' time. His English is fairly good and he is attending a special course in academic writing to help him with essays in English, but he needs to be able to read in English much more fluently and to do this he needs to improve his vocabulary dramatically. He will also have to understand lectures in English and, of course, communicate and socialise in his everyday life.

USEFUL LANGUAGE

a Discussing tips and suggestions
One thing that I think is very useful is …
I think he would benefit from …
He needs to concentrate on …
Her main priority should be …
She needs to find a way of …
This approach wouldn't work for everyone.
I think it really depends on the kind of person you are.
… -ing works for me.

b Describing your own needs and targets
One thing I'm good at is …
One of my worst faults is that I (never) …
My main aim is to …
… is one of my main priorities because …
For that reason, I'm aiming to …

Asha studied Russian for five years at school in London and spent four weeks on a study exchange programme in Moscow. She understands, speaks and reads Russian pretty well and is keen to keep it up and improve – she is sure that it will be useful to her one day although she is not exactly sure how yet. She cannot afford to pay for expensive lessons at a language school and is busy with a demanding university course.

Akiko is 33 and from Tokyo. She has just moved to San Francisco with her husband who has got a job in a company there. She has started English lessons, but they mainly focus on grammar and vocabulary, and as she studied English for eight years at school in Japan, she already knows a lot of this in theory. The problem is that her listening skills and spoken English are not very good. She would like to get out and get to know people, communicate with her daughter's teachers and friends, and even perhaps study, but she really lacks confidence in English. People think she is shy, but this is not really the case!

SHARE YOUR TASK

Plan a short summary of your needs and motivation as a language learner, and what you should do to progress, based on your answers in exercise 3.

Practise what you want to say until you feel confident.

Film/Record your summary.

Share your film/recording with your teacher and other students.

Writing
A report

1a Work in pairs and discuss. How many global brand cafés or restaurants can you think of?

b Which, if any, of the cafés and restaurants from exercise 1a do you sometimes visit? What traditional food do you cook/eat at home?

2a Read the report on how globalisation has affected eating habits in Warsaw, Poland. What aspects of the report are true of your town/local area?

b Choose the best linking word or phrase to complete gaps 1–9 in the report. More than one answer may be possible.

   1 as well / also / too
   2 Although / Despite / Even though
   3 As well as / Apart from / Also
   4 as well as that / other than that / apart from that
   5 on the other hand / although / even though
   6 Just / Alone / Only
   7 while / whereas / nevertheless
   8 even if / although / however
   9 this means that / this is because / this explains why

3 Decide which features apply to writing reports. Then try to add more of your own.

   • informal language
   • an introduction and a conclusion
   • clear, simple headings
   • use of the word 'I'

4a You are going to write a report for a lifestyle magazine on the effects of globalisation. Work in groups and discuss whether the ideas in the word web are true of your hometown/country.

b Choose one of the topics in the word web and think about how globalisation has affected your town/country in relation to this topic. Note down your ideas.

attitudes/beliefs: We know a lot more about how people think in different countries.

Introduction
The aim of this report is to describe how globalisation has affected eating habits in Warsaw and to consider how/whether traditional ways of eating have been affected.

Global brands
Globalisation is having a big impact on eating out in Warsaw. A significant number of global brand coffee shops and fast food restaurants such as Starbucks and Subway have sprung up in the last few years and the vast majority of people have no objection to using them. It should [1]_____ be noted that there are now many 'themed' global restaurants such as Hard Rock Café. [2]_____ all these places are traditionally seen as quite expensive, many people visit them on a regular basis.

Foreign restaurants
[3]_____ an interest in the mostly American global brands, it is generally true that Warsaw's residents are becoming more international in their tastes. Plenty of *bar mleczny* (milk bars) still exist, offering cheap, nourishing Polish food and a reminder of life as it used to be, but [4]_____, there are now restaurants offering food from many different cultures, including Indonesian, Brazilian and Indian. The food is frequently impressive, but [5]_____ the service can be disappointing – a fact mentioned by a significant minority of tourists on travel websites. Most young and middle-aged people eat out in an international restaurant at least once a month.

Eating at home
Poland has a tradition of high-quality, home-cooked food and, reassuringly, this is one aspect of Polish food culture that does not seem to be under threat from globalisation. [6]_____ a small minority of people eat ready meals at home [7]_____ most people claim to know how to cook traditional foods such as *pierogi* (dumplings).

Conclusion
In conclusion, it appears that [8]_____ globalisation is changing the way that people eat and drink when they go out, Warsaw's residents are still proud of their traditions and [9]_____ the culture of home-cooked food is still very much alive there today.

Listening
Varieties of English

1a 🎧 1.5 Listen to four radio news re[...] around the world. Where does each one c[...] nd what is the main event being descr[...]

b Listen again and note the key num[...] atistics. Work in pairs and compare answer[...] each story relates to globalisation.

2 The four reporters spoke American [...] tish English, Australian English and India[...] What differences did you hear between th[...] eties?

3a 🎧 1.6 **Pronunciation** Listen and co[...] pronunciation of different varieties [...] ou will hear each phrase below twice. C[...] r the difference in the pronunciation?

1 American English and British English:
   a all flights into and out of the area
   b share prices across the world
   c $15 billion
2 British English and Australian English:
   a sold all over Europe
   b a vote of confidence
   c announced that it was to close
3 Australian English and Indian English:
   a the vast majority of people
   b part of a natural process
   c 12,000 million tonnes of greenhouse gases
4 Indian English and American English:
   a scheduled to open this week
   b 20,000 branches
   c not everyone, however, is happy

b Listen again and repeat. Can you imitate the pronunciation of each variety of English?

4 Work in pairs and discuss. Which accent do you like best? Which do you find easiest to understand? Which are you most likely to come into contact with?

5 Write sentences using your notes from exercise 4 and the phrases in the table below.

The (vast) majority of About ... percent of Many/Not many (of) Very few (of) A small/significant minority (of)	people from my home town ... local residents ...
It is (generally) true that It seems/appears that It's obvious that Evidence suggests that	there is a growing interest in ... there are more and more ...

6a Organise your sentences from exercise 5 under headings, as in the report in exercise 2a. The main body of your report should have at least two sections. Then write the first draft of your report.

b Look at the checklist below and think about how your report could be improved. Swap reports with a partner and see if he/she agrees. Then write the final draft of your report.

- Does your report have an introduction and a conclusion?
- Does the introduction mention the aim of the report?
- Does the conclusion summarise the findings?
- Does the main body have at least two headings?
- Is the style appropriate to a formal report?
- Have you used plenty of linking words to tie the report together?

AFTER UNIT 1 YOU CAN ...

Discuss urbanisation and globalisation at a sophisticated level.

Introduce points in an argument using appropriate phrases.

Discuss the best ways of learning a language and describe your own learning needs.

Write a report.

Recognise different varieties of English.

02

STRONG EMOTION

IN THIS UNIT

- **Grammar:** Perfect verb forms; Cleft sentences
- **Vocabulary:** Feelings; Advertising and emotions; Idioms with *laugh*, *cry* and *tears*
- **Task:** Describe a story that provokes strong emotions
- **World culture:** Luxury Superbrands

Vocabulary and speaking
Feelings

1a Work in pairs and discuss. How do you think the people in the photos feel? Use the words/phrases in the box and your own ideas.

ashamed	apprehensive	disillusioned	scared stiff
devastated	wound-up	envious	relieved
desperate	disgusted	insecure	mortified
helpless	overjoyed	indifferent	shattered
cross	under a lot of pressure		sorry for himself/herself

b How do you think the people might have felt before/after the events in the photos?

2 Which words in exercise 1a suggest particularly strong emotions? Think of other adjectives that express strong emotions.

3 Work in groups. Choose five of the situations on page 17 and discuss the different emotions you would go through before, during and after these experiences.

> I think I would feel kind of / a bit / totally / incredibly …

> I'd feel a sense of (envy/disgust).

> It wouldn't bother me that much.

How would you feel?

- You've been learning to drive for months and, finally, the big day arrives: your driving test. Unfortunately, a few minutes beforehand you lock yourself out of your car and can't take the test.

- Your company/college offers you the opportunity to do a special course in the USA for nine months, away from all your family and friends.

- Your brother and sister-in-law ask you to look after their three pre-school children for the weekend while they go to a wedding. It turns out to be a wet, freezing weekend.

- You fail an important exam because you haven't done any studying. To make matters worse, all your friends seem to have passed with flying colours.

- A colleague you dislike is giving an important presentation. Her delivery is completely incoherent and she keeps going red and apologising. Members of the audience are sniggering openly.

- Things have been going fantastically well with your new boyfriend/girlfriend. Then, suddenly, he/she starts being late for dates or doesn't turn up at all. There's no good reason that you can see.

- You have finally got to play for the football team of your dreams. In the first half hour of the biggest match of your career, you score a vital goal, only to have it disallowed by the referee.

- You are in your mid-40s with three teenage children. Out of the blue, you and your husband/wife discover that you are having another baby.

4a **Pronunciation** Find single-word adjectives in the box in exercise 1a that match the stress patterns in the table below.

1 ●•	2 •●	3 ●••	4 •●•
desperate			
5 ••●	6 ●•••	7 ••●•	

b 🎧 2.1 Listen and check. Then practise saying the words.

5a Work in pairs and choose three words/phrases from the box in exercise 1a. Spend a few minutes inventing situations like the ones in exercise 3 to illustrate the emotions.

b Describe the situations to other students without saying the emotion you had in mind. Can they guess what the emotion is?

Expressing emotions across the world

by Melissa Thompson

Quite a few years ago, I took my first trip to Thailand to visit my boyfriend's family. I emerged from the airport to be greeted by a wall of heat unlike anything my pale English skin had ever experienced before, but that wasn't the only shock in store for me. After 20 minutes or so in the sweltering sun I started to complain: the flight had been exhausting, my feet were aching and so on. Quite suddenly, my boyfriend stopped me. 'It is not acceptable to show your emotions like that,' he whispered. 'You should try to smile.' I thought he was joking at first, but I soon realised he wasn't. In Thailand, the 'land of smiles', people go out of their way to put on a happy face for reasons I hadn't yet appreciated.

Ever since that trip, I've been trying to learn all I can about how people express emotions in different cultures and how those cultures shape what we feel. What I'd failed to grasp all those years ago is that negativity tends to be taboo in Thailand. The happiness of the group is put above that of the individual and one person's feelings are seen as closely linked to those of others. For that reason, my public whinging and whining was potentially offensive.

It's not just complaining which is taboo. In *collective* cultures like Thailand's, people who publicly express anger are seen as rude and unsophisticated. In more individualistic cultures like Europe or the USA, it is relatively common for friends and partners to have a brief slanging match, slam the door and then make up without too much harm being done. Anger has even been shown to be a successful negotiating strategy in business. In collective cultures though, losing your cool is definitely counterproductive.

This is not to say that you can't express negative emotions in Thailand. You simply do it much more subtly. Spend a bit of time in the country and you become aware of the myriad of different ways that you can smile: there's the I don't trust you smile, the that's a silly suggestion smile, the smile of genuine warmth and affection, and many others besides. I vividly remember the strained please don't ever do that again smile from my boyfriend's mother when I rested my feet on a chair (showing the soles of your feet is extremely rude in Thailand).

Emoticons give further clues to the differences. In the USA and Europe, people tend to use the mouth to indicate an emotion, for example, [:)] means happy and [: ( ] means sad, while in Asia, [^_^] and ['_'] carry these meanings, showing that the emotion conveyed by the eyes is much more important.

Personally speaking, I think of myself as quite an emotional person. I tend to get upset, sulk or laugh hysterically, depending on the situation. I can also be cynical, sarcastic and argumentative. I try to tone down my behaviour in Thailand ('when in Rome …', as the saying goes), but it's not always easy and I often get the feeling that people find me too volatile. However, what seems overly emotional to one person can seem reserved to another. A flatmate from Italy used to tell me how uptight I was because I didn't gesticulate and shout with the same carefree abandon that he did. So what's the truth? Is there a right way to behave, whichever culture you come from? Let me know your thoughts and experiences.

Readers' comments

Arun: Hi, Melissa. I'm kind of in the opposite situation to you. I'm Khmer, but I've married into an American family who are much more into expressing their emotions than people in my culture and I find some of their conflicts really make me uncomfortable. But I'm also able to see that the way my family behave can result in dishonesty. My mom will visit someone's house and smile and compliment everything, then when she gets home, she will say, 'There wasn't enough food!' or 'Why did they buy that sofa?' ♦

Karly: Great article, Melissa – really thought-provoking. I'm used to a culture where people generally let it be known if they're not happy, but when I was travelling in South East Asia, I found it much easier to be calm and laid-back. I found the Thai way of smiling, whatever, really suited me – in that respect, I was really able to embrace their culture. ♦

Andreas: You're right that in collective cultures like Thai and Japanese it's frowned on to express negative emotions like anger, but don't be fooled – the anger's still there! I've visited Japan and Thailand frequently on business and I often wonder what impact all this has on people psychologically – whether it's really bad for people to bottle up their feelings like this. Personally, it would drive me nuts! ♦

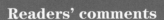

Reading

1 Work in groups and discuss. Which of the things below have you done recently? Why?

- shouted at someone
- laughed out loud
- hidden your feelings
- cried in public

2a Read the first paragraph of the article. Why do you think Thai people always appear happy?

b Read the full article and answer the questions.

1 Which emotions are taboo in Thailand and why?
2 How are strong emotions expressed?
3 What are the comment writers' opinions?

3 Read the article again and decide which three statements are not true. Underline evidence in the article to support your answers.

1 The author was surprised at what her boyfriend said.
2 Thai people make a great effort to smile.
3 In countries such as Thailand the individual is more important than the group.
4 In Europe and the USA getting angry is acceptable in certain situations.
5 Thai people never express negative emotions.
6 The author controls her emotional behaviour in Thailand.
7 Her Italian flatmate found her reserved.
8 Readers all believe the Thai way of expressing emotions is the best.

4 Find these colloquial expressions in the article or comments and explain them in your own words.

1 whinge and whine about something
2 have a slanging match
3 lose your cool
4 tone down your behaviour
5 be uptight
6 be laid-back
7 bottle up your feelings
8 drive someone nuts

5 Work in groups and discuss one or more of the questions below.

- Do you agree or disagree with the points made on the comments board?
- Do you generally express your emotions or do you tend to bottle up your feelings?
- Is it acceptable in your country to express negative emotions like anger?
- Do you think it is good to express negative emotions? In what circumstances?
- Have you ever experienced a culture where emotions are expressed differently from your own? What differences did you notice?

6 Read other students' comments and say if you agree.

Grammar review
Perfect verb forms

1 Read Simon's comment. Which country is he talking about? What cultural problems does he mention?

Simon: I definitely agree with you, Melissa. Many actions and gestures you usually take for granted can also have unexpected reactions. A few years ago we moved to Jakarta and [a]**we've been caught out in this way several times**. When we first arrived here, I noticed that people sometimes gave me angry looks in public and were sometimes rude to me at work. What I didn't realise is that [b]**I'd been standing with my hands on my hips** – something I did without thinking about it. The problem is, this is a sign of arrogance or aggression in Indonesia. This is just one example of many things [c]**we've had to learn since we moved here**, like not sitting with the soles of your feet showing, not touching people's heads, etc. Of course, [d]**we would like to have known these things before we came**, but since those first misunderstandings [e]**we've all been trying hard** to learn more about the culture of the country we're living in. [f]**By the end of the year, we will have been here** for five years and [g]**it's been a fascinating learning experience so far**. ♦

2 Work in pairs. Look at the phrases in bold in Simon's comment and underline the perfect verb forms. Discuss why a perfect form is used in each one.

3a In which phrase (a–g) does Simon use:

1 the Present perfect with an adverb which links the past to the present?
2 the Present perfect referring to a period of time which is incomplete?
3 the Present perfect with a phrase saying how many times it has happened?
4 the Present perfect continuous to emphasise the duration of the action?
5 the Past perfect continuous to show that an action happened before another in the past?
6 the Future perfect to link the present to a point in the future?
7 a perfect infinitive to emphasise that he is talking about a time further in the past?

b All perfect forms link two times. Which forms link: the past and present?; two points in the past?; two points in the future?

4 Complete the sentences with the correct form of the verbs in brackets. Discuss which are true for you.

1 I _____ (work) really hard recently.
2 This is the first time I _____ (study) the perfect aspect.
3 By the end of this course, I _____ (find out) lots of interesting things about my classmates.
4 I'd like _____ (start) learning English earlier.
5 I _____ (not have) a holiday for ages.
6 I was tired when I went to bed last night because I _____ (talk) to my friends all evening.

> **> Grammar extension bank, pages 116–119**

Listening and vocabulary
Advertising and emotions

1 Work in groups and discuss the questions below.

- Do you have any favourite adverts or any that particularly annoy you? Explain what you like/dislike about them.
- Look at the adverts in the photos. What are they advertising?
- How do you think the advertiser is trying to influence your emotions in each?

2a You are going to listen to a radio interview about how adverts appeal to our emotions. Before you listen, read the messages from the adverts below and decide whether the appeal is rational (R) or emotional (E).

1 This brand is good value for money.
2 This car has low fuel consumption.
3 Use this washing powder if you are a good parent.
4 People will envy you if you own this car.
5 This phone has the cheapest call tariff.
6 This beer is expensive, but you deserve a treat.
7 Wearing this T-shirt will make you feel like a cool person.
8 This isn't very good for you, but it's fun.

b 🎧 2.2 Listen and check.

3a Read the sentences and check the meaning of the words in bold. Then listen again and decide if the statements are true (T) or false (F), according to the interview.

1 Many adverts point out the logical **benefits** of a product.
2 There are important **differentiating factors** between makes of small cars.
3 Car ads appeal to people's **aspirations** in a range of different ways.
4 Many ads for phones and MP3 players aim to make people feel that they are part of their **peer group**.
5 Many adverts for luxury products try to persuade people that they should **pamper themselves**.
6 Health campaigns and adverts for charities often **deliberately set out to** annoy people.
7 Campaigning ads can **backfire** if they do not put their message across strongly enough.
8 Once an advert has been released, the advertisers **monitor** people's **responses** carefully.
9 Adverts for products that might be harmful are **heavily regulated** in many countries.
10 Humorous adverts for gambling **subtly flatter** people.

b Work in pairs and compare your answers. Explain why you think the statements are true/false.

4 Work in groups and discuss the questions below.

- Have you changed your opinions about the adverts in exercise 1?
- Can you think of any adverts you know that have the messages in exercise 2a?
- Do you think you are influenced by advertising?
- What kind of adverts tend to appeal to you?
- Has the interview made you feel differently about advertising? Will it affect what products you do/don't buy in the future?

PATTERNS TO NOTICE

Cleft sentences

1 🎧 2.3 **Complete sentence b in each pair so that it gives the same information as sentence a. Then listen and check.**

   1 a Most people prefer straightforward facts.
     b What _____ straightforward facts.
   2 a Charity ads often appeal to 'negative' emotions.
     b It's _____ 'negative' emotions.

2 **Read more examples, then answer the questions.**

   I didn't invite them. → **It wasn't me who** *invited them.*

   I began to suspect something. → **It was then that** *I began to suspect something.*

   You should tell her the truth. → **What you should do is** *tell her the truth.*

   I like the way she smiles. → **What I like (about her)** *is the way she smiles.*

   1 What is the difference in emphasis between the sentences in each pair?
   2 What changes are there in the construction of the second sentence?
   3 Where do we put the verb *be* after cleft sentences with *it* and *what*?
   4 Which construction also uses a relative pronoun?

5 Rewrite the sentences as cleft sentences. Begin with the word in brackets.

   1 You need a few days' rest and recreation. (what)
   2 Money is the thing people care about most nowadays. (it)
   3 We need someone to help us, not someone to criticise. (what)
   4 I like the way he always listens sympathetically. (what)
   5 His attitude towards other people really annoys me. (it)
   6 I don't understand why you had to lie to me. (what)
   7 I didn't decide to take a short cut across country! (it)
   8 The world needs love, peace and understanding. (what)
   9 Then everything became clear. (it)

6 Complete the sentences using your own ideas. Then work in pairs and compare your answers.

   1 What I really dislike about my city is *the terrible traffic and pollution*.
   2 What I like about my city is _____ .
   3 It's the _____ (in my country) that really _____ me.
   4 What I'd really like to do in my English class is _____ .
   5 It's _____ that I find really difficult in English.
   6 What my country needs is _____ .
   7 It was _____ who taught me to _____ .
   8 What I don't understand about _____ (a famous person) is why (s)he _____ .

Wordspot
Idioms with *laugh*, *cry* and *tears*

1a Work in pairs and complete the gaps with *laugh*, *cry* or *tears*. Which phrases do you already know? Which can you guess?

   1 a shoulder to _____ on
   2 be in floods of _____
   3 have the last _____
   4 _____ your eyes out
   5 be bored to _____
   6 it's no _____ing matter
   7 burst out _____ing
   8 burst into _____
   9 _____ your head off
   10 be close to _____

b Which two idioms from exercise 1a are illustrated in the cartoons?

2a Replace the phrases in bold with the correct form of an idiom from exercise 1a. More than one answer may be possible.

   1 I'm not sure you realise just how difficult parking is around here. **It's a very serious problem**.
   2 I don't know what the matter was, but when I went past her room, Linda was **crying a lot**.
   3 Despite bad reviews from the critics, the show was a success, so the director **was proved right in the end**.
   4 When I asked Bill where Tara was, he **began crying suddenly**.
   5 Tom was very sympathetic when Jan's dad died – he gave her **support when she was depressed**.
   6 I really enjoyed taking my nephew to the puppet show. He **laughed and laughed and laughed**.
   7 When we saw Ella in that ridiculous hat, we **suddenly started laughing**.
   8 The funeral was very moving – many people were **nearly crying**.
   9 It's such a sad story – I **cried and cried** at the end.
   10 I wish our teachers at school had made maths lessons more interesting. I was always **completely bored**.

b Work in pairs and compare your answers.

3 Choose four idioms from exercise 1a and think of a time when you felt or behaved like this. Then work in groups and explain what happened.

Task

Describe a story that provokes strong emotions

Preparation Listening and speaking

1a Think of stories that you know from a book, film or play that match the descriptions below.

- It makes me laugh.
- It moves me or makes me cry.
- It's scary or unnerving.
- It's thought-provoking.
- It has a strong feel-good factor.

b Work in groups and compare your answers.

2 Which of the features below do you think are most important in a story? Think of a good example for each feature from a story you know.

- The characters are convincing and you really care about them.
- There's lots of suspense and tension.
- It's full of action and moves at a fast pace.
- There are lots of clever plot twists.
- It allows you to escape into an imaginary world.
- The story is realistic and true to life.
- It convincingly recreates a period of history or a particular way of life.
- It has a happy ending.
- The ending is totally unexpected.
- The ending makes you cry.

3a 🎧 2.4 You are going to listen to someone describing a story they really like. Work in two groups.
Group A: Listen to story A.
Group B: Listen to story B. Answer the questions below.

1 What is the name of the story and where does it come from (a book, film, etc.)?
2 Where and when is it set?
3 What kind of story is it?
4 Is it told in detail or only in outline? Why?
5 Who are the main characters?
6 Which words/phrases in the box did you hear?

illegitimate daughter	floorboards	scream
police interview	radical group	mayor
adopts	ex-convict	uprising
false identity	heart beating	bishop
criminal justice system	insane narrator	

b Listen again and check. Make brief notes about the story as you listen.

4 Work in A/B pairs. Tell your partner as much as you can about the story you heard. It does not matter if you cannot remember every detail.

5 Read the phrases in the Useful language box. Which were used in the stories you heard? Look at audio script 2.4 on page 164 to check your answers.

The Tell-Tale Heart

FIGHT DREAM HOPE LOVE

HUGH JACKMAN · RUSSELL CROWE · ANNE HATHAWAY · AMANDA SEYFRIED · with HELENA BONHAM CARTER

Les Misérables

FROM THE ACADEMY AWARD-WINNING DIRECTOR OF

Task Speaking

1a Work alone or in pairs. Choose a story you like from a film, book or play to describe to the class. Check details of the story online if necessary.

b Spend about ten minutes planning how to describe your story. Ask your teacher for any words/phrases you need. Think about:

- what to include about the story in about two minutes. You should give enough detail to make the story interesting, but you can cut out unnecessary sub-plots, minor characters, etc.
- how much background information to give.
- the important characters and events of the story and the order in which they appear/happen.
- how the story makes you feel.
- whether or not you will give away the ending or leave it out so as not to spoil the story.

> Useful language a, b, c and d

2 Work in new pairs and practise telling your stories. Listen and give feedback about how clear the story is and which parts need more/less detail.

3 Take turns to tell your stories in groups or to the class. Which book/film/play that you have heard about would you most like to read/see?

Follow up Writing

1 Choose the story that you have told the class or another favourite story of yours. Write a brief plot summary for a website.

USEFUL LANGUAGE

a Introducing the story
It's set in (the future / ancient times / an imaginary world where ...).
It tells the story of ...
It's told in the first person.

b Describing the story
The story opens as ...
It's extremely long.
There are several subplots.
Little by little, you realise that ...
The tension builds up.
It's a bit ambiguous.

c Describing how it makes you feel
It's a very chilling story.
It makes you laugh out loud.
You have a strong sense of unease.
It fills you with a sense of despair.
It's very heartwarming.
Parts of it are heartbreaking / very uplifting.
It's so moving.
It leaves you with a feeling that ...

d The ending
It all ends happily.
The ending really makes you cry.

SHARE YOUR TASK

Practise retelling your story until you feel confident.

Film/Record yourself telling your story.

Share your film/recording with other students.

WORLD CULTURE

LUXURY SUPERBRANDS

Find out first

1a Work in pairs. Look at the list of luxury brands in the box below. What product is each one famous for? Can you add more names to the list?

Louis Vuitton	Rolls Royce
Gucci	Tiffany and Co
Chanel	Issey Miyake
Rolex	Vertu

b Do you or does anyone you know own any items produced by these brands?

2a Do the luxury brands quiz.

Luxury brands quiz

1. Which of the brands above has the highest global turnover?
   a) Louis Vuitton   b) Chanel   c) Rolls Royce

2. Which country is the largest market for luxury goods?
   a) China   b) France   c) the USA

3. How much is spent on luxury goods worldwide a year?
   a) around $3 bn   b) around $30 bn   c) around $300 bn

4. Which luxury brand company was started by a woman called Coco in Paris over 100 years ago?
   a) Gucci   b) Chanel   c) Tiffany and Co

5. Which luxury car brand started in the 1980s?
   a) Lexus   b) Rolls Royce   c) Ferrari

6. Approximately how many watches does Rolex make every day?
   a) 2,000   b) 200,000   c) 2 million

b Go online and check your answers or ask your teacher.

Search: luxury brands global turnover / largest market luxury goods / global sales luxury goods

View

3a Look at the words in the box. Tick the ones you think a company producing luxury brands would want to be seen as.

common   exclusive   high-end   mass-market   slick   tacky

b ▶ Watch the video about international luxury fashion brands and choose the correct word to complete each sentence.

1 The two men *would / might / wouldn't* willingly wear each other's belt.
2 Luxury brands make the most money from the *top / middle / bottom* of the pyramid.

4 Watch the video again and choose the correct answers. More than one answer may be correct.

1 a One of the men says that his belt has an unsophisticated image but he likes that.
   b The other man says that his belt is only suitable for women.
   c The presenter says that his belt is cheap and does its job.
2 What is the purpose of the top level of the pyramid model?
   a to build kudos
   b to make a lot of money
   c to appeal to the wealthy elite
3 What is the 'delicate balance' that Dana Thomas talks about?
   a keeping costs down and prices high
   b appealing to the elite while selling to the general public
   c making high fashion items while turning a profit
4 Which of these should luxury superbrands do?
   a maximise profits from the bottom of the pyramid
   b keep customers focussed on the top of the pyramid
   c make sure that products at the bottom of the pyramid are cheap

5 Work in pairs and discuss.

• Do the luxury superbrands appeal to you? Why?/Why not?
• Which ones appeal the most/least?

FIND OUT MORE

9a Which of these marketing techniques have you heard of? Do you know or can you guess how they work?

- stealth marketing
- ambush marketing
- celebrity endorsement

b Choose one of the techniques and go online to find out more about it. Try to find out:

- how that form of marketing works
- which companies have successfully used it
- what are the potential pitfalls in using it.

Search: stealth marketing /ambush marketing / celebrity endorsement

Present your research

10 Summarise what you have found out in a short presentation to your class. Use the prompts below.

- The topic of my mini-presentation today is ...
- This is a relatively new/tried-and-tested form of marketing. It involves ...
- Some of you may have heard of a company called ...
- This kind of marketing is not without risks. For example ...
- When used correctly, however, ... can be very effective because ...

Tip
Use a quote in the introduction to your presentation.
The topic of my presentation today is ambush marketing. As someone once said, 'Any publicity is good publicity,' and ambush marketing is a great example of this idea in action.

World view

6a Watch seven people talking about luxury brands. Do they approve (✓), disapprove (✗) or have mixed feelings (✓/✗) about them?

Name	Approve/disapprove/ mixed feelings?	Reasons, comments, examples given
Sophie		
Jurgen		
Keith		
Luis		
Clare		
Sayful		
Imogen		

b Compare answers in pairs. Can you remember any reasons, comments or examples that they gave?

7 Watch the film again and complete the second column of the table.

8 Discuss the questions in groups.

- Do you agree that luxury brands are a good thing because they give people something to aspire to or do you think they cause division and envy?
- Do you think that luxury brands spend too much money on advertising and are therefore bad value for money?
- Do you 'treat yourself' to luxury brands or do you regard them as a waste of money?
- What kind of luxury goods do you buy if any? In which cases do you go for 'value' products?

AFTER UNIT 2 YOU CAN ...

Describe and discuss emotions at a sophisticated level

Describe and discuss brands and the effects of advertising

Add emphasis to what you are saying using cleft sentences

Describe a story and how it makes you feel

Research online and give a short presentation about marketing

IN THIS UNIT

- Grammar: Time and tense; Inversion with negative adverbials
- Vocabulary: Money and enterprise; *worth*
- Task: Decide which project to back
- Language live: Describing quantities; Summarising statistics

Money,

Win the maximum prize of $2,000 by getting all the quiz questions correct!

For $100:

1. If something is so valuable that it cannot be bought, how can it be described?
   - A pricey
   - B worthless
   - C worthwhile
   - D priceless

2. Which of these is not a way of describing someone who hates spending money?
   - A tight
   - B flashy
   - C penny-pinching
   - D stingy

3. Which of these describes money given to a person in authority to get them to do something dishonest?
   - A a bribe
   - B an advance
   - C a deposit
   - D a fee

4. Tick (✓) the words that describe having a lot of money and cross (✗) the words that describe having little or none. (All answers must be correct to win the prize money.)
   - A skint
   - B loaded
   - C broke
   - D hard up

Vocabulary and speaking
Money and enterprise

1a Work in pairs and answer as many questions in the quiz as you can without using a dictionary.

b 🎧 3.1 Listen and check the quiz answers.

2a Answer the questions below using words/phrases from the quiz. Then work in pairs and compare your answers.

1. Have you ever:
   - been completely **broke**?
   - paid or been offered a **bribe**?
   - paid a lot of money for something that turned out to be **worthless**?
2. Do you know anyone who:
   - is always **in the red**?
   - is **loaded**?
   - is **flashy** with their money?
   - is very **stingy** with money?
3. What kind of people generally:
   - earn really good **tips**?
   - get high **pensions**?
   - receive large **alimony** payments?
   - **go bankrupt**?
4. What's happening at the moment in your country? Is there a boom or a recession? What do you think are the causes? Are the government making a lot of spending cuts?

b Think of three more questions using money words/phrases from the quiz. Ask other students.

money, money

5 Put the things that can happen to a business/businessperson in order from 1 (the most positive) to 5 (the least positive). (All answers must be in the correct order to win the prize money.)

A be in the red   C be in the black   E break even
B go bankrupt   D make a large profit

For $500:

6 Who receives the following from whom? (All answers must be correct to win the prize money.)

A a tip   C pocket money   E alimony/maintenance
B a pension   D a ransom

For $1,000:

7 Write R if the phrases are normally associated with an economic recession and B if they are normally associated with an economic boom. (All answers must be correct to win the prize money.)

A high unemployment   F high share prices
B high property prices   G high salaries
C a large government deficit H an increase in GDP
D businesses going bust   I economic expansion
E government spending cuts

---

3 Add the money words/phrases from the quiz to the word web below. Some can go in more than one category.

1 relating to the economic situation

2 relating to business finances

3 money paid in specific situations
ransom

8 describing how much money people have

money

4 relating to illegal activities with money

7 relating to pay

5 describing attitudes towards money

6 describing price

4a What do you think these sayings about money mean? Do you have any similar sayings in your language?

'Money makes the world go round.'

'Neither a borrower nor a lender be.'

'The love of money is the root of all evil.'

'Take care of the pennies and the pounds will take care of themselves.'

'The rich get richer and the poor get poorer.'

'Money can't buy happiness, but you can rent it for a while.'

b Choose one saying from exercise 4a that you agree with and one that you disagree with. Spend a few minutes thinking about why. Then work in groups to explain your ideas and find out what other students think.

But are they worth it?

Imagine that a person's height was exactly equivalent to their income so that people who earned, say, $25,000 a year were slightly taller than those who earned $24,000. Then imagine that every American adult walks past you in order of income, from lowest-earning to highest, all in the space of an hour. The first people to walk past you are the owners of loss-making businesses, the unemployed and those on the minimum wage – all of them invisible or tiny compared to a normal person. Surprisingly, after half an hour, people are still only waist-high and it is not until three-quarters of an hour has passed that the first average-sized person appears. Near the end of the hour, things start to get a little scary. With six minutes to go, people are 12 feet tall and in the final few seconds, as the 400 highest earners walk past, you realise that you can't see their heads because each one is more than three kilometres tall.

Hollywood stars command fees in excess of $20 million.

So who are these modern giants who measure their annual income in the millions? There are the Hollywood stars, of course, who can command fees in excess of $20 million per film, and professional footballers, the very best of whom can earn over €30 million a year in salary and sponsorship deals. But the world of finance and business can easily compete with these pay packets – and you don't even have to be successful. Dick Fuld, CEO of Lehman Brothers, earned $22 million in 2007, just before the company went bust, while Léo Apotheker, the short-lived head of Hewlett-Packard, is reported to have earned $23 million before being fired after just 11 months in the job. Dwarfing all these salaries is Tim Cook's pay for 2011. The head of Apple took home $378 million in cash and share options for a year's work – over a million dollars a day. So the simple question is: is it right that some people earn so much?

22,000 children die each day from factors caused by poverty.

The moral arguments against such extraordinarily large pay packets are obvious: in a world where 22,000 children die each day from factors caused by poverty, how can it be right that a few people get so much? There are plenty of practical arguments, too. Studies show that the more unequal a society is in terms of income, the more likely its citizens are to suffer from problems like drug addiction, mental illness and ill health. Plus, citizens of more equal societies are much more likely to be happy and to trust each other. In Japan, Sweden and Norway, for example, more than 60 percent of the population feel that they can trust their fellow citizens. In countries like the UK, the USA and Singapore, that figure falls to 15 percent.

And it's not even clear that higher pay leads to better performance. Research conducted by the renowned Massachusetts Institute of Technology (MIT) suggests that rewarding workers with huge bonuses can be counter-productive. In the study people were given a range of tasks to complete, physical and mental, and financial incentives for completing each one. The results showed that the incentives only worked when the tasks involved purely mechanical skills – equivalent, perhaps, to the tasks done by workers on a production line in a factory. When participants had to think and process information, incentives led to worse performance. And the higher the incentive, the worse the performance!

Many rich people use their incredible wealth to do great charitable things.

For others, however, remuneration is first and foremost an issue of freedom. Shouldn't we all be free to make as much money as we like? Isn't that what drives us to work harder and to innovate? And many rich people use their incredible wealth to do great charitable things. Bill Gates, one of the richest people alive, is using the $65 billion that he earned as founder of Microsoft to try to alleviate poverty and eradicate diseases like polio.

People are paid what they are worth, the argument goes, and if they weren't worth it, they wouldn't be paid it. Take film stars, for example. Statistics show that Natalie Portman films earn $43 for every dollar she is paid, so she justifies her high fees (at the other end of the scale, recently at least, is Eddie Murphy, whose films only bring in $2.30 for every dollar he's paid). Even the much-maligned Dick Fuld was once praised for the 14 years of incredible profit that Lehman Brothers enjoyed under his leadership.

In the end, whether you think it's fair that some people earn so much depends partly on the value you attach to money itself. It is, after all, just paper and there's no guarantee that it will solve your problems. As Arnold Schwarzenegger once said, 'Money doesn't make you happy. I now have $50 million, but I was just as happy when I had $48 million.'

Reading and speaking

1 Work in groups. Name two professions that you think are overpaid in your country and two that are underpaid. Give reasons.

2 Read the first two paragraphs of the article. What do you find most shocking? Think of one argument for and one against huge salaries.

3 Read the rest of the article and complete the arguments for and against high salaries.

for
1 freedom *People should be free to earn whatever is possible.*
2 innovation
3 charity
4 value/worth

against
1 morality *It's morally wrong when others are dying from poverty.*
2 social problems
3 trust and happiness
4 performance

4 Read the article again. Work in pairs and answer the questions below.

1 What happened to Lehman Brothers between 1993 and 2008?
2 What do Japan, Sweden and Norway have in common?
3 In what jobs do financial incentives work?
4 What causes does Bill Gates support?
5 What do the statistics show about Natalie Portman and Eddie Murphy?
6 What is humorous about Arnold Schwarzenegger's comment?

5 Find ten words/phrases in the article related to money. Add them to the word web on page 27.

6 Choose 'discussion' or 'debate'.

Discussion
Work in groups of three. Choose one question each and discuss, giving reasons.
- Do you think it is right that some people earn huge salaries?
- Is it possible for society to prevent people earning huge salaries? If so, how?
- Do you think financial incentives work?
- What professions do you think should/ shouldn't have performance-related pay?
- Do you agree that people in a society are happier if the gap between rich and poor is smaller?

Debate
Work in groups of three. Turn to page 107 and follow the instructions.

The RISE and RISE of Premier League incomes

It's every young football fan's dream that one day [1]**they'll be playing** for a top-flight football club and seeing themselves on TV every weekend. And with the highest paid European football players earning salaries of over €300,000 a week, it's easy to see why – even the average salary of €30,000 a week is not to be sniffed at! But it wasn't always like this. The late Scottish footballer Stewart Imlach, for example, [2]**had already played** for Scotland in the 1958 World Cup alongside the likes of Pelé when he was offered a €30-a-week salary by English club Nottingham Forest (about €450 in today's money). Things [3]**changed very little** until the late 1970s and 1980s, when the lifting of regulations allowed for freer trade of players across borders. Salaries during this time [4]**were increasing** steadily in order to attract the best players from abroad. Since then [5]**they've been rising** at an astronomical rate. Today's top-flight footballers [6]**earn** 50 times what they did in the early 1980s, with many, such as Lionel Messi and Cristiano Ronaldo, combining salaries with lucrative sponsorship deals.

So [7]**is** this upward spiral **going to continue** endlessly? Some argue that it shouldn't. 'Enough is enough,' argues Ted Muggerige, who [8]**is heading** a campaign to introduce limits on players' salaries. 'It's gone beyond a joke now, and with most top-division clubs facing heavy losses each year, the time has come for some sensible limits.'

Grammar review
Time and tense

1a Read the article about football salaries. What form are the verbs in bold?

  1 *Future continuous*

b Which time do the underlined verbs (1–8) in the article refer to? Complete the table.

Time	Verbs 1–8	Verbs a–h
past time		
present time/now		
future time	*they'll be playing*	*get paid*
general time		

2a Which time do the verbs in bold (a–h) refer to? Add them to the table in exercise 1b.

  a Could you lend me some money until I **get paid**?
  b Breaking news: Arsenal **sign** Diego for £20 million!
  c How would your life change if your salary **increased**?
  d A 20 percent increase? OK, I **accept**.
  e I **was wondering** how you'd feel if I asked for a pay rise.
  f Anderson **takes** the ball, he **shoots** ... he **scores**! Goal!
  g So, I **walk** into the interview and the first thing they **ask** me is how much I expect to earn!
  h I want to be able to retire when I**'m** 50.

b Work in pairs and discuss. Why are the verb forms in sentences a–h used?

3 Work in pairs. Student A: Turn to page 106. Student B: Turn to page 109.

> Grammar extension bank, pages 120–123

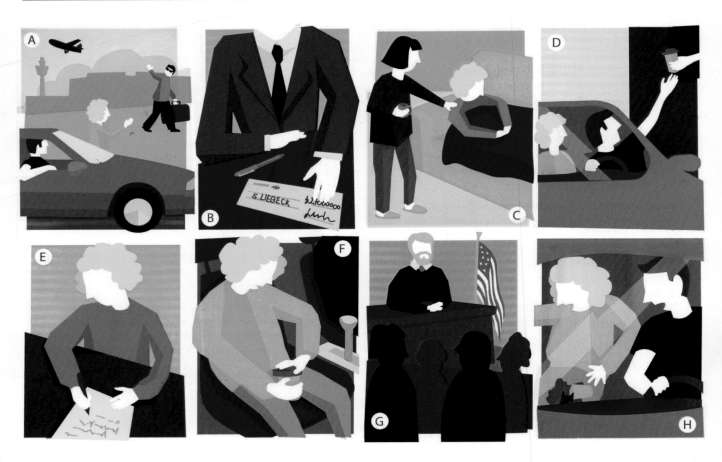

Listening
The case of Stella Liebeck

1a You are going to listen to what happened to Stella Liebeck, from New Mexico, USA when she ordered a coffee with her takeaway meal. Match the words in the box with the pictures.

tug	scalding	drop someone off	lid
damages	sue	horrified	jury

b 🎧 **3.2** Listen and put the pictures in order.

2a 🎧 **3.3** Listen to two people arguing about the case. What new information do you learn:

1 in favour of Stella?
2 in favour of the company?

b Who do you agree with?

3 Work in pairs and discuss the questions.

- What was Stella entitled to, if anything, in your opinion?
- Is it common in your country to sue for compensation? If so, what kind of institutions tend to be sued?
- What are the disadvantages of a 'compensation culture'?

PATTERNS TO NOTICE

Inversion with negative adverbials

1 🎧 **3.4** Put the words in the correct order to make phrases from the story. Then listen and check. Is this the usual word order in English?
   1 consult / did / a lawyer / only / Stella / then
   2 did / not once / her fault / it was / admit that / she
   3 all that money / have been given / no way / she / should

2 Inversion is used to give greater emphasis, particularly in formal situations. The adverbials in bold come at the beginning of a sentence and are followed by an inversion.
   Only then *did I understand what was happening.*
   Only now *can I appreciate the difficulties of the situation.*
   Not once *did he offer to pay.*
   Rarely/Seldom/Never before *have I experienced such kindness and hospitality.*
   No longer *will we accept these low standards.*
   Under no circumstances *should you wander around alone after dark.*
   On no account *must you overexert yourself.*
   Not only *did he take all our money, but he also betrayed our trust.*

3 The phrase *no way* (it's completely impossible) is also followed by an inversion. It is common in informal, spoken language.
   No way *will we be finished by ten.*

4 Make the sentences more formal. Replace the words in bold using the words/phrases in brackets. Make any other changes necessary.

1 Our country does **not** need to rely on foreign investment **any more**. (no longer)
2 You **certainly** should **not** borrow money without checking the interest rates. (under no circumstances)
3 **Now** we are **finally** seeing the benefits of the government's policies. (only now)
4 A change of government has **not often** had such a dramatic effect on the economic outlook. (rarely)
5 Frederick looked for his wallet to pay. **At that moment** he realised he had left all his money at home. (only then)
6 You **definitely** should**n't** reveal the details of your bank account over the telephone. (on no account)
7 This country has **not** witnessed such a serious financial crisis **before**. (never before)
8 **It's rare that** a politician admits publicly that he has made a mistake. (seldom)
9 George **had** to pay a large fine **and** he had to spend some time in prison **as well**. (not only … also)

5a 🎧 3.5 Listen to five people describing items a–e in an emphatic way. Match speakers 1–5 with the things they describe a–e.

a something you only understand or appreciate now you are older
b a time when you were happier than you'd ever been before
c something that visitors to your country or city should avoid
d a reason/reasons why you don't like someone
e something you think you definitely won't do or experience in the next year

b Listen again. Which negative adverbial does each speaker use?

6a Write a true sentence for items a–e in exercise 5a, using inversion with a negative adverbial.

b Work in pairs and compare your sentences.

Wordspot
worth

1a Match explanations a–f with the words/phrases with *worth* in six sentences below. Not all sentences have an explanation.

a very valuable
b deserving
c a very useful thing to work hard for
d I'm not sure whether or not it's useful
e show you can be useful
f useful and important

1 That vase doesn't look very exciting but it's actually **worth a fortune**!
2 Most of the stuff in that antique shop is just **worthless** junk.
3 I'm going to throw most of this stuff away – it's not really **worth keeping**.
4 I know it's really tough studying so much but one day, you see, it'll be **well worth the effort**.
5 I'm not that interested in making lots of money; I just want to find a job that's **worthwhile**.
6 Manchester United were **worthy** winners of the championship.
7 It's not the best museum I've ever been to, but it**'s worth a quick look**.
8 If you want some job advice, it might **be worth your while** to call my boss.
9 Have you got **five pounds' worth** of change?
10 Well, I'll give you my opinion, **for what it's worth**.
11 The situation was getting desperate – we only had **two days' worth** of food left.
12 If you want the job, you'll have **to prove your worth**.

b Work in pairs and think of your own explanations for the underlined words/phrases in the other six sentences.

2 Add the words/phrases in exercise 1a to the word web below.

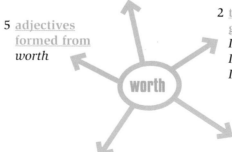

1 to describe monetary value
   It's worth about $1,000.

5 adjectives formed from worth

2 to say that something is good, useful or interesting
   It's worth a visit.
   It's worth thinking about.
   It's not worth it.

worth

4 idiomatic phrases

3 to describe a certain amount of something
   six hours' worth of recording time

3a 🎧 3.6 Listen and write your answers in random order.

b Work in pairs and explain your answers to exercise 3a using a phrase with *worth*.

Task

Decide which project to back

▶InvestinUs.com

Whether your project is creative, entrepreneurial or to help the local community, get the financial backing you need to get your project off the ground. Advertise your project on our website, invite online supporters to pledge anything from $20 to $500 and get off to a flying start!

Pick of this week's projects

1 Help us put on our play!

The play we wrote together last year, Afterwards, is a fast-paced, original look at the aftermath of a family tragedy and has already won first prize in a national playwriting competition. Now we want to take it to the International Youth Theatre Festival. We are a group of 17–20-year-olds, and are acting, directing and producing the play ourselves. We are funding our own travel to the festival, but need to raise money for entrance fees, costumes, props, venue hire, printing tickets, etc. Support our creative collaboration and you will receive free tickets to the opening night!

amount needed: $1,250
percentage raised: 20%

2 A treehouse for everyone to share!

We have got planning permission to build an imaginative, multi-level treehouse in our local park for use by the whole community – a place for children to have adventures, for families to picnic – in fact, for anyone who is young at heart! When completed, the tree house will showcase our talents and enable us to set up the business we have always dreamed of … building amazing tree houses! Support us and you will receive a 20 percent discount on your first treehouse order, as well as the knowledge that you have brought a little fun and imagination into the lives of our community!

amount needed: $1,000
percentage raised: 10%

3 Give a positive message!

I am a graphics student who has designed a range of stylish posters with positive, motivational messages. Now I need to print and market them to art shops and galleries around the country. Invest in me and you will receive a free motivational poster – and you will help turn my dream into a reality! And even more important: 20 percent of my profits will be donated to the mental health charity 'Think Positive', which has supported my brother so brilliantly.

amount needed: $850
percentage raised: 7%

4 Super kitchen!

A year ago we set up a profit-sharing cooperative making homemade soups, stir-fries and stews from our own kitchens, to supply the cafés, offices and college canteens of our city. Using local ingredients, we have developed healthy recipes, which are delivered to our customers' doors by bicycle. Not only do we offer low-cost healthy food to local people, we also help to keep local producers in business. The problem is that we have been so successful that we can't keep up with demand! We need to rent a commercial kitchen and equip it with fridges, cookers, etc. in order to produce enough of our fabulous food to keep all our customers happy! Support us and you will receive free recipe cards for our ten most popular dishes!

amount needed: $6,000
percentage raised: 36%

5 Ballroom dancing for deprived kids

The Dancing Shoes project, bringing ballroom dancing lessons to children who could not otherwise afford it, has already been widely praised in the national media. Dancing together successfully builds maturity and fosters self-confidence, teamwork and mutual respect. We aim to start up classes this year in three secondary schools in our local area and need to pay teachers, rent premises and reach out to young people in the area. We ask you to give generously to bring a little fun and happiness to disadvantaged young people who often have very little joy in their lives.

amount needed: $3,000
percentage raised: 49%

Preparation Reading and vocabulary

1 Read the introduction of the website *InvestinUs.com*. What are its aims and how does it work?

2 Now read about the five projects on the website. Summarise what each person or group wants to raise money for and why.

3 Work in pairs and check the meaning of the words in bold in the questions below. Then discuss the projects.

Which one(s):
- are very **entrepreneurial**?
- have already received **favourable publicity**?
- cannot **keep up with demand**?
- are partly **self-funded**?
- need help with **marketing costs**?
- seem very **collaborative**?
- seem to be **environmentally friendly**?
- are probably **non-profit-making**?
- are **community-based**?
- seems the most **innovative**?
- is **quirky** rather than practical?
- is likely to be the most **commercially successful**?

4 What are the benefits, material and altruistic, of supporting each project?

Task Speaking

1 Your group has a total of $500 to support the projects on the *InvestinUs* website. Think about the questions below. Ask your teacher for any words/ phrases you need.

- Which projects do you think are most worth supporting and why?
- Which are not worth supporting and why?

> Useful language a

2 Work in groups. Compare your ideas and try to persuade the other students which projects are most deserving and why. Decide how to allocate your $500.

> Useful language a and b

3 Present your group's decision to the class, explaining reasons. How much sponsorship did each project gain? Which projects were most/least popular? Why?

> Useful language c

SHARE YOUR TASK

Imagine you are giving feedback to the people behind one of the projects about why you have/haven't decided to support them. Plan what you will say.

Practise speaking until you feel confident.

Film/Record yourself giving your feedback.

Share your film/recording with other students.

LANGUAGE LIVE

Speaking
Describing quantities

1 Which phrases in the box could replace the quantities in bold in the sentences?

a vast number of	a handful	a dash
a huge sum of money	a while	a pinch
a small percentage	dozens of	
an enormous portion	a small quantity	
a great deal of time	the overwhelming majority	

1 The company spends only **two percent** of its annual budget on research.
2 Galvin was arrested when the police discovered **ten grams** of an illegal drug in his luggage.
3 **Over 40 million** people in the USA still do not have access to the internet.
4 I'd like a black coffee with just **0.2 ml** of milk.
5 I can't believe anyone can be so greedy! He ate **a kilogram** of potatoes and still had dessert!
6 In total, **95 percent** of people are in favour of reforming the tax system.
7 They could afford such an enormous house because they won **$5 million** in the state lottery.
8 Just add **0.001 grams** of salt to help bring out the flavour of the dish.
9 The council has spent **more than two years** looking into ways of saving money.
10 We have received **72** enquiries about our product.
11 It was disappointing that only **five or six** people attended the meeting.
12 You must be tired. Sit down and rest for **ten minutes**.

2 Complete the sentences to make them true using phrases in exercise 1.

1 _____ people in my country speak English.
2 Learning to speak a foreign language fluently requires _____ .
3 It's possible to win _____ money by _____ .
4 There are _____ female politicians in my country.
5 To become president you need _____ .
6 The government wastes _____ money on _____ .
7 A vast number of road accidents are caused by _____ .
8 I always add a dash of _____ to _____ .
9 The overwhelming majority of people my age have no interest in _____ .
10 It usually takes a while for me to _____ in the morning.
11 I often eat an enormous portion of _____ when _____ .
12 _____ tastes better with a pinch of _____ .

Writing
Summarising statistics

1 Work in pairs and discuss. What expenses does the average teenager have now that he/she didn't have 40 years ago?

The £9,000-a-year teenager

Most people assume that the cost of living has risen [1]_____ for everyone over time. However, they are mistaken. For some it has risen much more [2]_____ than for others, with teenagers (or their long-suffering parents) experiencing the biggest [3]_____ . [4]_____ , the yearly cost of a British 17-year-old's lifestyle has [5]_____ from £750 to £9,000 a year over the last 40 years – and those are the inflation-adjusted figures. That's a twelvefold [6]_____ .

[7]_____ the biggest expenses are food, housekeeping and clothing, but it's the things which weren't available in 1975 which really add to today's cost. For example, 17-year-olds these days clock up £420 on average for their mobile phone. On top of that, they spend around £200 on digital music. That's more than [8]_____ the £60 teenagers spent a year on vinyl back in 1975. [9]_____ is spent on things like sweets and trips to the cinema, despite the fact that both have increased [10]_____ . They now average around £6.50 and £7 a week [11]_____ .

[12]_____ , some things are cheaper now, such as games consoles, which have fallen [13]_____ from £1,200 in 1975 to £300 now, and transport, which has dropped [14]_____ in price. As most parents know, however, a games console in 1975 was a luxury, while for many of today's teens, it's closer to being a necessity.

2a Read the article and complete each paragraph with the words/phrases below. You do not need to use one of the words/phrases in each set.

Paragraph 1 steadily, overall, rise, dramatically, in contrast, increase, gone up
Paragraph 2 respectively, double, significantly, triple, by far, much less
Paragraph 3 similarly, slightly, in contrast, sharply

b Read the article again and make a list of useful phrases for describing trends and statistics.

risen steadily, risen dramatically, the biggest increase, …

3 Does anything in the article surprise you? What do you think is the same/different in your country?

4a Complete the sentences with words/phrases from exercise 2. More than one answer may be possible.

1 It costs _____ to fly abroad than it used to. Book ahead and you can get some bargains.
2 The cost of living has risen _____ over the last few years. It's at least 50% higher than it used to be.
3 The average price of a house or a flat has increased by 20% and 15% _____ .
4 _____ , people are spending more on film and music downloads and less on DVDs and CDs.
5 The number of people cycling to work has risen substantially in recent years. _____ , the number of people driving has fallen.
6 Inflation has fallen _____ from 4.9 to 4.8.
7 _____ the most popular toy last Christmas was 'Robodoll'. Nothing else came close.
8 There's been a big _____ in the number of people going abroad for work.
9 It's crazy how the cost of basics like bread has _____ or even _____ since last year.

b Work in pairs. Which statements in exercise 4a are true now? Rewrite three others to make them true.

5 Look at the monthly spending habits of single men and single women in the ta[...] Guess the missing numbers.

	Single men	Single [women]
electronics	€15	€ _____
personal care	€21	€ _____
clothing	€ _____	€66
pets	€16	€23.5
food shopping	€ _____	€133.5
going out	€15	€14
eating out	€102	€ _____

*#5 - project ans.
↳ SS write paragraph in pairs*

6 Complete article A with one word in each gap. Then check your answers to exercise 5. What, approximately, is each missing number in the table?

7a Work in pairs and look at bar chart B. What information do you find most surprising? Can you explain the reasons behind the changes?

b Write an article using the information in the bar chart. Use the two articles in this lesson to help you.

A Single men **VS** single women: *the truth about spending*

Men spend more on electronic gadgets and women spend more on clothes and make-up, or so the stereotype goes. But is it really true? According to a new report into the spending habits of single people, the answer is ... *yes*. To be more precise, men spend 50 percent more [1] _____ women on electronic products while women spend almost twice as much [2] _____ men on what is called 'personal care'. Personal care doesn't include clothing, where men spend [3] _____ third less than women.

So far, so predictable, but less easy to explain are the statistics around pets. Although the majority [4] _____ single people don't have a pet, women, on average, still spend nearly half [5] _____ much as men.

So where are men and women similar? The report shows that they spend similar amounts [6] _____ food shopping, roughly [7] _____ fifth of their total budget, and on going out, which is [8] _____ much smaller proportion of their total spend.

There is one other stereotype that seems to be true – some of the time, at least. Men spend 30 percent more [9] _____ women on eating out, suggesting either that men pick up the bill for women sometimes or that they have much bigger appetites!

B

How spending has changed for the average American: 1949 vs the present day

(Figures refer to spending on each area as a percentage of total spending.)

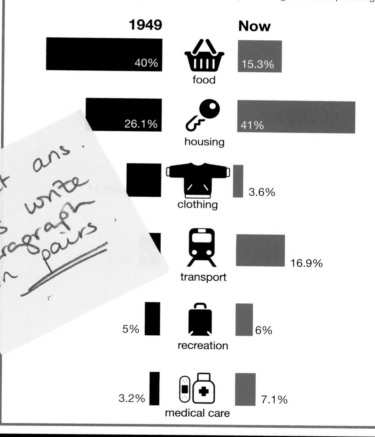

1949		Now
40%	food	15.3%
26.1%	housing	41%
	clothing	3.6%
	transport	16.9%
5%	recreation	6%
3.2%	medical care	7.1%

AFTER UNIT 3 YOU CAN ...

Discuss money and enterprise at a sophisticated level

Give emphasis in formal contexts using negative inversions

Discuss and persuade others of the merits of an idea

Describe quantities using everyday phrases

Summarise statistics in writing

04

SELF-HELP

Vocabulary and speaking
Self-improvement

1a Read the list of ideas for improving your life.

- taking up meditation
- getting counselling or therapy to deal with a personal problem
- training to run a marathon
- fasting or doing a radical detox programme
- doing voluntary work with the elderly, sick children, etc.
- taking up yoga or T'ai Chi
- taking up something artistic such as painting or creative writing
- having acupuncture to deal with a health problem
- having cosmetic surgery or laser treatment
- doing 'boot-camp style' fitness training
- becoming a vegetarian or vegan
- climbing a high mountain or taking up a high-risk sport
- giving up your job to work with poor people in a developing country
- going on a religious retreat
- joining a dating agency/website
- taking up a musical instrument
- having hypnotherapy to give up smoking, lose weight, etc.
- getting a massage

b Work in groups and discuss the questions.

- Which of these activities are popular in your country at the moment?
- Are any other forms of self-improvement popular?

3a 🎧 4.1 **Pronunciation** Listen to the words in the box. Focus on word stress, schwa sounds, silent letters, vowel/consonant sounds, etc. Then practise saying the words.

acupuncture	hypnotherapy	spirituality
counselling	laser	vegan
discipline	marathon	voluntary work
endurance		

b Listen again and check. How many did you say correctly? Practise saying the words you found difficult.

4a Read about three people who want to change their lives. Which activities in exercise 1 might help them? Can you think of any other suggestions?

Jasmine is in her early 30s and has a stressful, highly paid job. She often works late into the evenings and at weekends, then she can't sleep and ends up working even longer hours because she is being unproductive. She hardly has any time for a social life or relationship and often feels lonely.

Yara is a student in her second year at university, living away from home. She doesn't have many lectures and spends most of her time in her college room on her laptop, eating snacks. She is putting on weight, feels a bit depressed and is losing her confidence.

2a Read the comments and decide if they describe benefits (B) of self-improvement or doubts (D) about it. Which could be both?

1 It helps you to relax.   *B*
2 It doesn't work (for me).   *D*
3 It **improves your self-esteem**.
4 It **broadens your horizons**.
5 It helps you to **see a way forward**.
6 It **gives you a sense of perspective**.
7 It might **do more harm than good**.
8 It improves your **physical well-being**.
9 It improves your **mental well-being**.
10 The benefits are **purely psychological**.
11 The benefits are **superficial**.
12 It develops **self-discipline**.
13 It's very difficult to **keep it up**.
14 It makes you **believe in yourself**.
15 You might feel **overwhelmed**.
16 It develops your **spirituality**.
17 It makes some people very **uneasy**.
18 It makes you **think more about others**.
19 It **suits some people more than others**.
20 It pushes you and **tests your endurance**.

Ray had a busy career for 35 years, but now he has retired and, unfortunately, his wife died last year. His children have grown up and live far away. He feels lonely and depressed and does not know how to fill his time.

b Work in groups and compare your answers. Give reasons using phrases from exercise 2a.

> I think she should try something like hypnotherapy to help her to …

b Which activities in exercise 1 would you describe using the phrases in bold in exercise 2a? Work in pairs and compare your answers. Give reasons.

5 Work in new groups. Choose three activities from exercise 1 that you would be willing to try and three that you would not. Then explain why using phrases from exercise 2a and your own ideas.

Listening and vocabulary

Fitness

1 **Work in groups and discuss the questions.**

- Have you or any of your friends/family ever tried to get really fit?
- How did you/they go about it?
- What was your/their motivation?
- How successful were you/they?

2a **How are the people in the photos getting fit?**

b 🎧 **4.2 You are going to listen to Hannah (H), Ted (T) and Nicola (N) describing how they got fit. First, check the meaning of the words/phrases in bold below. Then listen and decide who:**

1 hired a **personal trainer**. *H*
2 had been **steadily putting on weight**.
3 ran a marathon.
4 needs to **tone up** his/her **muscles**.
5 uses a **fitness app**.
6 followed a **rigorous training programme**.
7 has worked out his/her **metabolic rate**.
8 uses his/her smartphone to check **nutritional information**.
9 was **motivated** by helping others.
10 has **manageable targets**.

3 **Work in pairs and discuss the questions below. Then listen again and check.**

1 What motivated each person to get fit?
2 How would you describe each person's level of motivation?
3 What aspect, positive or negative, of their training programme does each person mention?

4 **Work in groups and discuss. Whose training programme would suit you most/least, do you think? Why?**

PATTERNS TO NOTICE

Patterns with comparatives and superlatives

1 🎧 **4.3 Look at the patterns below and choose the correct answers. Then listen and check.**
   1 This is the *better / best* thing about the app.
   2 *More / The more* we talked about it, *more / the more* enthusiastic we got.
   3 There's nothing *worse / worst* than letting the other person down.

2 **Here are some other common patterns with comparatives and superlatives.**
   *Skipping is **one of the** quickest **ways of** getting your heart rate up.*

   *The older you get, **the less** energetic / **the more** unfit you get.*

   ***What could be more** satisfying **than** knowing that you have completed a marathon?*

   *Walking is **among the most** effective forms of exercise.*

How do you keep fit?

What are your top tips for getting fit?
Share them here – we'd love to hear
your suggestions!

■ **Carly**

Don't use being tired as an excuse. After a hard
day at work, do some exercise – ^{1}_____ more you
work out, the better you'll feel, instead of just
crashing on the sofa. ■

■ **Dan**

Try something new, like a sport. There's ^{2}_____
worse than doing exercise when you don't enjoy
it and the best ^{3}_____ about playing sport is that
you have fun and forget you're exercising! ■

■ **Connor**

Swimming is ^{4}_____ the most enjoyable types
of exercise you can do, and it builds everything
– strength, stamina and flexibility. Just make
sure you find a swimming pool that's heated! ■

■ **Nisha**

Don't give up! ^{5}_____ of the most common
reasons people don't get fit is because they quit
before they feel any of the benefits. Focus on
the future – what ^{6}_____ be better than knowing
you're healthy and getting fit? ■

■ **Chloe**

Don't overdo it, especially if you're just starting
out. The harder you work out at the start, the
^{7}_____ likely you are to get injured. And the
^{8}_____ thing about that is, you won't be able to
do any exercise! ■

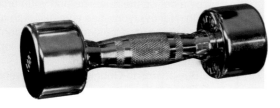

5a Complete the online forum entries with words from
the Patterns to notice box. Use one word in each gap.

b Work in pairs and discuss. Which tip do you
like most?

6 Write your own tip for the online forum using
structures from the Patterns to notice box.

Wordspot
Body idioms

1a Read the definitions in brackets and complete each
idiom with a part of the body.

1 be a _shoulder_ to cry on (= be a
sympathetic listener)
2 keep a straight _____ (= stop yourself
from laughing)
3 _____-raising (= very scary)
4 turn a blind _____ to something (= pretend not
to notice)
5 turn your _____ up at something (= treat
something with contempt)
6 _____-watering (= delicious, tasty)
7 up to your _____ in it (= totally overwhelmed
by work)
8 get your _____ round something (= understand
something difficult)
9 _____-rending (= extremely sad and moving)
10 have butterflies in your _____ (= feel very
nervous before you do something)
11 win _____ down (= win easily)
12 all fingers and _____ (= very, very clumsy)
13 pull someone's _____ (= make fun of somebody)
14 put your _____ in it (= say something that
upsets somebody)

b Which idioms do the cartoons illustrate?

2 Study the idioms in exercise 1a for a few minutes.
Which could relate to:

- food and drink?
- worry, sadness or nerves?
- embarrassing situations?
- humour?
- stressful situations?
- sport?

3 Work in pairs. Student A: Turn to page 107. Student
B: Turn to page 109. Take turns to ask and answer the
questions using body idioms.

Reading

1a How would you describe yourself now compared to when you were 15 years old?

> I'm more mature, but a bit less spontaneous.

b Work in pairs. Imagine you could go back in time and meet yourself as a younger person. What age would you go back to? What advice would you give yourself?

2a Read four letters from people to their younger selves and guess what job each person is doing now. How do you know?

b What else can you infer about each person? Compare your answers.

3 Read the letters again and match the statements below with the person who wrote about them in their letter. Underline evidence in the letters to support your answers.

1 It's good to think before you get angry.
2 Life gets easier as you get older.
3 In theory, it's easy to make money.
4 I had no time to play.
5 I took myself too seriously as a young person.
6 A good manager is kind to his or her workers.
7 Everything happens for a reason.
8 Someone important in my life died when I was young.
9 I didn't know how fortunate I was.
10 You don't need to follow all the rules all the time.
11 My writing wasn't as good as I thought it was.

4 Work in pairs and discuss the questions below.

1 Whose letter do you find most inspiring? Most humorous? The harshest?
2 Which letter is closest to the one you would write to your younger self?
3 Which of the four people would you most like to meet as their younger self? As an adult?

5a Work in pairs and check the meaning of the phrases in bold in the letters.

b Choose three of the phrases in the letters to give as advice to your younger self. Explain why you chose them.

6 Write your own letter to your younger self. Use your answers to exercises 1b and 5b to help you.

Dear Me...

...advice to my younger self.

Dearest Ria,

I am writing to tell you that you are beautiful and strong and deserve all the love in the world. You're only 15, but pretty soon everything is going to be turned upside down. The person that you hold dearest in life will be taken away from you. **Believe in yourself** and you will get through it. Try to remember that everything that is happening is just part of a much bigger picture and that somehow it will all make sense in the end. You're not really one for listening to advice, but here is some anyway: **treat everyone with respect** and demand it of them as well. Anyone can make a mistake once, but if someone lets you down twice, they're not your friend. There's more to life than you think, so try to **expand your horizons**. Most importantly, hold your mother tight and tell her you love her every day. She's right when she says you're too young to go out, so don't take it out on her. In fact, this little rule will help you a lot in life: **count to ten before you react**. I could tell you a lot more about your future and why it is that you love making your own clothes so much, but I think you've probably heard enough for now.
All my love,
Ria (aged 33)

Hey, Dude!
Greetings from the future you! First, a piece of heartfelt advice. **Lighten up!** I know you feel that no one really understands you right now and things can seem a bit dark at times, but the truth is that you're incredibly lucky to be born in the time and place that you are, **so make the most of it!** And PLEASE, PLEASE, PLEASE don't ever show your poetry to anyone! This may come as a shock to you, but it isn't much good and your future is not in this field. If you want a clue as to what you will be doing, then remember the time you found a cat which had been hit by a car on the roadside and you nursed it back to health. Not everyone has your skill with animals. And a word about your 'best friend' Mark: don't let him meet Sally or you'll regret it for a long, long time.
Adrian (aged 30)
PS Buy shares in Google when it's invented – that will help a lot!

Grammar review

Adjectives

1 Do the quiz. Add up your score, then work in pairs and compare your answers.

Adjectives quiz

1 Put the adjectives in brackets in the correct place in the sentences.

a You shouldn't feel if you do things for yourself sometimes. (selfish) **I point**

b Worry less about your appearance and you'll have a life. (great, personal) **2 points**

c Don't get if you don't always hear people say things about you. (upset, positive) **2 points**

d Don't always be rational – it's to listen to your voice. (inner, important) **2 points**

2 Choose the correct answers to complete the compound adjectives.

a It's a *well-knowing* / *well-known* fact that you're far too *easy-going* / *-gone*. **2 points**

b Pay attention to me, I'm a 50-*year-old* / *-years-old* version of you. **I point**

c Try not to get so stressed *up* / *out* when things don't go according to plan. **I point**

For two bonus points: think of two more adjectives formed from phrasal verbs (as in 2c).

3 Complete the sentences with adjectives formed from the nouns in brackets.

a You'd be more _____ (belief) if you told fewer lies. **I point**

b Don't be so _____ (drama) about everything. Things are never as bad as they first seem. **I point**

c Stay _____ (cheer) – you've got a lot to be happy about. **I point**

For two bonus points: think of two more adjectives which end in ways a–c.

4 Complete the adjectives with the correct prefixes. Look at the words in brackets to help you.

a Remember the time you were ___-confident (= too) and took a really big fall? **I point**

b You've been ___honest (= the opposite of) in the past, but it's never too late to change. **I point**

For four bonus points: think of four more prefixes which modify the meaning of adjectives and explain what they mean.

5 We use adverbs of degree (*very*, *really*, etc.) to change the meaning of adjectives. Choose the correct adverbs of degree.

a Sometimes your behaviour can be *very* / *completely* awful. **I point**

b It's *pretty* / *absolutely* hard being you sometimes. **I point**

c I know you're *a bit* / *not much* worried about your future, but you don't need to be. **I point**

For three bonus points: think of three more adverbs of degree which modify the meaning of adjectives.

Grammar extension bank, pages 124–127

Dear Jonah,

I'm 30 years older than you are right now, so I know a thing or two about life. Follow this advice and you'll do OK.

1 As your grandmother said, '**It's all right to fall, but don't stay down for too long**.'

2 As Mr Machionne said, 'Try to make everyone who works for you feel important.'

3 As your father said, 'Remember the 5 Ps: Planning and preparation prevent poor performance.'

4 As your future wife will say, '**Trust your instincts** and don't be afraid to think big.'

5 As your first boss said, 'Buy low, sell high. That's all you need to know to be a businessman.'

6 As Shakespeare said, 'Life is a tale told by an idiot, full of sound and fury, signifying nothing,' so enjoy it while it lasts!

Kind regards,

Jonah (aged 45)

Dear Jiao,

Right now your life is full of rules: do this, don't do that, say this, don't say that. You feel as though all you are doing is helping your parents and studying. Sweet Jiao, it will get better. You love to sing and act and you will get the chance. In fact, you will do it every day and people will pay you for doing it! There will still be rules, but you'll know when to break them. There will still be work, but you'll know when to rest. In fact, when it comesdown to it, only a few things matter. Respect your parents – they only want what's best for you. **Cherish the dead** – you're only here because of them. **Love yourself** – if you don't, who will? And finally, **follow your dreams** – they'll show you the way.

With love,

Jiao (aged 44)

Task

Decide who wins the award

Preparation Listening

1a Read about the Human Spirit award. What kind of achievements do you think it recognises?

b Work in groups. Look at the photos of the five finalists and the key words/phrases from their stories and guess why each person has been nominated.

2a 🎧 4.4 Listen to the stories and check.

b Work in pairs and discuss the questions below. Listen again if necessary.

- What is the background to each story?
- What exactly did the person do?
- Do we know why they did it or how they feel about it now?

Task Speaking

1a You are part of the panel which decides who wins the award. Make notes about the finalists' experiences and the ways in which they showed courage. Ask your teacher for any words/phrases you need.

  > Useful language a

b Put the finalists in order from 1 to 5 (1 = the person who most deserves the award). Make notes on the reasons you placed them in this order.

2a Work in groups and compare your arguments.

  > Useful language a and b

b Decide on the winner and the runner-up for the award.

3 Listen to the other groups' decisions. Are their arguments the same as yours? Have any of the arguments convinced you to change your mind?

HUMAN SPIRIT

is a popular TV series celebrating the exceptional mental, physical or moral courage of individuals in a wide range of situations. At the end of the series, the winner of the annual Human Spirit award is presented with a prize of $20,000 and there is a prize of $5,000 for the runner-up. These are the five finalists.

Camila Batmanghelidjh

- child psychologist
- drop-in centre
- underprivileged children
- care workers
- ex-gangsters

Jack Slater

- security guards
- attacked
- pinned to the ground
- CCTV footage

Follow up Writing

1 Write a short news article describing the awards ceremony. Use these guidelines to help you.

- Make the winner (and, to a lesser extent, the runner-up) the main focus of the article. Describe what he/she has achieved, why the panel chose him/her, and include some imaginary quotes from the delighted winner.
- Refer briefly to the other finalists and their achievements.
- Refer briefly to the TV programme and describe the atmosphere at the award ceremony.

> Useful language c

> Useful language c

USEFUL LANGUAGE

a Explaining your choice
He showed great courage/determination in the way he …
He could easily have (died).
She must have felt terrified about …
He sets a great example …
She is a positive role model for (young people).
He risked his life to …

b Comparing and expressing preferences
What particularly impresses me about … is (the fact that) …
Personally, I don't think he/she should have …
To me … stands out because …

c In your speech
We found it difficult to come to an agreement …
All the candidates' achievements were (impressive).
After a great deal of discussion, …
In the end we decided …
I am very proud to announce that the award goes to …

Lucy Gale
- collision
- level crossing
- steering wheel
- derailing
- prevented

Om Prakash
- burn injuries
- burning van
- a short circuit
- rescued

Martine Wright
- bomb attack
- coma
- rehabilitation
- Paralympic

SHARE YOUR TASK

Prepare a speech in which you announce the winner of the award.

Practise your speech until you feel confident.

Film/Record yourself giving your speech.

Share your film/recording with other students.

WORLD CULTURE

THREE MINUTES OF EXERCISE

Find out first

1a Work in pairs. Look at the health benefits listed below and say which you think are associated with exercise.

- lower cholesterol levels and blood pressure
- a reduced risk of heart disease
- a reduced risk of diabetes and cancer
- improved muscle tone
- a boost in self-esteem
- reduced stress
- a lower risk of depression and dementia
- improved mood
- weight loss
- a boost in energy levels
- better sleep patterns
- fewer colds
- an anti-ageing effect

b How many minutes of moderate-intensity aerobic exercise (e.g. walking or cycling) do you think the World Health Organisation recommends you should do each week?

2a Go online and check your answers to exercises 1a and 1b or ask your teacher.

b Work in pairs and discuss. Do you do the recommended amount of exercise? Why?/ Why not?

Search: proven health benefits of exercise / World Health Organisation recommended aerobic activity / exercise and blood pressure/heart disease, etc.

View

3a You are going to watch a video that suggests that we don't need to meet official exercise guidelines. Why do you think that might be the case?

b ▶ Watch the video and check your answers. Which summary of Professor Jamie Timmons' exercise regime is correct?

1 Three 20-second bursts of high-intensity exercise, once a week.
2 Three 20-second bursts of high intensity exercise, three times a week.
3 One 60-second burst of high-intensity exercise, three times a week.

4 Watch the video again and tick the three sentences that are true. Correct the false sentences.

1 The UK government recommends 75 minutes of moderate activity a week.
2 The three minute exercise regime involves three minutes of exercise three times a week.
3 Jogging activates less than half the muscle tissue of the three-minute exercise regime.
4 Professor Timmons advises buying equipment like running shoes.
5 Studies on the benefits of the three-minute exercise regime have been carried out in several countries.
6 Studies show that the three-minute exercise regime can bring all the benefits of three hours in the gym.
7 Michael Mosley finds the three-minute exercise regime surprisingly easy.

5 Do you think Professor Timmons exercise regime is a good replacement for official exercise guidelines? Would you try it? Why?/Why not?

World view

6a ▶ Watch George and Carol discussing the government's role in improving people's health. Who brings up the following topics?

fitness areas in parks	pregnant women
Saving public spending on health	Smoking
preventative medicine	trans fats

b What do they say about these things?

7a Watch again and decide if the following statements are true or false.

1 Carol worries about the government deciding how people should live their lives.
2 George thinks the government should stop people from smoking.
3 Carol seems to disagree with him at the beginning of the conversation.
4 She is concerned about products that people consume without realising.
5 George believes it is better to educate people to make decisions for themselves, rather than banning things.
6 Carol uses the example of fitness areas in parks to show that the government wastes money on public health.
7 They both agree that the government needs to target its spending carefully.
8 Carol thinks government spending on public health can save money in the long run.

b Work in pairs. Compare and explain your answers.

8 Discuss. Do you agree with the speakers? If you were the health minister, how would you improve your nation's health?

🛜 FIND OUT MORE

9a What do you know about the regimes or programmes below? What do you think each involves?

- The Paleo diet
- Bikram Yoga
- The 5:2 diet

b Choose one of these regimes and find out more about it. Prepare a short, informative presentation for your class covering the following points.

- how it works
- the benefits
- other interesting features
- what critics say

Search: Paleo diet / Bikram Yoga / 5:2 diet

Present your research

10 Give your presentation to the class. Use the prompts below to help you.

- I'd like you to imagine a diet/ regime where you ...
- To make matters worse, you are not allowed to ...
- That diet/ regime is called ...
- You might wonder why anyone would put themselves through this. Well, proponents argue that ...
- The supposed (health) benefits also include ...
- It's interesting to note that ...
- Critics claim that the regime ...
- To learn more you might want to check out ...

Tip
Involve your audience by asking them to imagine a situation related to the topic of your presentation.
I'd like you to imagine a daily routine where you get up at four in the morning and then, apart from a few breaks, spend 15 hours sitting doing nothing. How would you feel?

05

HOW YOU COME ACROSS

Speaking and vocabulary
Polite social behaviour

1   Read the text. Then work in groups and discuss the questions.

- What is Fowey Community School doing?
- What do you think of the idea?
- Do you know of anything similar in schools in your country?

> A Cornish school is giving teenage boys lessons in the art of etiquette. Something you might expect at an exclusive private school, perhaps, but Fowey Community School is a state comprehensive. Male pupils from the school have started a six-month course to learn key skills such as personal grooming, table manners and how to greet a lady. Female pupils at the school complain about the rudeness, bad language and personal hygiene of their male peers, but the boys are taking the lessons surprisingly seriously, spurred on, no doubt, by the hope that it might help create the right impression with girls. Their head teacher John Perry, however, has other motives. He believes that, along with good academic qualifications, it will also help them to impress future employers.

2   Write six things you were taught about good and bad manners by your parents/at school. Compare your list with other students'.

Is it the right thing to do?

- ? standing up when a boss, guest, etc. enters or leaves the room
- ? men opening doors for women and helping them to take off and put on their coats
- ? calling people you don't know very well by their first name
- ? dropping in at someone's house without being invited
- ? doing things on your phone when you are socialising with other people
- ? asking people how much they earn or how old they are
- ? a man paying for a woman's meal and drinks
- ? coughing, sniffing, sneezing or yawning without putting your hand over your mouth

- ? touching people when you talk to them, e.g. patting them on the back or putting your arm round them
- ? shouting, rowing or holding loud conversations in public places
- ? swearing or blaspheming in formal situations (such as a meeting)
- ? men whistling or shouting comments at women they find attractive
- ? couples kissing and cuddling in public
- ? arriving half an hour late to a social engagement (without a good reason)
- ? phoning people after ten o'clock in the evening

3a Check the meaning of the words/phrases in bold. Then underline three that can be used to describe polite behaviour.

- It's **disrespectful**.
- It **creates** a good **impression**.
- It's **inconsiderate**.
- It's **over the top**.
- It's a way of **showing respect** to older people.
- It might make other people feel **awkward**.
- It's **revolting**.
- It's **overly familiar**.
- It's considered **gentlemanly**.
- It's **sexist**.
- It's not **the done thing**.
- It's a real **turn-off**.
- It's **unhygienic**.
- It's **unprofessional**.
- It might seem **pushy**.
- It might be **offensive** to some people.
- It could be **misinterpreted**.
- It's completely **taboo**.

b Describe your ideas in exercise 2 using some of the words/phrases in bold in exercise 3a.

4a Social behaviour varies in different situations. Read the list above and decide:

- which of these is always/never acceptable.
- which depends on people's ages or the social context (e.g. at work, with friends, etc.).
- the right way to behave in these situations.

b Work in groups and compare your answers. Explain your opinions using phrases from exercise 3a.

5 🎧 5.1 Listen to five people talking about behaviour they find rude or unacceptable. Make notes about the questions.

1 What exactly is the behaviour that annoys them and why?
2 Do you agree with what they say? Why?/Why not?

6a You are going to give a short talk. Choose one of the topics below and spend a few minutes preparing your talk.

- the kind of rude behaviour that infuriates you
- the six most important things a child should be taught about manners
- good manners between men and women
- the social taboos in your country that a foreigner should know about

b Work in groups and give your talks. Explain your opinions, giving examples from your own experience.

Image

1 Miriam Glassman, one of New York's top image consultants, is standing in front of a rack of jackets in a designer clothes shop. 'Can you give me an idea of what you are looking for?' she asks Lucy, her client. 'Something hip and cool,' says Lucy, 'but it mustn't be too hip. I don't want to look like a fashion victim.' Glassman pulls some jackets from the rack and marches off to the changing room with Lucy, chatting about Prada and Hermès. Lucy is nine years old. Glassman, who charges $100 an hour, is not unique in working with such young clients. It is a growing trend and the reasons are obvious: we continually encourage our youth to be successful and success, as everyone knows, is partly down to having the right image. But when nine-year-olds hire image consultants, you have to wonder: could things have finally gone too far?

2 Some of the most image-obsessed people around are politicians. They know that everything about you – clothes, posture, voice and smile – influences what people think of you and hence has to be carefully managed. British Prime Minister Margaret Thatcher had to change her image before she could become electable – she was taught to speak in a less shrill voice and wear less frumpy clothes – and in the 1960 US presidential debate between Nixon and Kennedy, those listening on the radio believed that Nixon won, while those watching on TV believed Kennedy was the victor. The difference was that Kennedy was wearing make-up but Nixon wasn't, and the viewers were put off by his appearance. Even body fat can be important in this respect. A top-selling French magazine was widely criticised for removing President Sarkozy's 'love handles' in a photo of him paddling a boat. The magazine claimed it was unintentional, but suspicions remained that someone might have been trying to improve the president's image.

3 Of course, you need more than a Photoshop expert to ensure a good public image. Lady Gaga is said to have an entourage of up to 80 people who accompany her wherever she goes, mostly dedicated to looking after her tightly controlled image. Even fairly minor celebrities seek help from wardrobe and hair stylists, make-up artists, colour consultants, PR consultants and more just to manage their profile, and these professionals don't come cheap. Maria Moriati, stylist to some of Hollywood's A-listers, is said to be paid $10,000–20,000 a time to choose the clothes for a celebrity on a press tour. She will pack each outfit, label it and include detailed instructions on how to wear the clothes ('roll up the sleeves twice and undo the top button of the shirt'). But she doesn't expect any thanks – not from the men, at least. 'Male stars,' she says, 'won't admit that they have a stylist. It's not cool – a bit like women and Botox.'

4 It's not just celebrities who need an image boost every now and then. Whole cities, too, try to give themselves the marketing equivalent of a style makeover. They know that most of us don't have the time to think in detail about where we want to go on holiday and instead rely on a few simple preconceptions of what a place is like. Those preconceptions are easy to manipulate with an advertising campaign, a celebrity endorsement or a catchy slogan. Successful slogans include: 'New York: the city that never sleeps' and 'Malaysia: truly Asia'. But perhaps the marketing men needn't have bothered with 'Dannevirke: take a liking to a Viking' (for a New Zealand city founded by Scandinavians) or 'Keep Austin Weird' (for Austin, Texas)?

Reading and vocabulary

Image

1 Why is image important to politicians / celebrities / young people? In what ways do they try to manage their image?

2 Check the meaning of the words/phrases in bold. Then discuss the questions. Give reasons.

1 Would you rather hire an **image consultant**, a **make-up artist** or a **personal trainer**?
2 Would you rather pay for **Botox injections**, a **style makeover** or a **flattering portrait** of yourself?
3 Which would you least like to be seen as: someone who is **overdressed**, a **fashion victim** or someone having a **bad hair day**?
4 Would you rather be told you have good **posture**, **inner beauty** or **charisma**?

3 Read the article and match paragraphs 1–5 with headings a–f. You do not need to use one heading.

a The public faces of places
b Are we too obsessed with image?
c How image influences voters
d How to become an image consultant
e Can we change?
f Styling celebrities

4 Read the article again and decide which statements are true. Find evidence to support your answers.

Paragraph 1
a Glassman is successful in her field.
b Many young people hire image consultants.
c Image is the only thing that matters for success.

Paragraph 2
a Mrs Thatcher wouldn't have won the election if she hadn't changed her image.
b Nixon didn't look good without make-up.
c Everyone believed the magazine's explanation.

Paragraph 3
a Image is purely about good photos.
b Stylists, etc., can be expensive.
c Male Hollywood stars are proud of using stylists.

'Male stars,' she says, 'won't admit that they have a stylist. It's not cool – a bit like women and Botox.'

5 So, perhaps we should step back for a moment from our image obsession and focus on what is important? Ignore the gossip, ignore the hype, ignore the websites telling us to manage our online reputation and build our 'personal brand' and instead rely on facts rather than image to reach decisions. All very sensible, but is it realistic? How much research are we really going to do before deciding which celebrity we like or where to go on our next holiday? And going back to our image consultant, surely Glassman must have reservations about taking on clients as young as Lucy? Apparently not. 'I get so many calls from teens,' she says. 'School is a competitive place and image is important. Lucy is just taking control of hers.'

Paragraph 4
a Most people think carefully about where they go on holiday.
b Advertising can easily influence our holiday choices.
c Not all city slogans are effective.

Paragraph 5
a We need to worry less about image.
b Society's image obsession won't change any time soon.
c Glassman believes it's fine to work with young children like Lucy.

5 Work in groups and discuss the questions below.

1 Do you agree with Glassman that Lucy is 'just taking control' of her image or does what she is doing worry you?
2 How do you try to manage your image on your online profile, in your CV, etc.?
3 To what extent do you think success is about having the right image?

Grammar review
Modals and related verbs

1 Underline the modals in sentences 1–9 from the text. Match them with explanations a–j. One sentence has two modals.

1 Can you give me an idea of what you are looking for?
2 It mustn't be *too* hip. I don't want to look like a fashion victim.
3 Margaret Thatcher had to change her image before she could become electable.
4 Even body fat can be important.
5 Someone might have been trying to improve the president's image.
6 Male stars won't admit that they have a stylist.
7 Perhaps the marketing men needn't have bothered.
8 We should step back from our image obsession and focus on what is important.
9 Surely Glassman must have reservations about taking on clients as young as Lucy?

a the right/best thing to do
b an obligation coming from the speaker
c an obligation coming from circumstances outside the speaker's control
d a general theoretical possibility
e a possibility about the past
f a logical deduction
g (un)willingness
h a request
i ability
j something that wasn't necessary

2 Choose the correct answers to complete the rules.

1 Modals generally describe a *speaker's opinion / facts*.
2 Modal questions and negatives are generally *regular / irregular*.
3 Modals generally have *regular / irregular* past forms.

3 Explain the meaning of the verbs in bold in each pair of sentences using explanations a–j in exercise 1. What is the difference between the two verbs in each pair?

1 a **Can** you give me some advice about what to wear?
  b **Would** you thank Alison for the kind invitation?
  Both are requests; 'would' is more formal than 'can'.
2 a You **must be** John's niece – it's a pleasure to meet you.
  b You **can't be** Karina's mother, surely? You're far too young!
3 a Even in unexpected situations, Jon **could** stay calm.
  b Many people protested, but the minister **managed to** win the audience round.
4 a We **didn't need to wear** formal clothes – we just dressed casually.
  b Looking at other people, we realised we **needn't have dressed** so formally.
5 a You **shouldn't** worry about what you look like. How you behave is more important.
  b I don't think you **ought to** be late again – the boss is getting a bit fed up about it.
6 a Many people **won't admit** they've had plastic surgery.
  b She **wouldn't accept** that she was in the wrong.

> **Grammar extension bank, pages 128–131**

Listening and vocabulary
Communication

1 Read the statistics. Are you surprised? Why do you think so many people want to improve their communication skills?

> When asked in a survey, 60 percent of people said that they would like to improve their communication skills, 80 percent said that they had been shy at some point in their lives and 25 percent described themselves as chronically shy.

2 Read the list of situations oppposite. Choose three where you think you would feel shy or nervous and two where you think you would be confident. Then work in pairs and compare your answers.

3a Tick the activities below which are good ways to behave, cross the ones which are not good ways to behave and write a question mark if you are not sure or it depends.

- ○ circulate and make small talk
- ○ gabble nervously about whatever comes into your head
- ○ dry up because you can't think of anything to say
- ○ ask questions and make the other people feel at ease
- ○ make eye contact
- ○ crack lots of jokes
- ○ pause from time to time
- ○ talk over other people and dominate the conversation
- ○ become over-apologetic
- ○ giggle nervously
- ○ act cool and nonchalant
- ○ stumble over your words
- ○ listen carefully
- ○ get emotional
- ○ look stiff and uncomfortable
- ○ blush, shake or sweat

b Work in pairs and compare your answers. Use the phrases in exercise 3a to say:
- how you *would* behave in the situations in exercise 2.
- how you think you *should* behave in these situations.

How confident are you?

Do you sail through tricky social situations, or do you cower in a corner? How do you feel in these situations?

- ◎ socialising at a party where you only know one or two people
- ◎ suggesting a social arrangement (e.g. a drink) to a new acquaintance or colleague
- ◎ meeting your boyfriend or girlfriend's parents for the first time
- ◎ asking a friend or colleague to do you a big favour

- ◎ talking to someone you fancy for the first time
- ◎ talking about a subject you don't know much about
- ◎ socialising for the evening with a group of people you feel are senior to you (senior colleagues, your parents' friends, etc.)
- ◎ giving a ten-minute presentation to a group of 15 or 20 people
- ◎ making a light-hearted speech at a wedding or a party
- ◎ making a complaint (e.g. in a restaurant or shop)
- ◎ calling someone you should have called ages ago

4 🎧 **5.2** Listen to a radio interview with Rosemary Bailey, who coaches people in communication skills, and answer the questions below.

1 Which situations in exercise 2 does she refer to?
2 What tips does she give for the best way to behave in these situations?

5 Work in pairs. Which of the statements do you agree with? Can you remember what Rosemary said? Listen again if necessary.

1 People communicate less effectively with people they perceive as being very different from themselves.
2 In social situations, the more questions you ask, the better.
3 You should never pause during conversations with people you don't know very well.
4 You shouldn't look people in the eye for too long or you may give the wrong message.
5 When complaining, don't be distracted by listening too closely to what the other person is saying.
6 It's very useful if you summarise the other person's point of view at the end of your complaint.
7 Everyone naturally has good communication skills.

PATTERNS TO NOTICE

Patterns with abstract nouns and relative clauses

1 **In complex sentences, an abstract noun is often followed by a relative clause.**
People have problems communicating in **situations where** *they're unsure of who they're talking to.*

A lot depends on **the way in which/that** *you say it.*

2 **Notice how different nouns collocate with different relative pronouns.**
the part/place where …
a time when …
a period/the way in which …

Complete the sentences with the relative pronouns in the box.

which (x2)   why (x2)   where (x3)

1 There are many **reasons** _____ communication skills are important.
2 We have seen several **cases** _____ people have started arguing.
3 It is easy to reach **the point** _____ you become over-emotional.
4 There's **no reason** _____ you should feel uncomfortable.
5 We are going through **a period in** _____ communication is difficult.
6 No one is sure of **the extent to** _____ this will affect our business.
7 A key step to clear communication is **the part** _____ you summarise what the other person says.

---

6 Join the sentences using phrases from the Patterns to notice box. Begin with the words in bold. Make any changes necessary.

1 Make other people feel important. **Many** experts say that charm depends on how much you do this.
Many experts say that charm depends on the extent to which you make other people feel important.

2 Nervous people forget to smile. **There** are various reasons for this.
3 People talk too much because they are nervous. **I** have seen many situations like this.
4 Two people remember different things from the same conversation. **It** is quite common to come across cases like this.
5 People dread long conversations with senior colleagues at parties. **There** are a large number of reasons for this.
6 Everyone can calm down after an argument. **It** is essential to have a time like this.
7 How you stand or sit while you are talking is important. **People** often judge you unconsciously by this.
8 How people complain is important. **Many** people respond negatively to this.

7a Write an example from your own experience for each of the following.

- a period in your life when you wish you'd been more confident
- a reason why you've blushed in the past
- the way in which you start a conversation with someone you've just met
- the extent to which you feel confident communicating in English
- a situation where you've giggled inappropriately
- a case where someone you know was involved in a misunderstanding

b Work in pairs. Read your examples to your partner in random order. Your partner tries to guess which item from the list they relate to.

> Changing schools at the age of 14.

> Is that a period in your life when you wish you'd been more confident ?

Task

Deal with a problem tactfully

The flatmate from hell

Monica's parents are very protective and had always refused to allow her to attend university in a city 100 km away. However, when her aunt and uncle bought a flat there for her cousin Julia, they agreed to let her go, if she lived with Julia. Monica knew Julia was a bit spoilt, but they had always got on fine and Monica was happy to share with her. However, she has seen another side of her cousin since they started living together. Julia never invites Monica to join in when she has friends round and is selfish in all sorts of small ways.

She switches the TV over when Monica is watching something, plays music late at night when she knows Monica has early lectures next day and uses Monica's clothes, make-up and food without asking. She acts as if Monica owes her something, even though Monica's father is paying rent. Monica likes college, but living with Julia is spoiling everything and she feels she needs to speak to someone. But who? Her aunt and uncle can see no wrong in their daughter and she's afraid that her parents might make her go home. She's dropped hints to Julia, but Julia hasn't responded. She's been asking friends' advice.

He's dropped out and depressed

Eight months ago Richard, aged 22, failed his exams and dropped out of university. He got a job for three months, but was sacked for being unreliable. Since then he seems to have fallen into a deep depression – he refuses to look for a job or go back to college and hardly goes out. He's a very intelligent but highly sensitive young man and tends to fly off the handle if he feels he's being criticised. His father is losing patience rapidly and his mother is at her wits' end. You've known the family for years and are close to Richard. A few days ago his mother phoned you in tears, begging you to talk to him before his father does something terrible like throw him out of the house. You feel you must help and have asked friends for suggestions.

Preparation Reading and vocabulary

1 Imagine you have a difficult personal problem. Tick the things that are helpful. Give reasons.

Things you do	Things your friends/family do
• **talk** the problem **over** with friends • **get emotional** • **close up** and refuse to discuss it • start **resenting** people who try to help • **get defensive** • tell friends to **mind their own business** • **pull yourself together**	• try to be **supportive** • start **criticising** you • make you face facts • **drop hints** about what you should do • make **patronising comments** • **lose** their **patience** • make **tactful** suggestions

2 Work in pairs. Read about three difficult situations and summarise the problem in each case.

Task Speaking

1a Work in groups and choose one of the three difficult situations to discuss.

b First work alone. Make a list of all the options you can think of for handling the problem you chose. For each one, decide why it is (not) a good idea. Ask your teacher for any words/phrases you need.

> Useful language a and b

2 Work in groups and compare your lists. Discuss the questions below.

1 What are all the options for tackling the problem?
2 What would be the worst thing you could do, in your opinion?
3 What else should you avoid?
4 What is the best thing to do? (It could be a combination of ideas.)

> Useful language a and b

Her dream job is a nightmare

A year ago, your sister Anna, aged 25, landed her dream job in a publishing company and everyone was delighted. But after a few months she got involved in an on-off relationship with the boss, Paul, aged 41. She is besotted with him, and sometimes he is very attentive to her, but at other times he treats her as if she doesn't exist. He is also getting her to do a lot of extra work without paying her and constantly hinting at promotion which never happens. She knows other people in the office are talking and laughing about her behind her back and no longer feels comfortable there. Anna used to be a bright, fun-loving girl and sometimes still is, but at other times she looks washed-out and seems to have lost her confidence. Your parents are very worried about her and can't imagine what has gone wrong, but she has made you swear not to tell anyone about Paul. So far you have not broken her confidence, but you feel that you have to do something and have asked friends for advice.

3 Present your conclusions to the class. If you cannot agree, explain why and find out what the class think.

Follow up Writing

1 Choose one of the tasks below.

a Imagine one of the people above has written to an online advice website asking other people's opinions about the best way to behave. Write a posting giving your opinion.

b Work in pairs. Write a script for a scene in which you discuss one of the problems with the person involved. Does it go as you planned or does it all go wrong? How does it end up? Act out your scene for the class.

> Useful language c

LANGUAGE LIVE

Writing
Asking people to do things

1a Read three emails asking people to do something. What is the relationship between each sender and recipient?

b Work in pairs and choose the two phrases that can be used to complete each gap. Why is the other phrase inappropriate?

1 a I just wanted to ask you a quick favour.
    b I am writing to request your help.
    c Could you help me out?
2 a We would be very grateful if you would lend us
    b Would you mind lending us
    c Could we possibly borrow
3 a I can
    b I'm happy to
    c I would, of course, be willing to
4 a asap
    b as soon as possible
    c at the earliest opportunity
5 a You must
    b Could I remind you to
    c Could everyone please remember to
6 a As you know
    b As you are no doubt aware
    c As you can see
7 a if you haven't already done so
    b for the last time
    c at the risk of repeating myself
8 a Cheers
    b Many thanks
    c Kind regards
9 a I'd like you to help me because
    b Please excuse this unsolicited email, but
    c I hope you don't mind me getting in touch with you, but
10 a if you are up for it
    b if you are willing to take part
    c if you can help

2 Read the strategies for asking people to do things. Which are most effective?

1 Say *please* and *thank you*.
2 Explain why you are asking for the favour.
3 Say that you know it's a favour.
4 Pay the recipient a compliment.
5 Make sure that what you're asking for is reasonable.
6 Keep the email short and to the point.
7 Offer to do something in return.

A
Hi Nat,
Hope you and Lilliana are well! ^{1}___ We've got some guests coming to stay (Roberto's sister-in-law and her three children) and we just don't have enough bedding. ^{2}___ some sheets, pillows and duvets and a blow-up mattress if you have one? ^{3}___ pick them up whenever suits. Could you let me know ^{4}___ because they're arriving on Thursday (argh!)?
Cheers,
Ella

B
Dear all,
^{5}___ sign the leaving card for Anthony. ^{6}___ , his last day is Friday and we'll be having cakes around his desk at four o'clock. Also, ^{7}___ , could I remind you to contribute to his leaving present? The collection envelope is on Ruth's desk and she'll be buying a present on Thursday. Lastly, could you let me know if you'll be coming for a celebratory drink after work on Friday.
^{8}___ ,
Orlando Hobbs (Office Manager)

C
Dear Mrs Benteke,
^{9}___ a friend of mine gave me your email address. My name is Asha Dey and I am currently doing a degree in Marketing and Communication at the University of Portdown. I am looking for people such as yourself who are highly experienced in the field of PR to help me in my research. I realise that you are very busy, but I would be very grateful if you would agree to complete a short email questionnaire for me. It should take no more than 15 minutes and all answers are completely anonymous. Please let me know at the earliest opportunity ^{10}___ .
Kind regards,
Asha Dey

3 Which strategies from exercise 2 does each email use? Underline any other useful phrases in the emails.

4 Work in groups of three. Choose a different email each and write a brief reply. Then read your replies to the group. How well does each reply copy the level of formality/informality of the email?

5 Write an email for one of the following situations.

- You work for a small company. Write an email to your colleagues reminding them to inform you as soon as possible of their holiday plans.
- You are organising a charity auction to support a local hospital. Write an email to a local business owner (decide on the name/business type) asking him/her to contribute something for the auction.
- You have arranged an evening out with some friends (decide the day/time), but you have realised that you won't be able to make it. Write a group email to your friends asking if the evening out can be rescheduled and suggesting another day/time.

6a Work in pairs and swap your emails. Check your partner's work and comment on the use of phrases/ strategies from exercises 1 and 2.

b Write a second draft of your email, taking your partner's feedback into account.

Speaking
Getting people to do things

1 🎧 5.3 Look at the pictures of four situations in which one person wants another person to do something. Try to guess the situations. Then listen and check.

2a Which phrases in the box below are used for:
1 interrupting someone?
2 asking for help/persuading?
3 refusing to do something?
4 asking someone to wait?
5 agreeing to do something?

Are you in the middle of ... ?	Sorry to disturb you.
If you say so.	We would very much
I'll be right with you.	appreciate it.
I don't see why I should.	I must ask you not to ...
Can I ask a really, really big favour?	
Oh, all right then.	
Oh, go on.	
I wonder if you might be able to help.	
If you'll just bear with me for a minute.	
I'd be really grateful.	
Shall I come back later?	

b 🎧 5.4 **Pronunciation** Listen to the phrases from exercise 2a. Pay attention to the intonation. Then practise saying the phrases.

3a Describe the attitude of each speaker in exercise 1 using the adjectives in the box.

cooperative	annoyed	fairly polite	reluctant
extremely polite	casual	uncooperative	

b Look at audio script 5.3 on page 168 and underline the phrases that show the speakers' attitudes.

4 Work in pairs and prepare a short conversation (15–20 lines). Use the questions below to help you. Then act out your conversation for the class.

1 Who are the two people involved? (friends, relatives, colleagues, strangers, other)
2 Where are they? (at home, at work, travelling, in a public place (e.g. a café, a library), other)
3 What does Speaker A want Speaker B to do? (lend him/her something, help him/her to do something, stop doing something, run an errand for him/he)
4 What is Speaker A's attitude? (extremely polite, fairly polite, casual, other)
5 What is Speaker B's attitude? (cooperative/helpful, uncooperative/unhelpful, annoyed/reluctant)

AFTER UNIT 5 YOU CAN ...

Describe and discuss polite, tactful or inappropriate social behaviour at a sophisticated level

Describe and discuss image and communication skills

Ask people to do things in emails using appropriate levels of formality

Use a sophisticated range of conversational phrases to make requests

06

LIVE AND LEARN

IN THIS UNIT

- Grammar: Use and non-use of the passive; Particles which modify meaning
- Vocabulary: Education; Learning
- Task: Teach a practical skill
- World culture: Teaching happiness

Vocabulary and speaking
Education

1 Work in groups. Write the alphabet on a piece of paper and write at least one word connected with education next to each letter. You have two minutes.

2a Compare your answers with the quiz. How many of the same words did you get? Then complete the quiz with the missing words.

 b Turn to page 107 and check your answers. Check the meaning of any words in the quiz that you are not sure about.

The A – Z of learning

A is for **assessment, assignments,** [1]_academics_ (a collective word for people who teach and work in universities, i.e. lecturers and researchers).

B is for **biology, break time,** [2]_____ (an adjective to describe someone who is very clever academically).

C is for **coursework, curriculum,** [3]_____ (an adjective to describe education or subjects that you have to do).

D is for **degree, discipline, doctorate.**

E is for **entrance exam, exam results,** [4]_____ **school** (the American equivalent of 'primary school' in the UK).

F is for **faculty, fees, finals.**

G is for **grade, graduate,** [5]_____ **ceremony** (the special occasion when students formally receive their degrees from their university).

H is for **high school, higher education, history.**

I is for **infant school, intellectual, IQ.**

J is for **junior school, junior high school, junior lecturer.**

K is for [6]_____ (a German word used in English and meaning the same as 'nursery school').

L is for **laboratory, lecture, library.**

M is for **marks, mature student,** [7]_____ **degree** (a post-graduate qualification).

N is for **note-taking, numeracy, nursery school.**

O is for [8]_____ **exam** (a type of exam where you speak rather than write).

P is for **private school, professor,** [9]_____ (a student who has already obtained his or her first university degree).

Q is for [10]_____ (what you need to get a skilled job).

R is for **retakes, revision, rote learning.**

S is for **seminar, state school,** [11]_____ (a place at a school or university for gifted students, often with money attached).

T is for **thesis, truancy,** [12]_____ (the daily schedule of lessons at school or university).

U is for [13]_____ (a person studying for their first degree).

V is for [14]_____ **course** (a course that prepares you for a particular job).

W is for **work experience, workload,** [15]_____ (an interactive class which focuses on practical skills, e.g. in drama or art).

X is what you get for a wrong answer!

Y is for **Yale, yearbook.**

Z is for **zero tolerance, zoology.**

3 Read the statements below. Tick the ones that are true in your country, cross the ones that are not true. Write a question mark if you are not sure.

1 Full-time education is compulsory until the age of 18.
2 Class sizes in schools and universities are very large.
3 Students do a huge number of exams, retakes, etc.
4 You can do vocational courses as well as study academic subjects in all secondary schools.
5 Very few people choose to send their children to private schools.
6 A lot of qualifications are assessed partly by coursework.
7 Academics tend to be badly paid.
8 All children receive free nursery education.
9 Children start school too early/late.
10 Truancy and discipline are big problems in many schools.
11 University fees are very high.
12 Many people go abroad to do postgraduate courses.

4 Work in pairs and compare your answers.

5 🎧 6.1 Listen to four people talking about some of the statements in exercise 3. Which ones do they mention? What opinions do they give?

6 Work in pairs and discuss at least two statements from exercise 3. Ask questions to find out your partner's opinions.

> Do you think class sizes in universities should be reduced?

> What do you think should be done about truancy in schools?

Sorry to say this, but ...you're very smart!

How often have you said to a child, 'You're so smart!' or 'You're really good at drawing/music/running, etc.'? It is generally believed that praising children helps build their self-esteem. Believe it or not, however, you may actually be doing more harm than good when you say these things. The reason is simple: dozens of studies have shown that high achievers, whether in music, art, chess or whatever, learn at the same speed as everyone else. The only difference is that they spend more time with their nose to the grindstone, practising. To put it another way, they put in more effort. And while it is true that some children start out with more 'natural ability' than others, in the long run this natural ability is just not very important.

To prove this hypothesis, psychologist Carol Dweck divided 400 students into two groups and gave each the same simple puzzle to do. Afterwards, the first group were praised for their ability and told, 'Wow! You must be really smart!' while the second group were praised for their effort and told, 'Wow! You must be hard-working!' Following this, all students were allowed to choose which follow-up test to take: easy or hard. Only one third of the first group chose the hard test – they feared shattering the illusion of natural ability. But 90 percent of the second group, who had been praised for effort, chose the hard test. They wanted to prove that they did indeed put in more effort. In the follow-up test results, the first 'smart' group showed a 20 percent decline in performance, while the second 'effort' group showed a 30 percent rise. And all this based on six simple words of praise!

How to shrink your brain

Most people instinctively know that stress is bad for you, but just how bad is only now being properly tested. New research suggests that severe stress can actually cause the brain to shrink and result in problems dealing with difficult situations in the future. In the research, over 100 healthy volunteers aged 18 to 48 were given a brain scan to measure the amount of grey matter in their brain (grey matter is the outer part of the brain). Those who reported having gone through traumatic and stressful events in life, such as divorce, death or loss of their home due to natural disaster, were found to have lower amounts of grey matter in parts of the brain responsible for emotions, self-control and blood pressure.

According to Rajita Sinha, a professor of psychiatry at Yale University, 'The brain is dynamic and plastic and things can improve, but only if stress is dealt with in a healthy manner. If not, the effects of stress can have a negative impact on both our physical and mental health.' Previous research has shown that smoking and neglect in childhood can also cause changes in the levels of grey matter in the brain.

Who's the bird brain now?

Most parents would be pretty confident in saying their child was more intelligent than a bird. According to recent research, however, they may be wrong. A study conducted at Cambridge University pitted birds called Eurasian jays against children in a series of problem-solving tests. The tests, inspired by one of Aesop's fables, involved dropping stones or corks into a tube in order to raise the water level and claim a prize. From the age of eight upwards, children learned more quickly than birds that stones, which sink, work better than corks, which float. Before the age of eight, however, the children were no quicker than the birds.

One test, however, did prove that children at least think differently from birds. The researchers built a special tube with a hidden connection to a second one. When a stone was dropped into the first tube, it raised the water level in the other one where the prize was. It didn't make sense, but the children didn't worry too much and were able to claim the prize. The birds, however, just couldn't get the hang of it and failed, proving, researchers say, that birds are hampered by their expectations, while human children are better at putting their expectations aside.

Reading and Vocabulary
Learning

1 Read the statements and decide whether they are facts (F) or myths (M). Then work in groups and compare your answers.

1 We all have the potential to be a genius.
2 Stress is bad for the brain.
3 The more you praise a child, the better.
4 Humans are always more intelligent than animals.
5 Schooldays are the happiest days of our lives.

2 Read the articles and match one statement from exercise 1 with each article. Is the statement a correct summary of each article?

3 Read the articles again and decide which statements below are true.

Article A
a To become a high achiever, you always need natural ability.
b Low achievers learn at the same speed as high achievers.
c Praising effort leads to improved performance.

Article B
a All of the volunteers had experienced trauma.
b All the grey matter in the brain was affected.
c Stress doesn't always have a negative effect on the brain.

Article C
a The study used different kinds of birds.
b Children aged eight and older are definitely smarter than birds.
c Birds rely on their expectations of what will happen.

4 Work in pairs. Student A: Turn to page 106. Student B: Turn to page 108. Read the article and answer the questions.

5a Close your books and summarise your article to your partner.

b Now read your partner's article and look at the questions. Did your partner summarise it accurately?

6 Work in groups and discuss the questions.

• Which research did you find most surprising? Has any of it changed your opinions or future actions?
• Do you think any of the findings may be dubious?
• Do you think schoolchildren these days have a tough time? Why?/Why not?

Grammar review
Use and non-use of the passive

1a Choose the correct answers.

1 *It generally believes / It is generally believed* that praising children helps build their self-esteem.
2 Afterwards, the first group *are / were* praised for their ability ... (then) all students were *allow / allowed* to choose which follow-up test to take: easy or hard.
3 ... is only now *being / been* properly tested.
4 Those who reported having *gone / been gone* through traumatic events in life ...
5 A study *conducted / was conducted* at Cambridge University pitted birds against children.
6 When a stone *dropped / was dropped* into the first tube, it raised the water level in the other one.
7 ... proving ... that birds are hampered *with / by* their expectations.
8 These disorders are known *being / to be* caused by children internalising their anxiety.
9 This could *be / to be* caused by parents being away from their children ... or by children *being / are being* stressed at school.
10 Rather than *getting / being* their children assessed by a professional, ...

b Find the sentences in the articles here and on page 108 and check your answers. Which sentences contain non-passive forms? Are there any sentences where you are not sure?

2a In the sentences in exercise 1a, find examples of:

a past and present passive forms.
b a continuous passive form.
c a modal passive.
d a passive infinitive.
e a reduced passive where only the past participle is used.
f a passive where the auxiliary verb is not *be*.

b Read some reasons why the passive is often used. Find examples in exercise 1a to illustrate them. More than one reason may be true for each example.
a The subject of the verb is unimportant, obvious or unknown.
b To keep the focus on the object of the verb.
c The passive is part of the formal/journalistic style.
d The passive verb is part of a set phrase.

3a Complete the sentences in at least two ways using the passive form of the verbs in brackets.

1 Schoolchildren should/shouldn't ... (allow)
2 In my country, ... (generally / believe) that children/parents should ...
3 Most children nowadays ... (expect)

b Work in pairs and compare your sentences. Ask questions about your partner's sentences.

> **Grammar extension bank, pages 132–135**

> *Discipline was strict – there were loads of rules.*

> *My education helped to make me self-motivated and able to learn things for myself. The whole experience made me and a lot of other people feel rather aimless.*

> *It made you very mature and adult.*

> *The approach was very traditional; lots of rote learning and tests.*

> *My education was very well rounded and gave me a broad outlook on life.*

> *It was really fun, creative and motivating.*

> *I think my education really helped to make me focused and hard-working.*

> *Bullying was a real problem at my school.*

> *We didn't learn that much that was useful in real life.*

Listening and speaking

1a Read the people's comments about their different experiences of education.

b Work in pairs. Discuss the questions below.
- Which comments are positive, which are negative and which might be either?
- Which are true of your own education and which are not? Why?

2 Look at the photos of four people whose education was unusual in some way. Which comments in exercise 1a could relate to their education? Why?

3a 🎧 6.2 Listen to the first two speakers, Gina and Steve, and make notes about the questions below.

   1 What was their education like and in what ways was it unusual?
   2 What were the good and bad aspects mentioned?

b 🎧 6.3 Now listen to Eva and Lester and complete your notes.

c Work in pairs and compare your answers for all four speakers.

4 Work in groups and discuss the questions below.
- Which ideas in exercise 1a did the speakers express?
- Were you surprised by anything they said?
- Whose education would you most/least like to have experienced? Why?

Gina attended stage school until the age of 14.

Steve went to boarding school from the age of eight.

Eva went to a French–American bilingual school.

Lester was educated at home by his parents.

PATTERNS TO NOTICE

Particles which modify the meaning of verbs

1a Particles can add to the basic meaning of a verb without fundamentally changing what it means. Read the sentences below. What idea do the particles in bold add?

That about sums it up.

*I look **back** on my schooldays fondly.*

b Check your answers in section 2.

2a There are patterns in the way these particles are used. Here are some more examples.

around = pointless activity	*messing around, hanging around*
away = intently/for a long time	*chatting away, working away, typing away*
back = to the past	*think back, check back*
down (1) = becoming less	*slow down, calm down, die down*
down (2) = onto paper	*write down, take down, note down*
on = continue	*work on, carry on, drive on*
out (1) = to different people	*hand out, share out, send out*
out (2) = loudly/publicly	*speak out, shout out, call out*
up = complete or finish	*lock up, drink/eat up, tidy up*

b Particles like these can also be used simply to emphasise or clarify the direction in which someone or something moves.

around = in the vicinity	*drive/walk/stand around*
away = far from	*move away, run away*
back = from where it came	*come/go back, put/hand back*
in/out	*lift/put/carry something in/out, etc.*
off = to another place	*drive/walk/run/saunter/rush off*
up/down	*climb up/down a ladder*

5 Look at the pairs of sentences below. Sentence a shows the normal meaning of each verb. How does the particle in b modify the meaning?

1 a There was already someone **sitting** outside the door when I got to the classroom.
b We spent the whole day **sitting around** at home, watching old films.
2 a Do you know if it's legal for schools to **copy** YouTube clips?
b The teacher wrote the answers on the blackboard, and we all **copied** them **down**.
3 a My brother came to **see** me at the airport.
b My brother came to **see** me **off** at the airport.
4 a Lopez can't **play** in Sunday's match.
b After receiving treatment from the physiotherapist, Lopez was able to **play on**.
5 a Have you **read** any of Shakespeare's plays?
b The teacher chose Jane to **read out** Hamlet's speech.
6 a Did the teacher **give** you any homework?
b The teacher **gave out** the exam papers.
7 a We **used** grey paint for the bathroom ceiling.
b We've already **used up** the paint you bought the other day.
8 a People in this city are always **rushing** everywhere.
b Jan **rushed off** before I could tell her the news.

6 Add a particle to the appropriate verb to complete the sentences.

At first, you might find the book a bit slow, but if you read ^ *on* there's a lot more action.

1 It wasn't a serious accident, but we took each other's name and address.
2 I don't know why he was so upset – he just went without saying a word.
3 Helen hasn't given me my book. I'm not going to lend anything to her again.
4 I don't see why we shouldn't complain. I really think it's time someone spoke.
5 Didn't your mother ever tell you to eat your vegetables?

7a Complete the questions with a verb and particle that have the meaning in brackets.

1 What is something you always have to _____ _____ (put on paper) in order to remember?
2 What would make you _____ _____ (leave quickly) at the end of the lesson today?
3 How often do you _____ _____ (clean) at home?
4 When was the last time you _____ _____ (do nothing) at home all day?
5 If you wanted to get a new job, who would you _____ your CV _____ (email/post to lots of people) to?
6 What is a cause or issue you would feel strongly enough about to _____ _____ (say something publicly) about?
7 What do you do to _____ _____ (feel more relaxed) if something makes you angry?
8 Why might you _____ _____ (go to live in another place) from the area in which you live?

b Work in pairs. Ask and answer the questions.

8a 🎧 6.4 **Pronunciation** Listen and write down the sentences you hear.

b Listen again and notice how the particles at the end of the sentences are stressed, then practise saying the sentences.

Task

Teach a practical skill

Preparation Vocabulary and listening

1a Read the list of skills below. Tick the things you know how to do.

1 take a good photograph
2 edit a photograph digitally to improve it
3 start a car and drive off safely
4 iron a shirt correctly
5 make a good salad dressing
6 bath a newborn baby
7 mend a puncture on a bike
8 give emergency resuscitation
9 change the wheel on a car
10 do a manicure or pedicure

b Work in groups. Match the words/phrases in the box with the skills in exercise 1a.

nail file *10*	special lens	bubbles
spare tyre	crease	cuticles
focal point	ignition	patch
clutch	collar and cuffs	inner tube
jack	support the head	crop
press down	pump (something) up	toss
turn something upside down		

2a You are going to listen to an advert about how to give hands-only CPR (cardiopulmonary resuscitation). Before you listen, put the pictures in the correct order.

 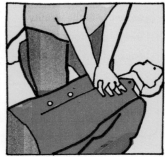

b 🎧 6.5 Listen and check. Then work in pairs. What else can you remember? Use the phrases in the box to help you.

be unresponsive	the heel of your hand
breastbone	pendant necklace
clasp your hands together	press down
a depth of 4–6 cm	your full body weight
cracked rib	

3a If necessary, listen again and check.

b Work in new pairs. Close your books and explain how to give CPR to someone who does not know. Use mime and gesture to help you.

USEFUL LANGUAGE

a Ordering your instructions
First of all, ...
You can prepare ... in advance.
The first thing to think about is ...
The first priority is to ...
At this point, you should ...
Something I should have mentioned earlier is ...

b Dos and don'ts
Make sure you always/never ...
Be very careful (not) to ...
Check that ...
The more you ..., the better/quicker/easier it will be.
The best way to ... is to ...
To do this, you should ...
One common mistake is to ...
Whatever you do, don't ...

c Checking you understand
So how exactly should you ...?
When you said ..., what exactly did you mean?
Could you just go over (the first/last part) again?
I didn't get the bit about ...

Task Speaking

1a Work alone or in pairs. Choose one of the skills you ticked in exercise 1a or a similar skill that you can explain in detail.

b Spend five to ten minutes planning how you will explain the skill to other students. Ask your teacher or use a dictionary for any words/phrases you need and make notes as necessary. Think about:

- any specialised vocabulary you need.
- any props or diagrams you could use to help you.
- how you can use gesture or mime to explain the skill.

> Useful language a and b

2 Find students in the class who don't know the skill that you can teach. Explain the skill and answer any questions.

> Useful language a, b and c

Follow up Writing

1 Write a short entry for a website.

- Explain a skill from exercise 1a or another skill.
- Write your instructions in short, clear steps.
- Think about any illustrations which would help to make the instructions clearer.

SHARE YOUR TASK

Choose a skill and plan a short presentation to explain it.

Practise your presentation until you feel confident.

Film/Record yourself giving your presentation.

Share your film/recording with other students.

63

WORLD CULTURE

TEACHING HAPPINESS

Find out first

1 Work in pairs. Can you guess the answers to the questions below? Go online to check your answers or ask your teacher.

1 What is Subjective Well-Being (SWB)?
2 Which countries report the highest levels of subjective well-being, according to the UN World Happiness Report?
3 Which of the following is true?
   a 15% / 25% / 40% of 20-somethings experience constant or regular stress. In the 1970s this was 15% / 25% / 41%.
   b The proportion of teenagers who feel anxious or depressed has halved/doubled/stayed the same in the last 30 years.
   c Facebook use increases/decreases/makes no difference to the well-being levels of young people.
   d At any given time, 1% / 6% / 11% of Americans over the age of 12 are taking anti-depressants.

Search What is Subjective Well-Being; UN World Happiness Report; levels of anxiety and depression in young people; effect of social media on young people's happiness; percentage of Americans taking anti-depressants

2 Discuss in groups.
   • Why do you think educationalists, politicians and other policy-makers are becoming interested in well-being?
   • How might they try to improve well-being levels?

View

3 ▶ Watch the video and decide if the statements below are true or false.

1 In South Tyneside they do not rate well-being as highly as academic success.
2 There are laws governing wellbeing in the area.
3 American schools started teaching happiness as a result of the project in Tyneside.
4 Lessons about topics like kindness are followed up with relevant homework.
5 The final speaker claims that the project has led to a reduction in teenage pregnancy and drug abuse.

4a Compare answers in pairs. Cany you remember the answers to these questions?

1 Which organisation in South Tyneside has taken on responsibility for well-being?
2 How did the project in the US school come about?
3 What example is given of a homework assignment related to a lesson on kindness?
4 What benefits are being felt from the American experiment?

b Watch again and check.

5 Discuss in groups.
   • Apart from kindness, what kind of topics do you think 'happiness lessons' cover?
   • Do you think lessons like these can make a difference to the future happiness of students?
   • Would you like to have received lessons like these? Why?/Why not?
   • Do you know of any similar projects in schools in your country?

World view

6 ▶ Watch Yvette and Tom discussing happiness and decide if the statements are true or false.

1 Tom thinks people were happier when they had more housework to do.
2 Yvette thinks people were happier in the past because they had stronger communities.
3 Tom thinks old people remember the past as being better than it really was.
4 Yvette thinks that people in developed countries are generally happy because their basic needs are met.
5 She thinks that people are looking for more complicated forms of happiness these days and this can cause problems.
6 They agree that modern media and the celebrity culture help to make people feel happier.
7 Yvette feels it is unrealistic to teach people to be happy.
8 She thinks that children's happiness is more the parents' responsibility than the schools.
9 She feels it is important for children to have a realistic attitude towards happiness.

b Compare answers in pairs. If the statements are false, can you say what the speakers actually said?

7 Watch again and check. Summarise in your own words the points that the speakers made.

8 Discuss. Do you think people today are happier than in the past? What are the most important things to teach children in order that they can lead happy lives?

FIND OUT MORE

9 Work in groups or individually. Choose one of the topic areas below to research online.

1 Is there a relationship between wealth and happiness? What relationship does research suggest? Is there any evidence of conflicting data?
2 What do the world's happiest (and saddest) nations seem to have in common? Where does your country come in the UN World Happiness report league tables? What about super powers like the US and China?
3 What is a typical curriculum for a 'well-being course' in school. What kind of tasks and assignments are pupils given? What benefits are claimed for them?
4 What are random acts of kindness? What effect do they have on well-being?

Search: relationship between wealth and happiness; the world's happiest countries; Well-being and Happiness programmes for schools; kindness research; random acts of kindness

Present your research

10 Summarise what you have found out in a short presentation to your class. Use the prompts below to help you.

- What I'd like to talk to you about today is …
- We need to start by defining what … is
- The facts make very interesting reading …
- The first thing that strikes you is …
- Some of the evidence is conflicting however …

Tip
Quote a few facts and figures but don't overwhelm your audience. Make sure that the facts you quote are relevant and up to date. *Recent research shows that 40% of young people experience constant or regular stress.*

AFTER UNIT 6 YOU CAN …

Describe and discuss the education system at a sophisticated level

Use particles to add a range of meanings to everyday verbs

Explain a practical skill in detail in speaking and writing

Research online and give a short presentation about well-being

07

TASTE

IN THIS UNIT

- **Grammar:** Adding emphasis with auxiliaries and inversion; Adverbs

- **Vocabulary:** Descriptive adjectives; Fashion, *look*, *sound* and *feel*

- **Task: Rant or rave**

- **Language live:** Writing an online review; Comment adverbials

Vocabulary and speaking
Descriptive adjectives

1   Work in pairs and look at the photos. Think of two adjectives to describe the style of the things/people in each.

2a   Which photo(s) do you think the groups of adjectives below describe?

1 cute, twee, sweet, childish
2 classic, vintage, outdated
3 sleek, minimal, stark, contemporary, ultra-modern
4 colourful, garish
5 outrageous, unconventional, fun, provocative
6 sophisticated, conventional, frumpy, chic
7 glamorous, tacky, vulgar, over-the-top
8 scruffy, messy, casual

b   Write + if the adjectives have a positive connotation, − if they have a negative connotation and *N* if they are neutral or could be either.

3   🎧 7.1 Listen to seven people talking about the photos. Work in pairs and discuss the questions.

- Which photo is each speaker describing? Which photo is not mentioned?
- Which adjectives from exercise 2a did they use? Which other adjectives did they use?
- Is each speaker's reaction positive or negative?
- Do you agree with their opinion? Why?/Why not?

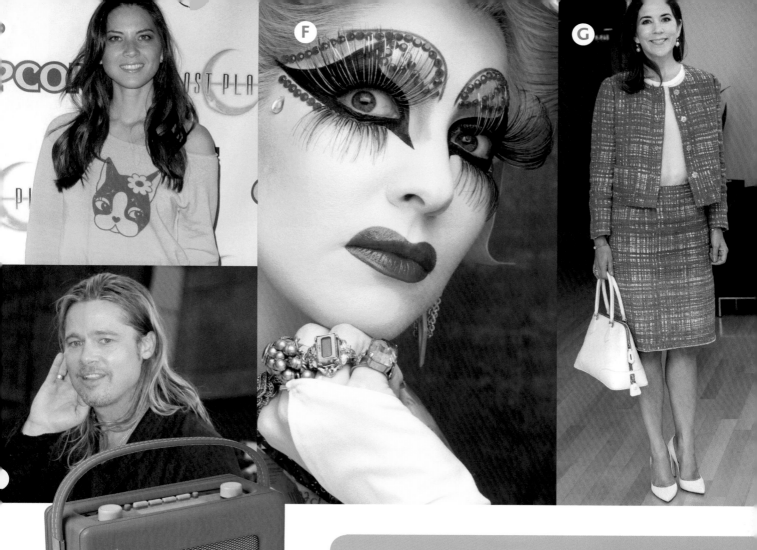

Would you ...

1 dye your hair bright purple or orange?
2 have your head shaved if you are a woman or grow your hair/beard very long if you are a man?
3 have your navel, nose or eyebrow pierced?
4 get a tattoo?
5 'invest' half a month's salary in a well-cut classic suit?
6 buy your clothes from a vintage or second-hand shop?
7 go to dinner in a restaurant wearing trainers?
8 buy a cute cuddly toy to put on your bed?
9 fill your home with vintage furniture, posters, etc.?
10 wear a shirt with a 'loud' psychedelic pattern?
11 wear leather trousers?
12 spend $150 on a top haircut?
13 decorate your home with abstract art?
14 paint your bedroom a garish colour, e.g. lime green or bright purple?
15 spend $500 on a painting or ornament that you love?
16 wear a T-shirt with a political slogan on it?
17 buy yourself a fancy sports car?

4a Read the questionnaire. Which of the things:

- would you never do?
- would you (secretly) like to do?
- have you already done?

b Work in pairs. Compare and explain your answers in the quiz using adjectives from exercise 2a and your own ideas.

> I would never go to a restaurant wearing trainers. I would feel really scruffy, as if everyone was looking at me.

> Really? I usually dress casually. I think it's fine unless it's a really smart restaurant.

Listening and vocabulary

Extreme fashion

1a Work in groups. Think of seven items of clothing/accessories that other students might not know. Use the word web to help you. You have two minutes.

1 upper body
  cloak

7 jewellery

2 head/hair

clothes/ accessories/ styles

3 whole body

6 underwear

4 lower body

5 feet

b Check answers with the class. Your group gets a point for every item that no one else thought of. Add any new words to the word web.

2 Which words in the box can you see in the photos? Guess if you are not sure. Add them to the word web above.

platform shoes	ankle socks	wig
glasses with big frames	leggings	corset
shoulder pads	jumpsuit	ponytail

3 You are going to listen to an expert talking about the history of fashion. Read the questions he answers. Which questions do the photos relate to?

1 In your opinion, what are the worst fashions of recent times?
2 Which was the most uncomfortable or harmful fashion in history?
3 How long does it take on average for a fashion to be recycled and why do some fashions keep coming back?
4 What was the biggest moment of change in fashion history?
5 What were the weirdest fashions in history?

4 🎧 7.2 Listen to the interview without the interviewer's questions. Match sections of the interview with questions 1–5 in exercise 3.

A _____ C _____ E _____
B _____ D _____

5 🎧 7.3 Listen and check. Choose the correct answer: a, b, or c.

1 It is definitely not a myth that
  a many 18th-century wigs had mice living in them.
  b people slept upright because of their wigs.
  c someone had a model ship built into their wig.
2 When 18th-century Americans and Europeans travelled to Japan,
  a Japanese people found their wigs very strange.
  b they seemed unaware that their wigs might seem strange to Japanese people.
  c Japanese and western people didn't like each other's hairstyles very much.
3 Corsets
  a were not worn outside Europe and America.
  b are typical of a certain type of fashion which weakened women physically.
  c forced women to only take very short steps when they walked.
4 According to the speaker, following the hippy movement in the 1960s,
  a people wore more functional, less decorative clothes.
  b the link between clothes and social status was strengthened.
  c people increasingly saw their clothes as an expression of their personality.
5 In the speaker's opinion,
  a only classic styles get recycled.
  b it's hard to explain why certain fashions reappear.
  c low-hanging pants will look cool in 20 years' time.

6 Work in groups and discuss one or more questions.

- People in the 18th century 'dressed in a lavish way to show off their economic status'. Is this true today? Give some examples.
- Do you agree that some fashion deliberately makes women physically weak? If so, why?
- Tony says that people today use clothes to reflect their personality rather than their social position. Think of some examples.
- Tony gives four examples of modern fashions he hates. What other fashions would you add?
- How much do you think fashion influences the way you dress? Do you consciously follow fashion?

PATTERNS TO NOTICE

Adding emphasis with auxiliaries and inversion

1 **How did the speaker use the auxiliary in brackets to give more emphasis to these sentences? What other changes are necessary, if any?**
  1 I think some of the stories told about them are in fact exaggerated. (do)
  2 That really happened! (did)

2 **Notice that we can add further emphasis using adverbs like** *certainly*, *definitely* **or** *really*.
  Women **certainly did** *suffer for the sake of fashion*.

  We **definitely do** *keep coming back to certain fashions*.

3 **We can also add emphasis by inverting the subject and auxiliary (usually in spoken English).**
  Am I *glad to see you!*

  Was I *surprised when I heard the news!*

---

7 Look at the verbs in bold and rewrite the sentences to add emphasis.

1 I**'m** pleased we left before the trouble started!
  Am I pleased we left before the trouble started!
2 I **felt** sorry for Charlie when I saw him yesterday.
3 This flat is a mess. I **think** you have a responsibility to help with the housework.
4 I'm absolutely exhausted! I **need** to get some sleep.
5 I'm sorry, but the way Gina behaves **annoys** me.
6 I know you think I don't like your cooking, but I **like** it.
7 I was **relieved** when the day was over!

8 🎧 7.4 **Pronunciation** Listen to some possible answers to exercise 7. Notice how auxiliaries and adverbs are stressed. Then practise saying the sentences, copying the stress.

Wordspot
look, sound and *feel*

1a Work in pairs and choose the correct answers.

1 Someone who resembles a famous person can be called *a lookalike* / *a lookout* / *an onlooker*.
2 To give someone a *muddy* / *dirty* / *grey* look is to look at them in an unfriendly or disapproving way.
3 If you look *up* / *up to* / *upon* someone, you admire and respect them.
4 A sound *bite* / *clip* / *grab* is a short phrase taken from a speech or interview that is broadcast on radio and TV.
5 If you sound *off* / *on* / *up* about something, you express strong opinions in an angry way.
6 The sounds produced artificially for film, radio or TV are called sound *affects* / *effects* / *efforts*.
7 The recorded music from a film is called the *soundband* / *soundplay* / *soundtrack*.
8 A *feel-fine* / *feel-good* / *feel-well* movie is one that makes you feel happy and optimistic.
9 If you're feeling particularly happy, you're feeling *on top of the mountain* / *at the top of the tree* / *on top of the world*.
10 If you have both positive and negative emotions about something, you have *assorted* / *combined* / *mixed* feelings about it.

b Which two idioms are illustrated in the cartoons?

2 🎧 7.5 Listen. In each sentence, the word *look*, *sound*, *feelings* or *feel* has been replaced by a beep. Write the missing words.

3 🎧 7.6 Listen and write answers to at least six questions on a piece of paper in random order. Work in pairs and explain your answers using the phrases in exercise 1a.

There's no accounting for taste – *or is there?*

What makes us love some things and hate others? We know that sometimes even the tiniest change can result in a huge difference in how we perceive something, so is there any rhyme or reason to our tastes and preferences? Here are three factors which play a role.

1 Conforming to expectations

In London a few years ago, two talented rappers called Silibil N' Brains took to the stage to perform at a music industry show for unsigned bands. They were an instant hit.

Their outrageous west-coast-American style, brilliant rap lyrics and couldn't-care-less attitude had the music industry's talent spotters falling over themselves to sign the pair. In a short space of time, Silibil N' Brains had a deal with a top management company, a contract with a major record label and an advance of £70,000 – and they hadn't even made a record. Before long, they were on tour with Eminem and out partying with Madonna. They were living the dream.

But rewind two years and the same two rappers were laughed off stage by the same talent spotters for singing the same songs. So what was the difference? Amazingly, it was their accent. You see, Silibil N' Brains weren't, in fact, from west-coast USA at all. Their real names were Gavin Bains and Billy Boyd and they were from Dundee in Scotland. During the first audition they had used their Scottish accents when rapping and it hadn't gone down well. 'They just laughed at us,' recalled Gavin, aka 'Brains'. 'We were heartbroken. We went back to Scotland with our tail between our legs.' The lesson for Gavin and Billy was that to succeed, you have to conform to expectations and at that time everyone expected rappers to be American.

2 The benefit of hindsight

Some people are simply ahead of their time. It's common knowledge that Vincent van Gogh sold only one painting in his lifetime – the other 900 or so were unknown and unloved until after his death. Monet's paintings, at least in his early career, were considered incomplete and ugly by critics at the time, while Vermeer, the painter of Girl with a Pearl Earring, even had to use his mother-in-law as a guarantor when he borrowed money – so unable was he to sell sufficient paintings! Now that public taste has caught up with these artists, more or less anything they touched has an astronomical price tag attached to it. Perhaps the reason is that it just takes a while to get used to something – after all, not all beauty is obvious at first sight.

One of the most loved and recognised tourist attractions in the world is the Eiffel Tower, but when plans for the tower were first proposed in the mid-1880s, Parisians protested loudly. Famous writers Guy de Maupassant and Alexandre Dumas described it as 'useless and monstrous' and 'a ghastly dream'. But when the tower finally opened, everyone changed their mind and declared it a stunning achievement. Everyone, that is, except for Maupassant, who frequently ate dinner in the tower's second floor restaurant because, he said, it was the only point in the city where he couldn't see 'this giant and disgraceful skeleton'.

3 A reassuring price tag

In a world where the range of products on offer can be completely bewildering, we often look to price as an indication of quality. We may think we prefer the expensive wine to the cheap plonk, but we may simply be influenced by the price tag. Even professionals can make this mistake. A researcher from the University of Bordeaux in France took an average bottle of red wine and poured it into two empty bottles, one with an expensive label and the other with a cheap one. Then he invited 57 wine 'experts' to taste the wine. Forty of them recommended the wine from the expensive bottle, describing it as 'agreeable', 'complex', 'balanced' and 'rounded', while the same wine from the cheap bottle was described as 'weak' and 'flat', with only 12 of the experts recommending it. The study made the researcher unpopular with the French wine tasters, but he did prove that price has a significant impact on taste.

A story from the world of business illustrates the connection between price and taste. A jewellery shop owner was keen to sell off some turquoise jewellery, which had been on display in her shop. Despite her best efforts, customers had shown no interest, so before going away on a business trip, she wrote a note to one of her sales assistants saying 'Everything in this display case, price x ½'. When she returned, she found, to her satisfaction, that all the jewellery had been sold and assumed that customers had been quick to snap up a bargain. It was only later that she discovered the real reason: the sales assistant had misread the note and had actually doubled the price of everything!

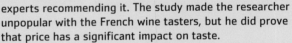

Reading

1 Work in pairs and discuss the questions.

- Do you have strong tastes in any of these areas?
  films   music   architecture   art   books
- How would you describe your taste?
- Do you feel confident about giving your opinion in these areas?

2 Work in groups of three. Read the introduction to the article and the three section headings. Predict what each section is about.

3a Student A: Read section 1 of the article. Student B: Read section 2. Student C: Read section 3. Re-read your section until you are ready to explain it.

b Explain your section to your group. Listen to other students' explanations and ask questions.

> Could you explain that bit again?

> Do you know why …?

4 Which explanation for *taste* do you find most convincing?

5 Read the rest of the article and answer the questions.

1 How do we know Silibil N' Brains were good actors?
2 How did the rappers feel about being initially rejected?
3 Why did Vermeer have to borrow money?
4 Where did Maupassant often eat and why?
5 Why was the French university researcher unpopular?
6 Why did the turquoise jewellery quickly sell out?

6 Read the quotes about taste. What do you think they mean? Which do you most agree with?

> I would rather be able to appreciate things I cannot have than to have things I am not able to appreciate.
> *Elbert Hubbard*

> Bad taste creates more millionaires than good taste ever does.
> *Charles Bukowski*

> Finding someone who has the same taste in music as you is like finding your soul mate.
> *Anon*

> If you do things because the crowd does them and like things because the crowd likes them, you shouldn't be surprised if your gravestone says 'Here lies one who was much like everyone else.'
> *Anon*

Grammar review
Adverbs

1 Put the adverbs in the box in the correct place in the sentences. Check your answers in the article.

even   amazingly   at that time   completely   finally
frequently   just   loudly   often   simply   well

1 Silibil N' Brains had a deal with a top management
   even
   company and they hadn't ^ made a record.
2 So what was the difference? It was their accent.
3 Their Scottish accents hadn't gone down.
4 'They laughed at us,' recalled Gavin.
5 Everyone expected rappers to be American.
6 Some people are ahead of their time.
7 When plans for the Eiffel Tower were first proposed, Parisians protested.
8 When the tower opened, everyone changed their mind.
9 Maupassant ate dinner in the tower's second floor restaurant.
10 The range of products on offer can be bewildering.
11 We look to price as an indication of quality.

2 Find at least one example of the following in exercise 1. More than one description may be possible for each adverb.

a a 'focus' adverb (used to focus attention on particular words) *even*
b a time adverbial
c an adverb of manner (telling us how something is done)
d an adverb of frequency (telling us how often something is done)
e an adverb of comment (adds the speaker's comment or opinion)
f an adverb of degree (tells us how much)
g an adverb that can collocate with either an adjective or a verb

3 Underline the adverbs in the sentences below. Which ones are true for you? Rewrite the others to make them true, using an appropriate adverb.

1 I'm working really hard at the moment.
2 Our teacher hardly ever gives us homework.
3 My sister can sing really well.
4 I'm terrible at cooking – I can't even make toast.
5 I've been studying English for ten years.
6 I really like where I live.

> **> Grammar extension bank, pages 136–139**

Task

Rant or rave

just took my breath away

fundamentally immoral

absolutely spectacular

awesome

a monstrosity

it drives me mad

disgusting

a real creep

totally gross

a waste of time

just magic

genius

tedious

Preparation Listening

1a Look at the words/phrases above. Do they express strong positive or negative feelings?

b Which words/phrases could be used to describe any of the things on the list below? Which could only be used to describe one or two?

- a fashion or item of clothing
- a song or style of music
- a shop or brand
- a building
- an activity
- a type of food
- a film or TV programme
- a famous person
- a topic of conversation
- a habit or type of behaviour
- a machine or aspect of technology
- something you hate that everyone else seems to love
- something you love that everyone else seems to hate

2 🎧 7.7 Listen to five people 'ranting' about something they hate, or 'raving' about something they love and answer the questions.

- What are they talking about?
- What category from the list does it belong to?
- Do they love or hate it?
- What reasons do they give?

3 Listen again and tick the phrases you hear in the Useful language box. Did the speakers use any of the phrases from the illustration?

Task Speaking

1 Think of a couple of things you hate (to rant about) and a couple of things you love (to rave about). Use the list above or your own ideas. Spend a few minutes preparing and ask your teacher for any words/phrases you need. Think about:

- what you especially love/hate about these things.
- specific examples of what you mean.
- what makes you feel like this.

2 Work in pairs. Talk about the things you have chosen and why.

a Describing strong feelings

I really love/hate the way …
There's one thing that really gets on my nerves …
The main thing I object to is …
What really appeals to me is …
One thing that I really can't stand/just love is …
It makes me absolutely furious!
The thing that really annoys me/drives me mad (about …) is …
There's nothing like it.
It seems very odd to me that …
He/She is so funny/appealing/annoying/infuriating.
I find … completely/totally/absolutely fascinating/disgusting.
I think … to be honest …

b Persuading others

I'm sure you agree that …
Like me, you've probably noticed that …
I'm sure you're aware of the fact that …

3a Choose the topic that you feel most strongly about and prepare to tell the class. Think about how to persuade the others to feel the same way you do.

> Useful language a and b

b Listen to other students. At the end vote on 'the most convincing rant' and 'the most convincing rave'.

Follow up Writing

1 Imagine that you have just read an online article about the topic that you have ranted or raved about. Write a paragraph or two on the comment board giving your opinion.

SHARE YOUR TASK

Practise a rant or rave (on the topic in exercise 3 or another one) until you feel confident.

Film/Record yourself giving your opinion.

Share your film/recording with other students.

LANGUAGE LIVE

Writing
An online review

1 Do you ever read/write online reviews? If so, what for? Which websites are well-known for them?

2 Read review A. In what order does the writer cover these points?

- the negatives
- location
- overall opinion
- the positives

3a The words in bold in review A are common adjectives that lack impact. Work in pairs and think of a more sophisticated alternative for each.

b Look at the words/phrases in the box. Did you come up with any of them in exercise 3a? Use them to replace the words in bold in the review.

> disappointing, to say the least
> within easy walking distance of
> gone out of their way
> fails to impress
> perfectly adequate
> impressive
> its big selling point
> positive

4 Read review B. Which phrases in bold are positive and which are negative?

5a Complete review C with words/phrases from exercises 3 and 4.

b Underline useful phrases related to music and albums in the review in exercise 5a.

6a Think of a film, album or hotel and make notes about it. Organise your notes into a logical structure and write the first draft of your review.

b Look at the checklist and think about how your review could be improved. Swap reviews with a partner and see if he/she agrees. Write the final draft of your review.

- Has your review got a logical structure (e.g. introduction, positives, negatives, overall opinion)?
- Have you described what you liked and didn't like?
- Have you mentioned specific features (e.g. the acting, a particular track, the staff)?
- Have you used sophisticated phrases rather than simple words?

A Reviewed 27th January ★ 15 people found this review he

'Great location, but ...'

The central location of Hotel Panoramic is **great**. It stands on a quiet square near restaurants and bars, but is **close to** most of the major tou attractions. Our first impressions when we arrived were quite **good**. The reception was clean and spacious and the rooms were **OK**. There were complimentary soft drinks in the mini-bar and the view from the balcony was **very nice**. It was only later that we began to have reservations. The breakfast was **not good** and the air-conditioning in our room packed up the second day. Although we were eventually upgraded free of charge a junior deluxe room, we felt the staff could and should have **done mor** resolve the issue. Overall, the hotel is **not great**, given the price, and th are probably better options out there.

B
Journey into suspense!

Reviewed 5th February   *18 out of 19 people found this review usefu*
112 min - Drama - Lena Ferova
★★★★

Director Mary Cassell's adaptation of Igor Shatov's novel *Journey Into Night* is a **thought-provoking** and, at times, laugh-out-loud funny film that, despite its flaws, **leaves a lasting impression** after the final credit have rolled. Set in Moscow in the early 80s, the film tells the story of Yuri Ignatiev, a spy who risks it all – and loses. Despite the fact that we learn Yuri's fate early on, *Journey Into Night* keeps us **on the edge of our seats** with a plot that is both **gripping and believable**, dialogue that is never **clunky** and cinematography that is truly **breathtaking**. The acting, however, **isn't quite up to the same high standards** and although Valery Yartsev's central performance is **mesmerising**, that of his co-star, Olga Grishina, chosen for her looks as much as her acting ability, it seems, is **slightly wide of the mark**. Despite being part-thrille part-action film, there is **a refreshing lack of** violence, although there are, to my mind, **a few too many** car chases. In short, however, this film is **not to be missed**.

C
Tell me about Better Days!
by Beata Majdan

Three years after her highly acclaimed debut *Tell Me*, Jolanta Toma's new album, *Better Days*, has been a long time coming. In my opinion, it has been worth the wait. The collection of new songs is [1] _____ and although not all are [2] _____ as *Tell Me*, they are [3] _____ nonetheless and there are certainly no filler tracks. As with the previous album, Jolanta's [4] _____ is her unmistakeable voice. She never [5] _____ with her raw talent and eclectic style, mixing jazz, folk, hip hop and R&B. Only one track [6] _____ , *Selfish Me*, which although [7] _____ , has slightly [8] _____ lyrics and [9] _____ repetitions of the chorus for my liking. Still, this is one of the standout albums of the year so far and definitely one [10] _____ . I can't wait to see what the next album holds. Hopefully, we won't have to wait another three years to find out!

★★★☆☆

Speaking
Comment adverbials

1 Look at the adverbial phrases in bold below. Which are used:

a to say that something is good news or lucky?
b to emphasise that what you're saying is true?
c to emphasise that something is unfortunate?
d to say that we hope something will happen?
e to emphasise that something is strange, surprising or coincidental?

1 **Amazingly enough**, it's the third time I've won £50 on the lottery this year.
2 **To be perfectly honest**, I've no idea why I bought it.
3 **I'm glad to say** that the after-sales service is very good.
4 **Quite frankly**, I've never seen an uglier pair of shoes.
5 **Thank goodness** there was someone there to help me.
6 **It's a good job** you didn't buy that computer.
7 **Much to my surprise**, it fitted like a glove.
8 **All being well**, the kids will like their presents.
9 **To tell the truth**, I didn't expect it to be so busy.
10 **Funnily enough**, he had the exact same model in grey.
11 Our room wasn't ready and **to make matters worse**, the hotel didn't even apologise!
12 **To my utter astonishment**, he produced a ring and proposed.
13 **I'm afraid to say** that it didn't leave a lasting impression on me.

2 🎧 7.8 Listen to two online reviews. What is being reviewed and what does the reviewer like/dislike most in each case?

3 Work in pairs. Which phrases from exercise 1 did the reviewers use? Complete the sentences below. Then listen again and check.

Review 1
1 _____ , you don't need to use a remote to operate this.
2 It's a great feature, but _____ , I don't use it.
3 _____ that they include one of those with the package.
4 I'm going to turn it on and, _____ , it's going to work.
5 Now, _____ , the sound quality is not the best in the world.
6 _____ , it's got one of the best pictures I've ever seen.

Review 2
7 They arrived today in the post and _____ I kept the receipt.
8 Firstly, _____ , the pockets are tiny!
9 _____ I didn't sit down on my white sofa because ...
10 _____ , one of the buttons fell off.
11 _____ , my friend bought exactly the same pair of jeans.
12 _____ , however, she likes her jeans.

4a Work in pairs and write a script for an online review of something that you both own. Use at least five phrases from exercise 1.

b Read your review to the class and listen to the other reviews. Which ones sound the most authentic?

AFTER UNIT 7 YOU CAN ...

Describe and discuss style, taste and fashion at a sophisticated level

Use auxiliaries to emphasis in informal contexts

Express strong opinions in spoken and written contexts

Use comment adverbials to add emphasis to your opinions

Write an online review

08

LIVE AND LET LIVE

IN THIS UNIT

- **Grammar: Describing typical habits; Infinitives and *-ing* forms; Compound phrases**
- **Vocabulary: Characteristics and behaviour; *just***
- **Task: Choose celebrities for a charity trek**
- **World culture: Running a large family**

Vocabulary and speaking
Characteristics and behaviour

1a Which of the following types of household do you think are most/least common in your country? Is this situation changing and if so, why? Work in groups and discuss.

- extended families and multi-generational households
- nuclear families
- single parent households
- childless couples
- groups of housemates/adults who are not related
- single people living alone

b Discuss the questions.

- Do you live or have you ever lived away from your family? Under what circumstances? If not, would you like to?
- What are/were the advantages and disadvantages of living alone or with friends rather than with family?

2a Read the descriptions of people you might live with and check the meaning of the words in bold. Then, for each, write:

1 = This would really get on my nerves.
2 = (Not great, but) it wouldn't bother me.
3 = I would like to live with someone like this.

- **a chatterbox** who likes constant company
- someone who is a bit **awkward socially** and **keeps themself to themself**
- someone who likes **messing around** and **cracking jokes**
- someone who is **irritable** or **on a short fuse**
- someone **laid-back** who never **lets things get to them**
- someone **highly strung** who **lives on their nerves**
- a **neat freak** or someone who's very **fussy** about hygiene, etc.
- someone who **leaves their stuff all over the place** and **won't do their share** of the housework
- someone **overbearing** and **arrogant** who **won't listen to other people's point of view**
- someone **hyperactive** who never sits down and **finds it difficult to unwind**
- someone who **lounges around** doing nothing for hours on end
- someone who **sulks** rather than **saying what is on their mind**
- someone **opinionated** and **outspoken**
- someone **unpredictable** whose **mood changes** for no apparent reason

b Work in groups and compare your answers. Does any other kind of behaviour drive you mad?

3a 🎧 8.1 Listen to five people describing a person they find/found difficult to live with. Who are they talking about? Which characteristics in exercise 2 do they mention?

b Listen again and make notes about why the speakers find/found these people difficult.

4 Choose three of the following people and think of three or four typical habits (good and bad) that each person has/had. Then work in pairs and tell your partner about them using the verb forms in the Patterns to notice box.

- someone you live with now
- someone you used to live with
- a colleague or acquaintance who irritates you
- a neighbour you don't/didn't like
- someone who looked after you a lot when you were a child
- a teacher from primary or secondary school

PATTERNS TO NOTICE

Describing typical habits

1 Notice the use of *will*/*would* and the Present/Past continuous + *always* to describe typical behaviour (good or bad).
Present habits:

She'll go off in a corner and sulk.

She won't pick up the phone.

She's always laughing.

He's always moaning.

Past habits:

One day he'd be really friendly and the next he'd be really down.

He was always picking things up and sighing.

2 Past habits (but not present habits) can also be described with *used to*.

He would swing from on extreme to another.

He used to go mad at me if I left things lying around.

3 The verbs *keep* (*on*) + *-ing* and *tend to* + infinitive are also common and can be used in both the past and the present.
- *Keep* (*on*) emphasises that the action is repeated frequently.

Sorry, I keep forgetting your name!

He just kept on asking her to marry him until, in the end, she said yes.

- *Tend to* is used with repeated actions and typical states.

She tends to speak very loudly.

My parents tended to be very strict.

Listening
Leaving home

1a Work in groups and discuss. What's the longest you've ever been away from home? What were the circumstances? How did you feel about it?

b List at least six reasons why people might leave home. What are the most common reasons?

2a Look at the photos and read the captions. Why did each person leave home?

b You are going to listen to the three people discussing their experiences. Look at the list of topics mentioned during the conversation. Who do you think talked about each one?

	Who mentioned it?	What did they say?
1 shooting a rifle		
2 ironing and sewing		
3 growing up in the country		
4 going to the beach		
5 teaching English		
6 being told what to do		
7 haircuts		
8 losing your individuality		
9 becoming more independent		

3a 🎧 8.2 Listen and complete the second column of the table in exercise 2b.

b Note down as many details in the second column as you can. Then work in pairs and compare your answers.

4 Work in pairs and discuss the questions below.

- Overall, were the speakers' experiences positive or not?
- Do you think doing military service/going to boarding school/being an au pair is a good thing or not?
- Which experience would you most/least like to have yourself?

At the age of 18, Peter left home for the first time to do military or 'national' service.

At the age of 11, Liz was sent to a boarding school where she lived during the term, only going home in the holidays.

After studying French at school until the age of 18, Catherine went to be an au pair in Brittany, northern France, where she stayed with a family and looked after their two young children.

Grammar review
Infinitives and *-ing* forms

1a Who said the following in the recording?

1 'It was an opportunity to go abroad.'
2 'I can't imagine anything worse than being in the army!'
3 'The parents really wanted them to learn English whilst I was there ...'
4 '... so one of my roles was to teach them English.'
5 'I don't like being told what to do.'
6 'You start doing those kind of things yourself ...'
7 '... without having to be told.'
8 'He looked as if he was ready to attack you.'
9 'Perhaps that was his way of coping in an alien environment.'
10 'Because I got used to studying ...'

b Look at audio script 8.2 on page 000 and check your answers.

2 Find at least one example of the following in the sentences in exercise 1.

a gerund:
a after a verb
b after a preposition
c as an object
d in the passive form

an infinitive:
e after a verb and object
f after the verb *be*
g after a noun
h after an adjective
i in the passive form

3 Work in pairs and discuss the difference in meaning between the pairs of sentences.

1 **a** We **stopped to have** lunch together.
  b We **stopped having** lunch together.
2 **a** I'm **trying to open** the door, but the key won't turn.
  b Why don't you **try opening** the door towards you?
3 **a** I'll **remember to tell** Jenny about the meeting.
  b I **remember telling** Jenny about the meeting.

4 Complete the sentences so they are true for you.

1 I can't think of anything worse than ...
2 I don't like being ...
3 In my job, my role is ...
4 I recently tried ...
5 I'd love to have the opportunity to ...
6 When I was younger, my parents wanted me ...

> **Grammar extension bank, pages 142–145**

Wordspot
just

1 Read the sentences and look at the word web. Which meaning (1–5) does *just* have in each sentence? More than one answer may be possible.

a If you ask me, men and women **just** think differently.   *4*
b That's **just** the point I was trying to make.
c You've **just** interrupted me for about the fourth time.
d Sorry about the noise – it's **just** our way of having fun!
e Marco's so rude! I smiled at him and he **just** ignored me!
f Ignore what Steve **just** said, he doesn't mean it.
g Oliver didn't mean to tear your book – he's **just** a baby.
h Have you phoned your sister? I'm **just** going to.
i Could I **just** have a quick word with you?
j I saw Carrie in the corridor **just** now.

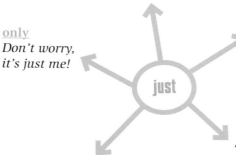

2 <u>exactly</u>
That jumper is just what I'm looking for.

3 <u>a short time (before or after)</u>
It's just before midnight.
He phoned me just after you left.

1 <u>only</u>
Don't worry, it's just me!

just

4 <u>for emphasis</u>
That's just typical of your mother!
It's just beautiful!

5 <u>with polite phrases</u>
Could everyone just wait here?
Can I just take your name?

2 Add *just* in the correct place in the sentences. More than one answer may be possible. How does *just* change the meaning of each sentence?

1 I'll take your coat for you.
2 I was so annoyed, I tore up the letter and walked out.
3 I'm looking, thank you.
4 The weather was perfect for my birthday party.
5 These shoes are what I need.
6 I'll be a few minutes and then we can go.
7 Look! I've found that receipt you were looking for.
8 Lunch is a sandwich. I hope that's OK.
9 Would you mind holding this for me, please?
10 I've got enough money to pay!

3 🎧 8.3 Listen to some possible answers to exercise 2 and compare them with yours.

4 Work in pairs. Student A: Turn to page 108. Student B: Turn to page 110. Take turns to ask and answer the questions.

Reading

1   Read the quotes about men, women and relationships. Which do you like best/least? Work in pairs and compare your opinions.

> 'I married beneath me – all women do.'
> *Mae West, 1930s film star*

> 'A man in love is incomplete until he is married. Then he's finished.' *Zsa Zsa Gabor, Hungarian-born American actor*

> 'All women become like their mothers. That is their tragedy. No man does. That is his.'
> *Oscar Wilde, Irish playwright*

> 'My wife and I were happy for 20 years. Then we met.' *Rodney Dangerfield, US comedian*

2a   You are going to read an extract from a book about men's and women's behaviour. Which characteristics in the box below do you:

   1 associate more with women?
   2 associate more with men?
   3 associate equally with both?
   4 think it is impossible to generalise about?

a tendency to be competitive	a love of gadgets
an ability to ignore mess	a tendency to feel guilty
a lack of self-confidence	a fear of failure
a desire for approval	a sense of superiority
a tendency to nag	a fear of commitment
an inability to make decisions	a need for attention

b   Work in groups. Compare and explain your opinions.

3a   Read the extract and complete it with *man/men* or *woman/women*. Then work in pairs and compare your answers. Finally, turn to page 108 and check.

b   Which characteristics in exercise 2a are described in the extract? Which sex are they associated with?

4a   Read the extract again and answer the questions. Underline examples in the text to support your opinions.

   • Which points in the extract did you find particularly true/particularly unfair?
   • Is the text biased against either men or women, or is it equally critical of both?
   • Are such generalisations about men and women meaningful or is this just sexual stereotyping?

b   Work in groups. Compare and discuss your answers.

A bluffer's guide to men and women

Approval

[1]_____ are suckers for approval. They want to feel that [2]_____ have noticed them and need them. Best of all would be if [3]_____ admired them. They would also like it if they trusted them, but that would probably be asking too much.

Conversation

The average [4]_____ uses 10,000 words a day in speech; the average [5]_____ finds 4,000 perfectly adequate. Around the house, a [6]_____'s conversation is especially economical, often reduced to grunts and utterances of one syllable. Telephone calls are for the transmission of essential information, not for gossiping or the exchange of confidences. For [7]_____ , all information is essential. 'But what were you talking about?' a bemused [8]_____ may ask a [9]_____ who has just spent two hours on the phone to someone they saw only that morning.

A good cry

Although it is nowadays officially acceptable – even desirable – for [10]_____ to cry, they will never be a match for [11]_____ . They will never understand how [12]_____ can, in the right circumstances, claim to enjoy 'a good cry'. Tears make [13]_____ very uncomfortable because they feel something is expected of them, but they don't know what.

Nagging

It is important to remember that a [14]_____ does not nag, but reminds. This point cannot be made too often. [15]_____ are simply being made aware of the fact that they have not done what they said they were going to do and therefore need to be prompted regularly, otherwise it won't get done.

Friendship

Friendship is enormously important to [19]_____ . [20]_____ want friends to play with (for example, as tennis partners or as people with whom to watch the Cup Final), whereas [21]_____ want friends to talk to. They have friends the way [22]_____ have hobbies.

Housework

These days [16]_____ can and do cook, iron and vacuum, and have even been known to clean the bath. But surveys show that [17]_____ still spend four or five times as long on domestic chores as their helpful spouses. The fact is that [18]_____ can tolerate a greater degree of grime and disorder before they even notice it. They have the advantage of being thick-skinned – they approach the state of the house rather like the Three Wise Monkeys: 'see no evil, feel no evil, smell no evil'.

Guilt

[23]_____ feel guilty about everything, all the time. They feel guilty about their weight, their appearance, their careers, their mothering skills, the whiteness of their washes. Above all, they feel guilty about not being perfect. They read articles in glossy magazines about 'having it all'. Then they read about the folly of sacrificing quality of life and peace of mind to Superwoman ideals and feel conscience-stricken about that, too.

Commitment

[24]_____ find it hard to commit themselves to a relationship. Getting them to do so is like getting hold of the soap in the bath. For [25]_____ , the very idea of commitment is uncomfortable – after all, the verb 'to commit' is used for suicide or being sent to an asylum. They harbour the distinct fear that marriage will change them. [26]_____ only hope that it will.

Shopping

The majority of [27]_____ dislike shopping. It not only means spending money, but making snap decisions. They like armchair-shopping first, studying advertisements and comparing prices before going out and buying a car, a house or an international corporation. A mega waste of time, as far as [28]_____ are concerned, is window-shopping. This they do not understand at all. The joy of staring at goods which cannot be bought because the shop is closed is quite beyond their comprehension.

PATTERNS TO NOTICE

Compound phrases: *a lack of ...,* *a tendency to ...,* etc.

1 **Complex characteristics and feelings are often described by compound phrases. Find some more examples of patterns a and b in exercise 2a.**

  a noun + preposition + noun
  a **fear of** *failure* a **lack of** *self-confidence*
  a **need for** *attention* a **desire for** *approval*

  b noun + infinitive
  a **tendency to be** *competitive*
  an **ability to ignore** *mess*

2 **Notice that the first noun is often qualified by an adjective.**

  a **total** *lack of confidence*

  a **strange** *ability to ignore mess*

  an **enormous** *sense of superiority*

5a 🎧 **8.4 Listen and complete the common compound phrases.**

  1 a sense of *security*
  2 a _*big*_ fear of _____
  3 a love of _____
  4 a tendency to _____
  5 a _____ need to _____
  6 an _____ desire to _____
  7 an _____ lack of _____
  8 a _____ sense of _____
  9 this need for _____
  10 this _____ ability to _____
  11 a _____ sense of _____
  12 a _____ inability to _____

b 🎧 **8.5 Pronunciation Listen to the compound phrases. Then listen again and repeat, copying the stress pattern.**

6a Using the ideas in exercises 2a and 5a, think of:

  1 at least two things that everyone experiences sometimes.
    a lack of self-confidence, ...
  2 at least two things that are more characteristic of men than women.
  3 at least two things that are more characteristic of women than men.
  4 one thing that tends to be more characteristic of young people.
  5 one thing that tends to be more characteristic of elderly people.
  6 something you yourself feel or have experienced.
  7 something you have never felt or experienced.

b Work in groups and compare your answers.

Task

Choose celebrities for a charity trek

OPERATION EDUCATE

Operation Educate is an international charity aiming to provide buildings and essential equipment to schools in poor areas around the world. To raise money and to increase its public profile and status, the charity is organising a 'celebrity safari trek' from the northern coast to the southern tip of Africa, which will be featured regularly on daytime TV. Hopefully, this will attract lots of media coverage and large donations from the public.

Six celebrities will cross the continent in a trip lasting two months. They will drive a 4x4 and camp or sleep in huts at night, with only basic facilities for much of the trip, and there will also be regular canoeing and trekking, some of it over rough terrain, so a moderate to good level of fitness is required.

Basic survival training will be provided, as well as guides for special parts of the trip, but for much of the two months the group will be driving, navigating and living by themselves. They will also film themselves and one of them will be responsible for reporting back to the media at home (this person could make an important difference to the overall amount of money raised).

It is important from the point of view of image and sponsorship that no one drops out of the trek and that the group is seen to function as a team. There will be a group leader who will be responsible for dealing with unforeseen problems, conflicts within the group, etc.

The highlight of the trip will be a four-day climb up Mount Kilimanjaro, to be undertaken by three of the celebrities in the company of a camera crew. This will feature on numerous TV shows and will undoubtedly have the greatest impact in terms of publicity and fundraising. The celebrities undertaking this climb will need good to excellent levels of fitness.

The roles

The Operation Educate committee have to decide:

1 which six celebrities will make the final team.
2 who will be the 'reserve' in case anyone drops out.
3 who will be the media spokesperson.
4 who will be appointed overall group leader.
5 which three of the final six will do the Kilimanjaro climb.

Preparation Reading

1 Read about Operation Educate and the charity safari trek it is organising. Then work in pairs and summarise:

- what Operation Educate aims to do as a charity.
- the aims of the safari trek and how it will work.
- the most important characteristics and attributes that the celebrity participants need.
- what other decisions have to be made by the organising committee.

2a Turn to pages 110–111 and read about the celebrities whose names have been put forward. Underline the factors that make them suitable/valuable for the trip and circle the negative factors.

b Work in pairs and discuss. Which celebrities:

1 are most/least suitable from a fitness point of view?
2 might have psychological issues/lack the necessary mental stamina?
3 seem to have obvious leadership qualities?
4 will be most useful from a fundraising/publicity point of view?
5 will be good/bad at dealing with the media?
6 might help to broaden the appeal and get a wider range of the public interested?
7 are likely to be in conflict with each other?
8 will get on best as a group?

Task Speaking

1 Work in groups. Spend a few minutes deciding who you will select for roles 1–5 in the text. Ask your teacher for any words/phrases you need.

2 Work in new groups. Compare and explain your choices and try to reach agreement about who should go and in what role.

> Useful language a and b

3 Present your conclusions to the class. Explain any issues that you could not agree on and say why you disagreed.

> Useful language c and d

WORLD CULTURE

RUNNING A LARGE FAMILY

Find out first

1a Work in pairs. Can you guess the answers to the following questions?

Families around the world

1 Can you match the descriptions to the numbers in the box? (there are two extras)
a. The average number of children per family in the US in 1800
b. The average number of children per family in the US in 1900
c. The average number of children per family in the US in 2000

| 10 | 7 | 3.5 | 1.86 | 0.9 |

2 What is the average number of children per woman worldwide?
4.45   3.45   2.45   1.45

3 Which two statistics in the table below do you think have been swapped round?

Average number of children per woman in 2013 in:			
China	1.55	Saudi Arabia	2.21
India	2.55	Singapore	0.79
Italy	6.17	Somalia	1.41
Poland	1.32	Turkey	2.10
Russia	1.62	UK	1.90

4 How many children are there in Britain's biggest family?

b Check your answers online or ask your teacher.

....

Search: size of an average US family in 1800 (etc.); total fertility rate worldwide 2013; Britain's biggest family

....

2 Discuss in groups. Is there anything in the information above that surprises you? Why?

View

3 You are going to watch a video about a family with 13 children. What kind of practical problems do you think they might have in organising their daily lives?

4a ▶ Two of the statements in each question below are true. Watch part one of the video and identify the false statement.

1 Time and motion study is a way of ...
   a ensuring that workers don't waste effort.
   b keeping factory production moving fast.
   c ensuring that production costs are high.
2 Frank Gilbreth ...
   a analysed the movements of bricklayers and managed to increase their productivity by 50%.
   b had worked in the building trade himself.
   c applied his theories at home too.
3 The Shaw family ...
   a had 13 children over 17 years.
   b get up and off to school in less than 45 minutes.
   c operate in a way that can be compared to factory production processes.
4 The time and motions expert admires ...
   a the uncomplicated way the family does things.
   b the fact that everyone is highly organised.
   c the preparation done before the children get up.

b Compare answers in pairs. Can you correct the false sentences? Watch again and check your answers.

5 ▶ In part two of the video the time and motion expert gives his feedback on the family. What do you think he will say? Watch and check your answers.

6 Discuss these questions in groups.

   • Do you admire the way the Shaws run their family?
   • Would you like to be part of such a large family? Why?/Why not?

World view

7a ▶ Watch five people from different countries talking about how families are changing. For each person, answer the questions in the table.

Name and country	How are families changing in their country?	Do they think family ties are getting stronger or weaker?
Abigail, Britain		
Sayful, Bangladesh		
Luis, Spain		
Ciara, Ireland		
Paulona, Hong Kong		

b Compare answers in pairs. Can you remember what reasons and examples they give to explain their answers?

8 Watch again if necessary to check your answers.

9 Discuss these questions.

- Are families getting smaller in your country?
- What are the most important reasons for this in your opinion?
- Do you think family ties are getting stronger or weaker?
- Which comments in the film also apply to families in your country?
- In what ways are these changes affecting people's lives?

FIND OUT MORE

10 Work in groups or individually. Choose a topic below to research online.

- How fast is the world' population growing? What is it now and what is it expected to be in the future? When is it expected to peak? What problems will this cause? Which countries in the world will suffer most from over-population?
  Have any other countries introduced this policy?
- Which countries in the world have a declining population? What problems does this bring and what are the solutions?
- What are the benefits and problems of having a youthful population? What kind of countries are experiencing this and what are the solutions?

Search: growth of the world's population; over-population; declining/ageing/youthful population.

Present your research

11 Summarise what you have found out in a short presentation to your class. Use the prompts below.

- Over the next (50 years) the population is expected to grow /shrink by …
- It is estimated that by (2030) …
- As a result of this …
- The benefits/main problems are that …
- One solution is to …

Tip
Make your presentation more dynamic by asking rhetorical questions. Questions to which you do not expect an answer from your audience help your presentation flow more naturally. *So, as you probably know, the world's population is growing, but how fast is it growing and what problems will this cause?*

AFTER UNIT 8 YOU CAN ...

Describe habits and social relationships at a sophisticated level

Describe complex characteristics and social behaviour

Discuss and select from a shortlist and present your choice to an audience

Research online and give a short presentation about family and population around the world

The shape of things to come

10 future trends to look out for – big and small

1. Unmanned flying vehicles, or drones, costing just a few hundred pounds, **are set to** become part of our everyday life in the next few years. Plans **are underway** to use drones, equipped with high-definition video cameras, for tasks ranging from delivering takeaway meals and parcels, to tracking and deterring illegal poachers of rare species such as rhinos and tigers.

2. Robots could soon **have the capacity to** write news articles, generating stories from online data (headlines, statistics and tweets) with no human input required. It is estimated that up to 20 percent of all news content could be written by 'robo-writers': football reports have already been successfully generated in this way.

Vocabulary and speaking
Describing future developments

1a Work in groups. You are going to read an article predicting some future trends. What do you think might be said about these topics?

- transport
- diet
- the environment
- the media
- business and services
- society generally

b Read the article and check your predictions in exercise 1a.

2 Check the meaning of the words/phrases in bold in the article and in the comments below.

- 'I think this could transform our lives in certain ways.'
- 'It's unlikely to catch on in the long term.'
- 'This is already happening and I think it will gain more and more in popularity.'
- 'It's interesting, but I don't think it will ever become a reality.'
- 'I think this will emerge as an important trend.'
- 'I don't think this would be sustainable in the long term.'
- 'It depends on market forces.'
- 'I think this will meet with a lot of resistance.'

3 So far they have been slow to **fulfil their potential**, but it is predicted that in the next five to ten years the sale of electric vehicles will **take off**, and that by 2020 more than 45 million electric bicycles, cars and buses will be sold annually. This, in turn, will **pave the way for** new concepts such as 'pay-by-the-kilometre' motoring. And so-called 'smart cars' will offer the option of hands-free driving, moving autonomously through modern cities.

4 A new product has been patented that could **revolutionise** the way you eat: breathable food. The idea is that you inhale calorific foods, such as chocolate, from a lipstick-sized inhaler, enabling you to enjoy much of the flavour without consuming any of the calories!

5 After decades in which cheap **air travel has seemed to be the way forward**, the next decade or two will see the rise of global high-speed rail networks connecting not just cities, but continents. Huge **infrastructure** projects could make rail travel between Europe and China or Moscow and the Middle East a real possibility, as rail increasingly becomes a driver of **economic growth**.

6 Priority queuing, a concept already familiar if you travel with budget airlines, could soon **change the face of the service industry**. The idea is that you pay extra to save time, allowing you to use a faster motorway lane or jump to the front of the queue in a theme park, for example, and effectively creating two tiers of service.

7 The global middle class, interconnected by a **massive boom** in internet use and mobile devices, is set to increase to some five billion by 2020. Astonishingly, between 2006 and 2012, the number of university-educated people in the world increased from one percent to seven percent, due largely to **a huge expansion** of higher education in China and India.

8 Global **consumer demand will have a huge impact on natural resources** like water, meaning that big companies such as soft drinks manufacturers will have little choice but to **adapt and invest** in greener options. **Sustainability** will simply become smart business.

9 As new markets and opportunities in China and India **emerge**, it is expected that educated professionals from Europe and the USA will flock to Asia in what some call 'a reverse brain drain'.

10 Cyber wars fought by cyber soldiers may sound like fantasy, but military experts around the world accept that this science fiction scenario is likely to **become a reality**. This so-called 'fifth battlefront' (alongside land, sea, air and space) will centre round the control of information and will mainly involve espionage and hacking.

3a Which comments in exercise 2, if any, reflect your own reaction to the trends described? What are the possible consequences of these things happening?

b Compare your ideas with other students.

4 Are the pairs of phrases similar (S) or different (D) in meaning? Explain any important differences.

1 become a reality/meet with resistance   *D*
2 gain in popularity/catch on   *S*
3 emerge/adapt
4 a massive boom/a huge expansion
5 have a huge impact on/change the face of
6 natural resources/infrastructure
7 pave the way for/be underway
8 market forces/economic growth

5 Complete the table. Use a dictionary to help you if necessary.

Verb	Noun	Adjective
¹ boom	boom	² _____
emerge	³ _____	⁴ _____
⁵ _____	expansion	⁶ _____
	potential	⁷ _____
revolutionise	⁸ _____	⁹ _____
¹⁰ _____	sustainability	¹¹ _____

6 Work in groups. Make five predictions of your own about future trends using the vocabulary in exercise 4.

> I think Brazil will emerge as one of the most important economies in the world.

Grammar review

Future forms

1 Read predictions 1–10 and find examples of:

  a *will* to make a prediction.
  b *going to* to make a prediction.
  c two present phrases that convey a future meaning.
  d a modal in a past form used to talk about the future.
  e a future modal.
  f a future passive form.
  g the Future continuous.
  h a 'future in the past'.
  i the Future perfect (or a 'past in the future').

  1 Scientists expect that humans will generally live to be over 100 years old.
  2 Asteroids might be mined for minerals by a private mining company.
  3 As soon as we discover a cure for AIDS or cancer, a new disease is bound to appear.
  4 With the growth of the internet, it was generally thought that people would be working from home, but recent research suggests that people need 'face time' in the office.
  5 A digital currency is set to become widely used and accepted.
  6 If current CO_2 emissions continue, the Arctic is going to be completely free of ice in the summer months.
  7 At some point in the next 50 years, a computer will have been created that is more intelligent than humans.
  8 In the next few years, doctors will be prescribing medical apps for patients.
  9 Technology is emerging that could make fully controllable prosthetic limbs the norm.
  10 People will be able to physically touch each other through their smartphones.

2 Work in pairs and discuss the questions.

  1 Why is *will* used in sentence 1 and *going to* in sentence 6?
  2 Why is the Present simple used after *as soon as* in sentence 3?
  3 How does sentence 4 describe 'the future in the past'?
  4 How does sentence 7 describe 'the past in the future'?
  5 Which sentence describes something that will happen in the normal or expected course of events?
  6 Why isn't *can* used in sentence 10?

3 Work in groups. Which of the predictions in exercise 1 do you think will happen? Have any of them already come true?

▷ **Grammar extension bank, pages 144–147**

Listening and speaking

Living by numbers

1 Look at the things in the box. Tick the ones that you keep careful track of and underline the ones that you don't track but would like to.

- calories consumed
- how much sleep you get
- money spent
- countries and cities visited
- number of days sick in a year
- time spent studying/working
- holiday days you've had this year
- thoughts and feelings (e.g. in a journal)
- mood
- weight
- coffee consumed
- steps taken in a day
- time spent online
- money in the bank
- miles driven in your car

2 Do you or does anyone you know use special tools (e.g. software, phone apps, notebooks) to track this kind of information? Do you think it's a good idea? Why?/Why not?

Describing current trends

1 To describe trends, we often use the Present continuous with verbs like *become*, *get* (*better/worse*), *develop*, *change*, *increase*, *improve*, *deteriorate*.
Self-tracking **is becoming** *mainstream.*

2 These forms are commonly accompanied by adverbs like *rapidly*, *quickly*, *slowly*, *increasingly*, etc., which give more detail.
While most of us **are increasingly feeling** *like we're drowning in a sea of data …*
This trend **is rapidly changing** *what we know and how we live.*

3 We also use comparative forms and phrases like *more and more*.
Modern technology is making it **easier and easier** *for them to collect data.*
More and more *people are doing it.*

5 Work in groups and discuss the questions.
- Do you think that self-tracking is a waste of time or that the more you know about yourself, the better you can become?
- Would you wear a tiny video camera that recorded every moment of your life? Why?/Why not?
- Do you think self-tracking will become mainstream in the future? What will we track and how?
- What do you think are the negative effects of self-tracking?
- Do you agree that knowledge is power? Can you give examples?

6 Write about the trends in your country in the areas below. Use the phrases in the Patterns to notice box to write five sentences that you think are true and three that you think are false.
- the job market
- education
- transport
- holidays and travel
- people's health
- technology
- the media

Public exams are becoming increasingly difficult.

The quality of TV programmes is deteriorating rapidly.

Computers are getting more and more sophisticated.

7 Read your sentences to other students. Can they guess the false ones?

3a 🎧 9.1 Listen to the first part of a TV programme about people who use data to track many aspects of their lives. Do they mention any of the things in exercise 1a?

b Work in pairs and answer the questions. Listen again if necessary.
1 What do most of us rely on to answer questions about our lives?
2 What makes self-tracking more possible now?
3 What two gadgets does Kevin Briar have and what do they track?
4 What does Lucy Granger's database track?

4a 🎧 9.2 Listen to the second part of the programme, in which two people debate self-tracking. Take notes, then summarise the basic points that each person makes.

b Work in pairs and compare your answers. Listen again if necessary.

Reading and speaking

1 **Work in groups and discuss the questions.**

- Which science fiction films, novels and TV series are you familiar with?
- What predictions about the future have they come up with? (Think about technology, society, etc.)

2 **Read the title of the article. Predict some of the ideas the author will talk about. Read and check your predictions.**

3 **Read the article again and decide if the statements are true (T) or false (F). Underline evidence to support your answers. Then work in pairs and compare your answers.**

1 The author starts by suggesting that many science fiction predictions have come true.

2 Predictions about travel and domestic automation have been particularly inaccurate.

3 Video calls have made communication with your family much more rewarding.

4 The author thinks that we do not sufficiently appreciate how amazing modern technology is.

5 Science fiction predictions about medical advances make the reality rather disappointing.

6 The author is very impressed with what Dean Kamen's prosthetic arm can do.

7 The three science fiction predictions from the end of the article have all come true.

4 **Find the words/phrases in the article. Can you guess what they mean?**

- inception (line 8)
- clunky (line 19)
- utter (line 29)
- outstrips (line 30)
- pinprick-sized (line 36)
- amputees (line 39)
- non-invasive (line 40)

5 **Work in groups and discuss. Do you agree or disagree with the author's points below?**

- video calls are still rather unsatisfactory.
- computers 'utterly dominate' our lives.
- we are too complacent about the wonders of modern technology.
- technological advances in the field of medicine are the most impressive.
- a 'point of view' gun would be very handy in arguments.

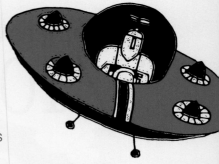

From fantasy to reality:

How science fiction has influenced technology

by Adam Rutherford

Instead of cruising in on a hoverboard, I rode my bike to the office today. The bicycle was invented in the 19th century. Almost the whole journey was on a form of tarmac, invented at the end of that same century. Instead of taking a pill for breakfast, I had a bacon roll, cooked using gas.
5 Science fiction has lied to us.

Making predictions is tricky, especially about the future, as physicist Niels Bohr quipped. In science fiction, you can't escape that challenge, though. Since the inception of the genre in the 19th century, writers have tirelessly imagined the things to come: gadgets that humankind will invent to make
10 life easier. But in so many instances, those promises have not come to pass. The biggest disappointments are in travel – jet packs, hoverboards and flying cars are yet to fill the skies. Air travel has become significantly cheaper and wide-reaching, but only using distinctly 20th-century technology: commercial aeroplanes are much the same as they were 50 years ago.

15 Automation is what science fiction frequently delivers, but its arrival in the real world has been unpredictable. Domestic robots with a degree of intelligence are yet to materialise, though robotic vacuum cleaners are commercially available – even if they are fairly hopeless. Video calls have now arrived – sort of – but conferencing on Skype is still clunky. In mobiles, video call technology
20 is now available, so when your dad rings to update you on his vegetable patch, he'll be able to see your look of perplexed boredom.

The truth is that we quickly forget the astonishment of invention: our wonderment is soon replaced with complacency. We should try to stay in that period of awe. It is astonishing that the contents of every book ever written
25 can be stored in a box the size of a coffin. Or that you can carry 10,000 albums on an object kept in your pocket. Or that almost all the information in the world can be accessed almost anywhere at any time. All these actions are dependent on the emergence of the microchip and its place in computers. Yet sci-fi didn't predict the utter dominance of the computer in running our lives.

30 But the real area where reality far outstrips predictions is medicine. Sure, fiction would describe humans as 'disease-free' or 'with access to panacea', but without going into detail. Both are still absent, but the progress made in maintaining life is breathtaking. With relative ease, we can sequence anyone's genome, giving a read-out of our entire genetic code. This means we can
35 pinpoint the underlying genetic cause of thousands of diseases in minutes. We can perform complex surgery by making pinprick-sized holes in the flesh.

Dean Kamen, inventor of the Segway personal transporter, has been working on a robotic prosthetic arm with 14 degrees of freedom (normal arms have 21) for amputees for several years now, and it is astonishing. I saw a video
40 demo last year in which an amputee soldier strapped on the arm (it is non-invasive, so all the electrical connections are done via skin contact), and then proceeded to not only pick up a screw between thumb and forefinger, but screw it into a hole. The arm costs many millions of dollars, but technology is emerging that could make fully controllable robotic prosthetics the norm.

45 Photosensitive implants now exist that can replace damaged cells in the retina and can thus restore sight to the blind. While the inventions of science fiction can show great ideas we'd like to happen, nothing surpasses the inventiveness of people in the real world.

Things science fiction got right

(and some that would be handy)

Touch screens

Crew members of the Starship Enterprise in *Star Trek: The Next Generation* (1987) would read everything on a buttonless, colour-screen tablet. But before that, in 1978, Arthur Dent negotiated the universe with *The Hitchhiker's Guide to the Galaxy*, an interactive touch screen book that contained all the useful (and useless) information in the universe.

Automatic doors

In 1899, HG Wells wrote in *When the Sleeper Wakes* that two men 'turned obediently … and instead of going through the archway, walked straight to the dead wall of the apartment opposite the archway. And then came a strange thing; a long strip of this apparently solid wall rolled up with a snap, hung over the two retreating men and fell again.' The first automatic door was not installed until 1960, but now they are ubiquitous.

'Point-of-view' gun

For his screenplay adaption of *The Hitchhiker's Guide to the Galaxy*, Douglas Adams added a new weapon to sci-fi's arsenal. Fed up with ending spousal arguments with the phrase 'You just don't get it, do you?', the Intergalactic Consortium of Angry Housewives invented a gun that would allow the shot person to see things from the perspective of the shooter.

Word web (way)

route/direction
ask the way = ask for directions
lead the way = go ahead/first
1 _____ =
discover the route somewhere
2 _____ =
be familiar with the route somewhere
3 _____ = arriving soon

manner/method
This is **the best way** to cook beef.
I hate **the way** he laughs.

other
No way!
= Absolutely not!
By the way(used to change topic)
9_____ =
take extra trouble to do something
8 _____
= much too (big)

get what you want
have your own way
= have things as you want them

blocking or avoiding
be/get in the way
= block the path
get 4_____
= stop blocking the path

describing progress
the way forward
7 _____
= in progress
6 _____
= make it possible for something to happen

position/situation
the wrong way round
= reversed
5 _____ = reversed

way

Wordspot *way*

1a Choose the correct phrases.

1 Many people believe that high-speed rail travel is **out of the way** / **the way forward** / **under way** for public transport.

2 I've only just started work on this report. **By the way** / **No way** / **In a bad way** will it be finished tonight.

3 When they get lost, men are more reluctant to **ask the way** / **find their way** / **know the way** than women.

4 You shouldn't let children **go out of their way** / **have their own way** / **get in the way** all the time or they will grow up spoiled.

5 Apparently, the taxi is **in the way** / **on the way** / **paving the way**.

6 That shirt is the **wrong way up** / **the wrong way round** / **way too big for you** – try a smaller size.

b Complete the word web with phrases from exercise 1a.

2a Complete the conversations using a phrase with *way*.

1 **A:** Can I get past, please?
  B: Oh, I'm sorry, are my bags _____ ?

2 **A:** Oh, dear! I think we're lost.
  B: Why don't you stop and _____ ?

3 **A:** What do you think we should buy Sophie for her birthday? How about a doll?
  B: _____ ! She's 14 years old. She's _____ for dolls!

4 **A:** Were the staff nice at the hotel?
  B: Oh yes, they really _____ to make us feel at home.

5 **A:** OK, we'll drive to the restaurant. Do you _____ ?
  B: I'm not sure I remember it. You'd better _____ and we'll follow behind.

6 **A:** When will the new cinema complex open?
  B: They expect the work to be _____ by the beginning of next month.

7 **A:** How many children does Geraldine have now?
  B: Three. And there's another one _____ !

8 **A:** Is this how I put the ink cartridge in?
  B: No, you've got it _____ . Here, let me do it.

b 🎧 9.3 Listen and check.

Task

Present a fantasy invention

Preparation Listening and speaking

1a Read the description of *My Fantasy Invention* on the web page below. How does the show work?

b Work in pairs. Now read the list of recent entries on the web page and guess what each invention might be.

2 🎧 9.4 Listen to five people presenting their fantasy inventions and answer the questions.

    1 Which inventions from the list in exercise 1 are they talking about?

    2 What, roughly, would each invention be like? How would it work?

3 Why does each speaker think their invention would be useful and to whom?

4 Listen again and tick the phrases you hear in the Useful language box.

5 Work in pairs and compare your answers. Discuss the questions below.

- Which speakers do you think are most/least persuasive? Why?
- What questions would you ask about each invention if you were on the panel?
- Which would you vote for? Why?

My Fantasy Invention

My Fantasy Invention is a radio programme in which contestants describe a fantasy invention to a panel of experts and the studio audience and try to persuade them of the practical or entertainment value that the invention would have. The inventions do not need to be technically viable. The panel asks questions and at the end of the show the audience votes on the fantasy invention they would most like to own.

Recent entries

- an adult-use playground in the park
- an AnnoyanceTeleporter
- an AnythingFinder
- a bed that can fly at night
- a BusStopper
- a CalorieNeutraliser
- a camera to film your dreams
- a car with no seats/pull-up seats from the floor
- glasses which give you information about what you're seeing around you
- foot-massaging shoes
- a flying car
- a housework robot

- a LazybonesEjectorBed
- a measurement photo app
- a MindReader
- a phone app to monitor what percentage of a conversation you have been talking vs listening
- a solar-charged phone
- a remote control to switch off/turn down the volume of someone who's speaking to you
- a smart coat hanger to match up outfits
- a TailgateLoser
- a teleporter
- a wearable life coach device

Task Speaking

1a Decide which fantasy inventions on the list most appeal to you or think of some ideas of your own. Think briefly about what the inventions would be like, how they would work and what the benefits would be. Ask your teacher for any words/phrases you need.

b Work in groups and compare your answers. Decide which ideas are the most appealing/practical.

2a Work alone or in pairs. Choose one idea that you have discussed to develop further and present to the class.

b Spend five to ten minutes planning what you will say. Think about:

- what the device will look like.
- how it will work (this does not have to be technologically feasible).
- what the benefits will be.
- a name for it if it does not already have one.
- the potential market for it/who it will appeal to.
- any obvious objections that might be raised and what you can say to counter them.

> Useful language a and b

3 Work in pairs and practise your presentation. Be as persuasive as possible.

> Useful language b

4a Imagine that the class are the panel/studio audience. Take turns to present your inventions.

b As you listen to the presentations, think of any questions/drawbacks that you would like to bring up. Ask/Respond to each other's questions. At the end, vote on the invention that you would most like to own.

> Useful language c

Follow up Writing

1 Write a short article for *Future Technology* magazine introducing your invention. Describe:

- its name and what it can do.
- what its potential market is.
- the drawbacks that have so far been identified.
- your own assessment of how likely it is to succeed. (You don't have to be realistic.)

USEFUL LANGUAGE

a Describing your invention

My invention would be very (simple).
It would be (a small device) that …
It would fit in (your pocket).
There would be a chip/camera built in that would …
You would simply (press a button/point it at …).
It would look rather like (a remote control).
You would be able to control (the speed) …
It would be about the size of (a button).

b Presenting the benefits

How many times have you (wished you could …)?
Just think of the advantages of being able to …
(This idea) makes perfect sense.
It would particularly appeal to (parents/students).
It would be a great way of (socialising).
It would save stress and time.
I think there could be a real market for it.

c Considering the drawbacks

In practice, I think … would …
It wouldn't be very fair for people who (can't afford it).
I think it would cause chaos.
I think it could actually make the situation worse.
You would never be able to …
For me the main drawback would be …
I think it would meet with a lot of resistance from (environmentalists).

SHARE YOUR TASK

Expand your presentation, taking into account the objections/questions raised by other students to your original presentation

Practise your presentation until you feel confident

Film/Record yourself giving your presentation

Share your film/recording with other students

LANGUAGE LIVE

Speaking
Explaining technical problems

1 What are you like at dealing with technical problems? What would you do in each situation below?

* Your computer is running very slowly.
* Your mobile phone can't find a signal.
* The printer at work/in college has jammed.

2a 🎧 9.5 Listen to three people describing technical problems. What is the problem in each case?

b Work in pairs and complete the sentences. Then listen again and check.

Conversation 1
1 It won't connect to the _____ .
2 The computer just can't find my wireless _____ .
3 It throws up an _____ message.
4 The screen freezes and I have to _____ .
5 Have you backed up all your files to an external _____ disk?

Conversation 2
6 I didn't print out a _____ copy, but I've got the confirmation email.
7 If you _____ down to the bottom, you can see it.
8 Have you installed any _____ software?
9 I had to _____ the operating system.
10 It asked me to set up an account and _____ a new password.
11 It's _____ a couple of times.
12 Have you _____ the phone?

Conversation 3
13 The drawer's _____ – I can't open it.
14 The screen is _____ – nothing's happening.
15 I'm so sorry, madam, this till is very _____ .
16 Hold down 'Clear' and _____ 'Delete'.
17 It's a process of _____ and error.
18 Turn it _____ and turn it _____ again.

3 Work in pairs. Discuss the questions below.

1 Which of the following do/don't you do? Why?
* sometimes print out a hard copy of your emails
* back up all your files
* install antivirus software
* use a process of trial and error to solve problems
* create a new password for each new account
* always update to the latest operating system

2a Do you have hardware which does the following?
* runs slowly
* often freezes
* jams a lot
* is temperamental
* sometimes crashes or needs rebooting
* sometimes throws up error messages

b What type of hardware is it? What do you do to resolve the problem?

4a Work in pairs. Imagine that a friend asks you for help with his/her tablet computer which is running very slowly. List all the questions you could ask. Use the phrases in exercise 2b and your own ideas.

When did the problem start?

Have you installed any new software?

b Act out the conversation.

> Could you help me? My tablet is running very slowly.

> When did the problem start?

Writing
Demanding urgent action

1 Have you ever had to take or send anything back that you bought in a shop or online? What were your experiences?

2 Read the emails and answer the questions.

1 What is each complaint about?
2 Which email is more effective? Why?

A

My dear Sir,

I am writing to you about a most unfortunate topic, one which, I'm sure, will greatly upset you. The topic, naturally, is a complaint and I must clearly request that action is taken as a matter of extreme urgency. I must inform you that I will be paying close attention to the outcome and as these days the internet is a popular way to make public one's complaints, unless I am satisfied by your response, I will write bad things about you on the web. Your repair to my tablet computer, as must now be clear, did not achieve the result I was seeking and thus I am again in contact with you. Not only that, but postage costs and technical support telephone charges are also very high.

I look forward to hearing from you.

Yours respectfully,

Mr Boris

B

Dear Uxis Printers,

I am emailing you concerning the above order for a PhotoSmart printer which I purchased on 20th May. I am very dissatisfied with the printer and the quality of service I have received.

A few days after I bought the printer red streaks started to appear on all my documents and the printer began to throw up error messages. I called your Technical Support helpline, at a cost of 35p a minute, and was advised to remove all the cartridges and perform a reset of the printer. This I duly did, but it made no difference to the problem. After a further call to the helpline and another sizeable phone bill, I was advised to send the printer to the Repairs Department. The Repairs Department held on to my printer for over three weeks before finally returning it to me yesterday. Unfortunately, the fault has not been fixed and every document that I print still has red streaks running through it.

In summary, I have spent £160 on what I thought was a top-quality printer, been charged £10 on calls to your helpline, spent several fruitless hours removing cartridges and trying to fix the problem myself, spent a further £10 on postage costs, waited over three weeks for a repair and still do not have a printer that works. As a consequence, I would like you to immediately reimburse in full the cost of the printer and the expenses I have incurred so far. I would also like you to arrange a courier to collect the printer at a time that is convenient to me.

I look forward to hearing from you in the next few days.

Kind regards,

Philip Le

3a Which email, A or B:

1 fails to get to the point?
2 has a logical organisation?
3 uses overly dramatic, personal language?
4 tells the story in clear, neutral language?
5 makes clear what is being asked for?
6 uses an inappropriate greeting/ending?
7 makes a personal threat?
8 offers a win–win situation as a solution?
9 frequently uses the passive to describe what happened?
10 uses unnatural vocabulary/collocations?

b In what order (1–5) does email B do these things?

1 State what action is being requested.
2 State simply the reason for the email.
3 Summarise the experience from the customer's side.
4 Give a time scale for a reply.
5 Give a history of the problem.

4 Underline any phrases in email B which you think are useful. Then work in pairs and compare your answers.

5a You are going to write an email complaining and demanding urgent action. First turn to page 108. Underline the information which you will include in your email.

b Organise the information into a logical structure. Look at exercise 3b to help you. Then write the first draft of your email.

6 Work in pairs and exchange emails. Comment on the language and structure in each other's email. Is it appropriate and effective? Write your final draft.

AFTER UNIT 9 YOU CAN ...

Describe change, trends and developments at a sophisticated level

Present an original idea to an audience and field queries

Explain technical problems precisely

Write an informal email demanding action in response to a complaint

10

TRUTH AND LIES

IN THIS UNIT

- Grammar: Phrases with *as ... as* + verb; Ellipsis and substitution
- Vocabulary: Truth and lies; *well*
- Task: Detect the lies
- World culture: Cyber crime

Sorry, my alarm clock didn't go off.

Wish you were here!

You won't feel a thing, I promise.

Don't cry – your rabbit's in rabbit heaven.

Sorry, but the dog ate it.

I do care, but I just need some space.

Vocabulary and speaking

Truth and lies

1 Look at the pictures showing six common 'white lies'. Work in groups and discuss the questions below.

- Who might say these things to whom, in what circumstances and why?
- What other things do people often tell white lies about? Think of three more common white lies.
- Do you ever tell white lies like this? Can you remember an occasion and what happened?

2 Read situations 1–13 and decide who is lying and who is telling the truth. Are there any cases where this is not clear?

Is it ever OK to lie?

1 A invites his old friend B to dinner along with some people that B can't stand. So, on the afternoon of the dinner, B texts A to say that he has a stomach bug and won't be able to come.

2 A husband asks his wife why she thinks he is putting on weight. She has thought for years that he is inactive and drinks too much beer and tells him so **bluntly**.

3 A tells B **a rumour** that C and D, both in relationships with other people, are having an **illicit** affair. B only half-believes the story, but tells several other people anyway.

4 A woman asks her best friend if the colour of her new dress suits her. Her friend doesn't think it does, but says it looks great.

5 A woman has a terrible morning in which everything seems to go wrong. She retells the story throughout the day to various friends, each time **embellishing the facts** to make it more amusing. By the end of the day, it has changed considerably!

6 A man who has been going out with his girlfriend for two years meets and falls in love with another woman. However, he does not finish with his girlfriend, who is **under a false impression** that they are going to get married.

7 A little girl tells her mother that her brother has eaten some sweets which their mother had told them not to eat.

8 A child has broken his mother's favourite vase, but when she asks, he says the cat did it.

9 **Testifying under oath**, a mother tells a court of law that her teenage son was at home with her on the evening that he was actually stealing a car with his friends. As a result, her son **gets away with** the crime, although his friends are sent to prison.

10 For her doctoral thesis, a student copies some sections from an obscure book that is now out of print and **passes it off** as her own work.

11 A man goes round calling on old-age pensioners, selling them **bogus** home security systems for hundreds of pounds. The security systems are completely useless.

12 A man makes a perfect copy of a painting by a famous artist, which is sold to a private collector for a large amount of money.

13 A group of young men set up some photos of what are supposed to be aliens. Thousands of people **are taken in** and they end up selling their pictures to several newspapers.

3 Match phrases a–m with situations 1–13 in exercise 2. More than one answer may be possible.

a telling **a white lie**   4
b spreading malicious gossip
c making an excuse
d exaggerating
e telling tales
f committing perjury
g **conning** people out of money
h telling a fib
i plagiarism
j **cheating on** someone
k committing forgery
l carrying out a hoax
m telling a few **home truths**

4a Read the situations in exercise 2 again and decide which comment below best reflects how you feel about what the person did.

- It was more **tactful** to lie than to tell the truth.
- It was wrong to **deceive** others, but it didn't **do** much **harm**.
- What this person did was **immoral**, but understandable.
- Personally, I wouldn't **trust** someone who behaved like this.
- This was immoral and **unscrupulous**.
- other

b Work in pairs and compare your answers. Discuss the questions using the words in bold in exercises 2, 3 and 4a to explain your answers.

- How would you have behaved in situations 1–6?
- In situations 7 and 8, which child would you punish or tell off and why?
- Which crimes in situations 9–13 are the most/least immoral?

5 Add the words/phrases in bold in exercises 2, 3 and 4a to the word web below.

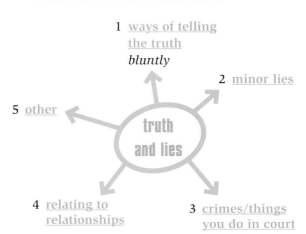

1 ways of telling the truth
bluntly

2 minor lies

5 other

truth and lies

4 relating to relationships

3 crimes/things you do in court

97

Listening
Living a lie

1 Work in pairs and discuss the questions.

- What do you think are some of the qualities of a good undercover police officer?
- What do you think are some of the things undercover officers must never/always do?
- Would you make a good undercover officer? Why?/Why not?

2a You are going to listen to the true story of an undercover officer, Jon K, who spent seven years spying on environmental activists. Which words/phrases in the box do you think apply to Jon K and which to the activists?

provide intelligence	a new identity	vegan
be set up by the police	protest banners	infiltrate
charged with a crime	unconventional	sue the police
have your conviction overturned		

b 🎧 10.1 Listen to the first part of the story of Jon K and decide if the statements are true (T) or false (F). Correct the false statements.

1 Jon's father was an undercover officer.
2 Jon spent as much time as possible with his family.
3 Jon was chosen to join the new police unit because he already looked like an activist.
4 He was nicknamed Johnny Cash because of his skill as a climber.
5 Jon agreed with many of the aims of the environmental protestors.

3a You are going to listen to the second part of the story. Which of these sentences do you think are the reason Jon began to question which side was right? More than one reason may be correct.

1 He was attacked by the police.
2 He fell in love.
3 He was charged with a crime.

b 🎧 10.2 Listen and check your answer to exercise 3a. Answer the questions.

1 What happened at the protest in Edinburgh in 2004?
2 What happened to Jon's marriage?
3 Who did Jon find it most difficult to lie to?
4 Why did the police arrest over 100 people?
5 Why did Jon suspect he was being set up?

4 You are going to listen to the final part of the story. Predict what you think will happen.

5 🎧 10.3 Listen and answer the questions.

1 Why did Jon come under suspicion from activists and the police?
2 Why did Jon resign?
3 How was his true identity uncovered by his activist friends?
4 What was Jon's chance for redemption?
5 Who sued the police and why?

6 Work in groups and discuss the questions.

- Who do you sympathise with most in the story?
- Who do you think was most to blame for what happened?
- What do you think the outcome of the two cases against the police should be? What damages, if any, would you award?
- What advice would you give to a friend who wanted to become an undercover police officer? An environmental activist?

PATTERNS TO NOTICE

Phrases with *as ... as* + verb

1 Complete the sentences from the story.
  1 Jon always seemed to have _____ much money as he _____ .
  2 He had to get out _____ soon as he _____ .

2 Notice these similar patterns.

(verb) +	as much as as many as as soon as as fast as as long as as often as as far as	+ person +	want/ wanted like/liked can/could need/ needed

You can eat **as much as you want.**

Run **as far as you can,** *then stop.*

7 Answer the questions using phrases from the Patterns to notice box.

1 What does this sign outside a restaurant mean: 'Buffet: all you can eat for €10'?
You can eat as much as you want.
2 You're at a very boring party. Your partner asks when you can leave. What do you say?
3 How many cigarettes can you buy at the airport? There are no limits.
4 I can't give you a lift all the way home, so how far should I take you?
5 How long should I spend doing my homework?
6 Oh dear, I can't eat all this! Do I have to eat it all?
7 How often did you go swimming when you were on holiday?
8 It's very urgent that I see you. How soon can you get here?
9 How many people can I invite to my birthday party?
10 Can't you two walk any faster?
11 How long can I keep the computer games you lent me?

Wordspot

well

1 Look at the word web. Underline any uses of *well* that you were not previously aware of.

2 healthy (= adjective)
look/feel well
Get well soon

3 *well-* + past participle
well-built
well-thought-out
well-dressed

1 satisfactorily or successfully
The concert went well.
Did you sleep well?

4 an interjection in speech
Well, maybe he's right.

well

8 phrases to congratulate people
Well done!
Well tried!
Well played!
Well said!

5 for emphasis
well before dawn
well behind us
well worth doing
well aware

7 *as well* (as) = in addition (to)
I'll have some of this cheese as well, please.
As well as being very talented, she's very hard-working.

6 to add probability with *may, might* and *could*
He may/might well be at home today.
Future generations may/could well see things very differently.

2 As an interjection, *well* can have subtly different meanings. Match the meanings in the box with uses 1–8.

for emphasis	to pause
to accept a situation	to show surprise
to show anger/annoyance	to express doubt
to show you've finished	to continue a story

1 Well, well! Fancy Andy and Laura getting married!
2 Well, you know what I think – I completely agree!
3 Well, I think she could have phoned and apologised!
4 Well, maybe. What do other people think?
5 Well, let me think.
6 You know what you told me about Erica the other day? Well, after I spoke to you, I saw her in the supermarket and …
7 Well, if you're sure that's what you really want …
8 Well, I think that's it then.

3a Work in pairs. What do the *well-* + past participle adjectives in the box mean? Use a dictionary if necessary.

well-balanced	well-educated	well-looked-after
well-behaved	well-written	well-paid
well-built	well-informed	well-prepared
well-chosen	well-fed	well-read
well-dressed	well-known	well-thought-out
well-earned	well-laid-outt	

b Which of the adjectives in exercise 3a should these things/people be? Compare your answers with other students.

- books
- children
- shops
- exam candidates
- teacher
- a holiday
- babies
- a potential husband/wife
- everyone

4 Put *well* in the correct place in the sentences to add emphasis.

well
1 I think all of you are ^ aware of the difficulties we have faced recently.
2 By the time we got home, it was after eight o'clock.
3 Personally, I think the end results have been worth the effort.
4 As you know, you are not allowed to smoke in here.
5 By the time they arrived – over two hours late – I was truly fed up.
6 Marta is ahead of the other students in the class.
7 The Chinese were using paper money before people in the West.

HOW DO YOU KNOW IF SOMEONE IS LYING?

1 HOW THE ANCIENT CHINESE DID IT

The Chinese used rice. An examination for truthfulness might go something like this: 'Is your name Chiang?' (They know the guy's name is, in fact, Chiang.)

'Yes.'

The interrogators hand Mr Chiang some rice. They have already counted the number of rice grains.

'OK. Put this handful of rice in your mouth. Hold it for three seconds. Spit it out.'

Then they count how many rice grains come out.

'Did you steal the chicken?'

'No.'

'OK. Put this handful of rice in your mouth. Hold it for three seconds. Spit it out.'

Again, they knew how many grains went in, and they count how many come out. If more grains come out after the question about the stolen chicken than came out after the 'easy' question, where the suspect truthfully gave his name, they know he's lying. How? The stress of being caught lying makes the suspect's mouth drier. Fewer grains stick. More come out. Mr Chiang stole the chicken.

2 MODERN LIE DETECTORS

Modern lie detectors, also known as polygraphs, rely on the same basic principle – that lying causes bodily changes which can be detected and measured. Having agreed to do the test (if the test is done under duress, the extra stress caused makes the test unreliable), the suspect is connected to three devices measuring blood pressure, breathing rate and electrodermal response (the increased amount of electricity which flows to the skin when we sweat). Increased activity in these areas suggests increased stress, which means the subject might be lying. Lie detectors have been widely used in the USA since the 1950s, but they remain controversial and their results are not always accepted by courts. Nowadays, polygraphs are used by the US police, the CIA and the FBI to screen job applicants, but private employers are not allowed to subject job candidates to polygraph examinations, except in a few high-security industries like pharmaceuticals and money manufacturing.

3 YOUR VOICE

Cheaper and faster than a polygraph, the Voice Stress Analyser, or VSA, is based on the premise that our voice changes when we are under stress – when we're lying, for example. The VSA detects the changes and will work on a telephone, tape-recording or from the next room via a wireless mike or bug. The analyser monitors the subject's voice patterns and inflections, and electronically evaluates their relative stress patterns to determine if they are lying or not. Now you can even buy a 'Truth Phone', so when your other half rings to say they're working late at the office, you can immediately know if it's true or not! Research indicates this technology is not very precise at picking up deceitfulness.

4 HESITATION

The period of time between the last word of an investigator's question and the first word of the subject's response is known as 'response latency'. Research tells us that the average response latency for subjects who are telling the truth is 0.5 seconds, whereas the average latency for liars is 1.5 seconds. This is because the subject is mentally considering whether to tell the truth, part of the truth or a complete lie. Latencies of two or three seconds should be regarded as highly suspicious; in other words, he who hesitates … is probably lying!

5 BLUSHING

According to researchers in the USA, when someone lies, you get an instantaneous warming around the eyes, commonly known as 'blushing'. Dr James Levine of the Mayo Clinic in Rochester, Minnesota, speculates that people who lie are afraid of getting caught. 'That fear triggers a primitive response to run away. Blood goes to the eyes so that the liar can more efficiently map out an escape route,' he says. A high-definition, heat-sensing camera can detect such blushes. The new technology has proved more reliable than conventional lie detectors and could offer a new tool for mass security screening at places like airports, office buildings and high-profile events.

Reading and speaking

1 Work in groups and discuss the questions.

- Do you know anyone who is a habitual liar? What kind of things do they say?
- In which jobs is it particularly important that you are trustworthy?
- Are there any jobs in which it is an advantage to be a good liar?
- What characteristics does a good liar need?

2a Work in pairs. List ways in which people often give away the fact that they are lying.

not looking you in the eye, …

b Read the article about lying. How many of the ways you listed are in the article? What other ways are mentioned?

3 Work in pairs. Read the article again and decide which statements are true. Give reasons. More than one answer may be true.

1 a Lying makes it harder to spit out the grains of rice.
   b Lying makes it easier to spit out the grains of rice.
   c The rice makes your mouth go dry.
2 a Lie detectors can only work if used voluntarily.
   b Lie detectors rely on various forms of physical data.
   c Lie detectors are reliable in the vast majority of cases.
3 a You don't have to be in the same room as the subject to use the VSA.
   b The VSA measures how stressed you are rather than whether or not you're lying.
   c The main advantages of the VSA are its cheapness and reliability.
4 a People hesitate before lying because they need to prepare their lie.
   b The latency period more than doubles when people are lying.
   c The less hesitation there is, the less likely it is that you're lying.
5 a People blush as the result of a primitive 'fight or flight' instinct.
   b Special machinery is needed to detect these blushes.
   c This technology is already in use for security screening at airports.

4 Think of a word/phrase that could replace the following words/phrases in the article without changing the meaning.

- examination (section 1)
- hand (section 1)
- bodily (section 2)
- under duress (section 2)
- premise (section 3)
- other half (section 3)
- picking up (section 4)
- mentally considering (section 4)
- getting (section 5)
- high-profile (section 5)

5 Work in groups and discuss the questions.

- Did you find any of the techniques surprising?
- Which seem to be the most/least reliable?
- In what circumstances do you think such tests should be used? What objections can you think of?
- Have you ever been in a situation where you were telling the truth and nobody believed you?

Grammar review
Ellipsis and substitution

1a Read the conversation and shorten the parts in bold. You may have to change some of the words.

A: Have you finished with the paper?
B: Hang on – I'm just reading an article about lie detectors.
A: Oh yes, ¹**that article about lie detectors**. I started reading it this morning, but ²**I didn't finish reading it**. Is it interesting?
B: Yes. Apparently, <u>you</u> can tell someone's lying because <u>they</u> can't help blushing.
A: ³**Do they realise they're blushing**?
B: No, ⁴**I don't think they realise they are blushing**. Tell me, do you ever blush when you talk to me?
A: No, of course ⁵**I don't ever blush when I talk to you**. That's because I never lie to you.
B: Is that true?
A: ⁶**Of course it's true**. ⁷**I never lie to you and you never lie to me**, right?
B: So, why are you blushing now, then?

b 🎧 **10.4** Listen and check.

2 Who do *you* and *they* underlined refer to in the conversation? Could you substitute these with any other pronouns?

> **Grammar extension bank, pages 148–152**

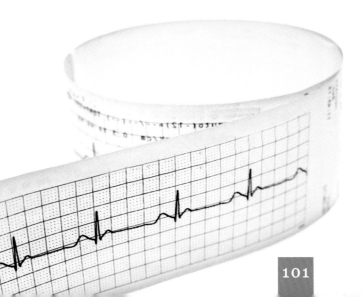

Task

Detect the lies

Family and relatives

How you spent last weekend

Things you love

Things you hate

Things you own

Famous people you've met

Lie detector!

Places you've been

Your education/jobs you've done

Past relationships

Skills and abilities you have

Illnesses/accidents/allergies you've had

Unusual experiences you've had

Preparation Listening

1 Work in pairs. Read the rules of *Lie detector!*, then explain in your own words how it works.

Lie detector! Rules

- In groups, take turns to choose a topic to talk about.
- Once a topic has been used, other players cannot use it.
- Talk for approximately one minute about the topic. You should mainly tell the truth, but try to slip in three lies in the course of the minute.
- When you have finished, the others can ask up to five questions about what you said.
- The others guess what the three lies were. They get a point for every lie they guess correctly.
- You get a point for every lie you get away with!

USEFUL LANGUAGE

a Making statements
I know this is hard to believe, but ...
You may not believe this, but once ...
Believe it or not, ...
As a matter of fact, I ...

b Checking information
Tell us a bit more about ...
Where/What/Why exactly did you ...?
Can you explain exactly when/how you ...?

c Deciding which statements are true
This one can't possibly be/must be/might be ...
There's no way she could've ...

2 🎧 **10.5** Listen to some people playing the game and answer the questions.

1 Which category is each player talking about?
2 What does he/she say?
3 What were the three lies? Which ones did the other players guess?

Task Speaking

1 Work alone. Decide which six categories in the game you would most like to talk about and what to say. Think about:

- plausible-sounding lies that you can tell.
- truths you can tell that sound unlikely and might fool your partners. (Remember you may have to talk about some categories that you have not chosen.)

> Useful language a

2 Work in pairs or groups and play the game. Who got the most points?

> Useful language b and c

SHARE YOUR TASK

Choose the category you feel most confident talking about and prepare a one-minute talk, either telling the truth or lying.

Practise your talk until you feel confident.

Film/Record yourself giving your talk.

Share your film/recording with other students. Can they guess correctly when you were telling the truth?

CYBER CRIME

Find out first

1a Work in pairs. Look at the list of ways in which people sometimes make fraudulent insurance claims. Can you add any ideas?

- Sell a car for scrap and claim it was stolen.
- Exaggerate the value of household items on a home insurance claim.
- Following a burglary, claim for items that were not actually stolen.
- Falsely claim for unnecessary medical treatment following a minor accident.
- Set fire to the offices of a failing business in order to claim the insurance.

b Work in pairs. Why do you think insurance companies want to prevent this kind of fraud?

2a Work in pairs. Do you know or can you guess the answers to these questions?

1 How do insurance companies try to prevent people making fraudulent insurance claims?
2 How do they detect the small percentage of fraudulent claims amongst the majority of genuine ones?

b Go online and check your answers or ask your teacher.

Search: detecting insurance fraud / suspicious insurance claims / preventing insurance fraud

View

3 ▶ Watch the video about how insurance companies detect fraudulent claims then answer the questions below.

1 How does the software communicate with the phone operator?
2 What is Steve Hayes' job now and who did he work for previously?
3 What does the man on the phone do in the end?

4 Watch again and answer the questions.

1 What do HR and SNS stand for?
2 What methods were used to assess claims before this software?
3 What is the person on the phone trying to claim for?
4 How does Steve try to catch him out?

5 Work in pairs. How do you think lie-detector technology might be used in the future?

FIND OUT MORE

8 Choose one of the crime-prevention methods from the search box and find out more about it. Prepare a short informative presentation for your class. Cover the following points where appropriate.

- what it is
- benefits / examples
- how it works
- what critics say

Search: CCTV / surveillance society / facial-recognition software / predictive policing / DNA evidence / technology and crime-prevention

Present your research

9 Give your presentation to the class. Use the prompts below to help you.

- Most of you will have heard of ...
- Some of you may not have heard of ...
- But / So what exactly is it? Basically, it's ...
- So how widespread is its use? Well, ...
- And what are the benefits of using this technology?
- Critics often argue that ...
- My own feeling is that this technology ...

Tip
Write important words, quotes, facts, etc., on cue cards which you can use to help you remember what you want to say. But don't read from the cards and always look at your audience.

World view

6a ▶ Watch six people discussing whether or not technology will make crime easier or more difficult in the future. Match the people in the box to the ideas below.

Eben   Heather   Imogen   Keith   Jurgen   Ciara

1 Social networking makes it easier for criminals to get together.
2 The pace of technological advance makes the prospects of crime very worrying.
3 The internet makes new types of crime easier, however technology should make it easier for the police to trace criminals.
4 The internet is such a great unknown that it is hard to predict how it will turn out.
5 Certain traditional crimes may become more difficult for criminals to get away with.
6 Criminals themselves are still finding out what is and is not possible.
7 Everyday entertainment devices make it possible to track where you are.
8 In order to prevent cyber crime we are in danger of losing personal rights and freedoms.

b Compare answers in pairs and then watch again to check. What other points and examples do the speakers mention?

7 Discuss. Do you think technology will make crime easier or more difficult? Are you worried about cyber crime in the future?

AFTER UNIT 10 YOU CAN ...

Describe and discuss truth and deceit at a sophisticated level

Use ellipsis and substitution to sound natural and fluent

Describe and discuss internet crime

Research online and give a short presentation about crime and technology

Communication Activities

Unit 1: Reading and vocabulary
Exercise 5, page 9
Student A

Read about Songdo. What are Songdo's answers to the problems of urbanisation?

Songdo

Songdo in South Korea is a brand new city for 65,000 residents and 300,000 workers which is being built entirely from scratch on reclaimed land. It has been planned as a green city in both senses of the word: it is 40 percent open space and it emits one-third of the greenhouse gases of a typical, similar-sized city. Songdo is also a technologically smart city, with electric water taxis, tubes that suck rubbish directly to a central processing facility and millions of wireless electronic sensors everywhere that transmit information to a control room. This information will allow the city to turn off street lights when a road is deserted, for example, or to change the traffic lights to ease congestion.

But perhaps the most surprising technological innovation is the installation of video conferencing screens in every home, office, shopping centre and public building so that video calls can be made whenever and wherever residents want. Songdo's planners hope to render unnecessary much of the day-to-day travelling that we do, such as visiting the doctor and going to see friends.

Songdo is a bold concept, and at an estimated cost of $35 billion, it is far from cheap, but plans are in the process of being drawn up for 20 more such cities across China and India, using Songdo as a template. The ultimate aim, for the planners and builders of Songdo, is to mass-produce cities.

Unit 1: Listening and speaking
Exercise 2a, page 10

Pronunciation guide

A rough (rʌf)-coated, dough (dəʊ)-faced, thoughtful (θɔːt) ploughman (aʊ) strode through (uː) the streets of Scarborough (bʌrə); after falling into a slough (ʌf), he coughed (ɒf) and hiccoughed (ʌp).

Unit 1: Listening and speaking
Exercise 2a, page 10

The following two language facts are false.
- *More English words begin with 't' than any other letter – about 25 percent of all words.*
  (16 percent of all words, begin with 't', not 25.)
- *' ... doctor-speak to simplify communication between doctors.'*
  (There is no such thing as 'doctor-speak'.)

Unit 3: Grammar review
Exercise 3, page 29
Student A

1 Read your sentences to Student B. Student B says which time they refer to: past, present, future or general time.

  1 I wish I **wasn't** so tired all the time.
  2 When I **woke up** this morning there **was** snow everywhere.
  3 A man **walks** into a bar ... ouch!
  4 This time next week I**'ll be lying** on a beach.
  5 Her flight **arrives** at 7:52.
  6 Sorry, Lily can't come to the phone right now – she**'s having** a shower.

2 Listen to Student B's sentences and say which time they refer to.

3 Look at both sets of sentences. Say why the verb forms in bold are used.

Unit 6: Reading
Exercise 4, page 59
Student A
  1 What does Professor Allan Snyder believe?
  2 What does the brain zapper do?
  3 What did the experiment prove?
  4 What are the drawbacks of the brain zapper?

Releasing genius

Scientists have long speculated that so-called 'idiot savants' with extraordinary mental powers (such as the character played by Dustin Hoffman in the film *Rain Man*) may offer a glimpse of what all of us are capable of. Professor Allan Snyder of the University of Sydney supports this view and believes that it may be simply a question of 'switching off' the conscious part of the brain. 'I believe that each of us has non-conscious machinery to do extraordinary art or mathematical calculations, achieve extraordinary feats of memory.'

Dr Robyn Young of Flinders University, Adelaide, has tried to prove the theory by using an electronic brain zapper on 17 volunteers in an attempt to release their artistic and mathematical skills. In a technique known as 'transcranial magnetic stimulation', Dr Young used the zapper to switch off the conscious part of the volunteers' brains, then gave them tasks to complete in order to assess their skills in calculation or drawing. The process, unfortunately, did not turn them into instant geniuses, but five of the volunteers showed some improvement in their performance. According to Dr Young, the technique could eventually be used to help children learn to read or adults to learn a new language. There are, however, some unfortunate side effects to the brain zapper and it may do as much damage as good. 'We had a hard time recruiting volunteers to get their brain zapped,' admitted Young. 'One guy got lost on his way to work the day after the experiment.'

Unit 3: Reading and speaking
Exercise 6, page 29

1 Find another team to debate against and choose a topic. Use the topic of the article you've just read or choose from the list below. Decide which team is 'for' and which is 'against'.

> 1 Most countries either don't have a minimum wage or, if they have one, it is too low. A higher minimum wage should be introduced now.
>
> 2 The income tax rate is too high and should be reduced now.
>
> 3 A university education should always be free.

2 Read the instructions on how to stage a debate.

Debating is a team event, so speakers should always try to work together as a team. Speakers debate a 'motion', i.e. the chosen topic in the form of a clear statement. Each team needs a 'team line'. For the 'for' team, the team line is to explain why the motion is true. For the 'against' team, the team line is to explain why the motion is false. It is the job of each speaker to reinforce the team line.

The order and roles of the speakers

1 The first speaker for the 'for' team speaks for two minutes. He/She presents the team line and some of the arguments to support it.

2 The first speaker for the 'against' team speaks for two minutes. He/She presents the team line and some of the arguments to support it.

3 The second speaker for the 'for' team rebuts the arguments of the other team and presents the rest of the arguments to support the motion.

4 The second speaker for the 'against' team rebuts the arguments of the opposing team and presents the rest of the arguments against the motion.

5 The third speaker for the 'for' team presents a summary of the arguments to support the motion, rebuts all the arguments for the other team and restates the team line.

6 The third speaker for the 'against' team presents a summary of the arguments against the motion, rebuts all the arguments for the other team and restates the team line.

Remember, when you rebut an argument, it is not enough to say that it is wrong. You must explain why it is wrong. Never criticise the speaker – only their arguments.

3 Decide who will be the first, second and third speakers and what they will say. Try to predict what the other team will say and how you can rebut their arguments.

4 Stage the debate. The audience should listen and then vote for a winner based solely on the quality of the team's debating skills.

Unit 4: Wordspot
Exercise 3, page 39
Student A

Read your questions to Student B. He/She answers the questions using body idioms. (Example answers are in brackets.)

1 Say this phrase another way: 'I just couldn't understand what he was saying.' (*I just couldn't **get my head around** what he was saying.*)

2 How can we describe a film, story or poem that is very sad? (*It's **heart-rending**.*)

3 What reason could you give for not going out because you've got so much work to do? (*I'm **up to my eyes** in work.*)

4 Djokovic won the tennis final 6–0, 6–0. He won ...? (*He **won hands down**.*)

5 It's clear that your friend is still very upset about a recent break-up, but has no one to talk to about it. What does he/she need? (*He/She needs **a shoulder to cry on**.*)

6 What might someone have just before they have to address a huge audience? (***Butterflies in their stomach**.*)

7 Our cat will only eat one type of cat food. What does she do when we give her another type? (*She **turns her nose up** at it.*)

Unit 6: Vocabulary and speaking
Exercise 2b, page 56

Answers

2	brainy	9	postgraduate
3	compulsory	10	qualification
4	elementary	11	scholarship
5	graduation	12	timetable
6	kindergarten	13	undergraduate
7	master's	14	vocational
8	oral	15	workshop

Communication Activities

Unit 8: Wordspot

Exercise 4, page 79

Student A

Take turns to ask and answer the questions.

- When did you last receive a present which was just what you wanted? What was it?
- What do you usually do just before you go to sleep at night? What about just after you wake up?
- Do you usually eat a big meal at lunchtime or just a snack? What about in the evening?
- Have you ever had a holiday that was just perfect? Why? What happened?

Unit 8: Reading

Exercise 3a, page 80

1	Women	11	women	21	women
2	men	12	women	22	men
3	men	13	men	23	Women
4	woman	14	woman	24	Men
5	man	15	Men	25	men
6	man	16	men	26	Women
7	women	17	women	27	men
8	man	18	men	28	men
9	woman	19	women		
10	men	20	Men		

Unit 6: Reading

Exercise 4, page 59

Student B

1. Who was the subject of the study? Where was it conducted?
2. What were the findings of the study?
3. What might be the causes of the children's stress?
4. What might be a solution?

Young kids, big worries

Today, 20 percent of modern children suffer from forms of anxieties so severe that they should be classified as psychiatric disorders, say scientists from the University of Maastricht. The researchers interviewed 290 primary school children from the Netherlands aged between eight and thirteen; one in five of them was beset with worries so serious that they affected their ability to lead normal lives. For example, many had trouble sleeping or were afraid to leave their homes; others had problems interacting with their peers. 'Nobody is sure exactly why this is, but these disorders are known to be caused by children internalising their anxiety,' said child psychiatrist Peter Muris. This could be caused by parents being away from their children for long periods or by children being stressed at school. A parent who does not spend time with their child could miss out on the fact that the child has the problem, meaning it can go untreated and get worse. Rather than getting their children assessed by a professional, it could just be a case of parents needing to spend more time with their children.

Unit 9: Language live: writing

Exercise 5a, page 95

1

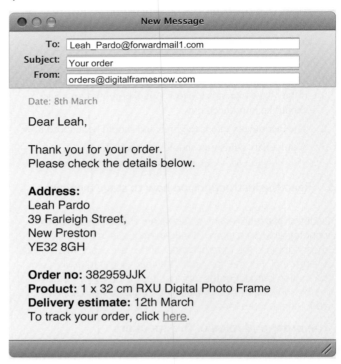

2

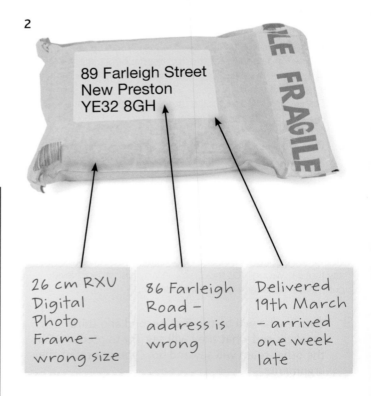

Unit 1: Reading and vocabulary
Exercise 5, page 9
Student B

Read about Medellin. What are Medellin's answers to the problems of urbanisation?

Medellin

Medellin, Colombia's second city, used to have one of the highest crime rates in the world, but thanks to a variety of initiatives, crime has dropped by 80 percent. Surprisingly, one part of the solution is cable cars. Since 2004, the city has invested over $60 million building a system of cable cars to connect the so-called 'barrios' to the centre of the city. The barrios – poorer residential areas – are located in the hills around Medellin and the cable cars, which are efficient and affordable, have reduced some journey times from two hours to seven minutes.

The radical thinking behind the cable cars is to integrate the poor into the city, rather than forcing them to the edge of it and thereby excluding them. Libraries and crèches have been built around the cable car stations, allowing mothers to leave their children close to home while they go to work in the city. The side effects of this project have been to reduce pollution and crime, and to turn what was previously a no-go area into a tourist destination.

The cable cars are, of course, not the only reason for Medellin's renaissance. New and impressive public buildings, designed by local architects, have restored a sense of pride in the city and even the poorest slum housing is now being supplied with water and electricity. Medellin still has challenges to overcome, but already it is being seen as an example to other cities around the world of how to cope with the problems of urbanisation.

Unit 8: Wordspot
Exercise 4, page 79
Student B

Take turns to ask and answer the questions.

- What have you just finished doing at work or school? Is this what you usually do?
- What changes would you need to make to where you live to make it just right for you?
- Have you ever eaten something that was just awful? Have you eaten it again since?
- Does it take you a long time to get ready to go out or just a few minutes?

Unit 3: Grammar review
Exercise 3, page 29
Student B

1   Listen to Student A's sentences and say which time they refer to.

2   Read your sentences to Student A. Student A says which time they refer to: past, present, future or general.

   1   Where **are you going** for your next holiday?
   2   We now **go over** to our financial correspondent for a report on ...
   3   Unemployment **rises** by three percent in the final quarter.
   4   I'll call you as soon as I **arrive**.
   5   It's high time you **started** taking your job more seriously.
   6   By the time I passed my driving test, I**'d been having** lessons for over a year.

3   Look at both sets of sentences. Say why the verb forms in bold are used.

Unit 4: Wordspot
Exercise 3, page 39
Student B

Read your questions to Student A. He/She answers the questions using body idioms. (Example answers are in brackets.)

1   My brother went on a frightening water ride at Water World theme park. How did he describe it? (*It was **hair-raising**!*)
2   We had a delicious, appetising meal. How did we describe it? (*It was **mouth-watering**!*)
3   My friend is trying to convince me that he's engaged to a film star, but I don't believe him. What do I say to him? (*You're **pulling my leg**!*)
4   He looked so ridiculous dressed in that wig that we had to laugh! What couldn't we do? (*We couldn't **keep a straight face**.*)
5   What might a corrupt police officer do when he sees something illegal happening? (*He might **turn a blind eye**.*)
6   When I asked him how his wife was, he said she'd left him. What did I do? (*You **put your foot in it**.*)
7   A waitress keeps dropping things all over the place. How could you describe her? (*She's **all fingers and thumbs**.*)

Communication Activities

Freddie Finn (55)

DJ and TV presenter, a household name, with powerful connections in the media. His jokey, jovial manner makes him very popular with the public, but behind the scenes he has a reputation for being overbearing and egocentric. He famously smoked heavily, but since suffering from a heart attack three years ago he has taken up power-walking and his doctors say that he is fit enough to make the trip.

Alex Lane (20)

Member of the super-popular boy band Slur. He has a huge following amongst teenage girls and will attract a lot of publicity for the trip. Despite his glamorous image, he is said to be extremely shy and awkward socially, although kind-natured and willing to learn. He cannot drive.

Viv Shepherd (26)

Professional cyclist, popular with the public since her surprise Olympic gold medal win last year. Those who know her describe her as sweet-natured, but highly strung and psychologically fragile; she has had well-publicised emotional problems in the past. Super-fit.

Angelique (29)

Ex-model and reality TV star, famous for dating footballers and minor pop stars. She is constantly appearing on the covers of celebrity magazines, but is known to be tough, shrewd and energetic, with a good eye for publicity opportunities. She describes herself as 'mouthy' and people tend to either love or hate her. She is said to be interested in going on the trip to improve her image and has already appeared on a number of TV shows declaring how passionately she cares about education in poor countries. She is good at horse-riding and skiing.

Mo Sharif (34)

Ex-charity worker and journalist, who is now chief foreign correspondent on the national news. Known to the public for his high-profile reports on the plight of children in war zones, and an expert on African affairs, he has well-known left-wing views. Colleagues describe him as level-headed and highly intelligent, but he is also known to be impatient and some people claim he is arrogant. He has publicly expressed his contempt for celebrity culture and people who appear in celebrity magazines. He says he is quite fit, but does not do any regular exercise.

Nadia Doran (52)

Member of Parliament and ex-lawyer. She is known for her outspoken, even outrageous and rather right-wing opinions. The leader of her party has publicly dissociated himself from her and she is a frequent figure of fun in the media, although people who know her well say that newspapers treat her unfairly and that she is actually smart, kind and warm-hearted, if rather headstrong. She is known to be super-energetic and jogs daily. She has been married three times.

Ricky Lowe (39)

Extremely popular comedian, with an excellent TV manner. He is said by friends to be as easy-going and fun in private as he is on TV. He is known for his charity work, especially with children, and has appeared in a number of previous TV fundraising events. He is, however, considerably overweight and does not exercise.

Apricot Albany (22)

Daughter of an internationally famous rock guitarist and his supermodel wife. Apricot is 'famous for being famous'. In the past she has had well-publicised problems with drugs and alcohol, but is said to have been 'clean' for the last nine months and for the last two months has been working as a charity volunteer in India. If she is chosen for the celebrity trek, her father has promised to perform a free concert in aid of Operation Educate, which would be of considerable value to the fundraising and publicity effort. She cannot drive and has been quoted as saying that she hates all forms of sport and fitness. She is currently dating the ex-fiancé of Angelique (left).

Lena Chang (45)

Multi-millionaire international businesswoman. Although she appears frequently as a 'talking head' on business and financial programmes, she is not especially well-known to the public in general. She is, however, well-known and powerful in the business world and could bring lots of valuable sponsorship. Insiders are full of praise for her negotiating and people skills and describe her as quietly charismatic and highly determined. She has promised that one of her companies will provide building materials and equipment to the schools, in return for publicity during the trek. She describes herself as averagely fit, but does not do any regular training.

Bishop Martin Okoro (68)

Internationally renowned figure. Respected by people of all religions for the way in which he has promoted peace and tolerance, his courtesy and good humour have made him a favourite on TV, too. The bishop is passionate about education in developing countries and his association with the project would bring real international kudos. He has no known health problems apart from high blood pressure and is said to be fit and energetic for his age. His other commitments mean that he could only join the trip for the first month.

01 LANGUAGE SUMMARY

CONTINUOUS VERB FORMS

General

1   We use continuous verb forms to describe actions which we see happening over a period of time.
*I hear you're **doing** a cookery course.*
*We **were watching** an interesting series about murders.*
*I've **been trying** to phone you.* (= over a period of time)
*When you finish work, we'**ll be waiting** for you outside.*
With simple verb forms we are not interested in this sense of duration.

2   We may also see the situation as:
  *   temporary.
      *We'**re staying** with my uncle while our house **is being decorated**.*
  *   happening around a point of time.
      *At 12 o'clock James **was** still **working** on his computer.*
      *Don't phone me at 12:00. I'**ll be having** a meeting.*
  *   involving change or development.
      *She **was getting** more disobedient every day.*
      *There's no doubt the world's climate **is changing**.*
  *   incomplete.
      *We **were having** a very interesting conversation.*
      (= before you interrupted)
      *I've **been reading** Nelson Mandela's autobiography.*
      (= but I haven't finished it)

NOTICE!

- The idea of incompletion is especially important with continuous perfect forms. Simple perfect forms emphasise completion
(= and therefore the result of the action).

  *The local council **have spent** a lot of money on new roads.*
  (= Now they are finished.)

  *We'**d downloaded** some files from the internet.*
  (= This is completed.)

- Continuous perfect forms emphasise the action itself.

  *The local council **have been spending** a lot of money on new roads.* (= This is how they have been spending their money – perhaps the roads are not complete.)

  *We'**d been downloading** some files from the internet.* (= This was how we spent our time, but perhaps we didn't finish.)

---

3   The continuous infinitive (*be/to be + -ing*) also emphasises that an action is in progress at a particular time.
*Wherever you go nowadays, everyone seems **to be speaking** English.* (= They are speaking English when you hear them.)
  *   Compare this to:
      Wherever you go nowadays, everyone seems to speak English. (= They are generally able to speak English.)

Exercises 1–3, page 114

Special uses of continuous forms

1   *ALWAYS* + continuous form
  *   *always* + the simple form simply indicates that something happens regularly.
      *I **always start** work early.*
  *   However, *always* + the continuous form is also common. This stresses the repetitiveness of the action and often indicates that the speaker finds the repeated action surprising, strange or irritating.
      *Stanley **was always dreaming** up strange schemes to make money.*
      *Christian'**s always smiling**.*
      *I'**m always locking** myself out.*
  *   We use *constantly*, *forever*, *continually*, etc. in the same way.
      *How can I be expected to work if you'**re constantly interrupting**?*
      *My parents **were continually criticising** me.*

Exercise 4, page 114

2   **Past continuous for polite requests**
    We can use the Past continuous to make requests more polite and tentative.
    *I **was wondering** if you could recommend a good restaurant.*
    *I **was hoping** you might help me with this application form.*

3   **Present continuous for future arrangements**
  *   The Present continuous is commonly used to describe arrangements for the future.
      *They'**re opening** that new hypermarket next week.*
      *What **are** you **doing** over Christmas?*
  *   In this case, either there is a future time phrase in the sentence or it is clear from the context that we are talking about the future. (See Unit 3 and Unit 9 Language summaries, pages 120 and 144.)

4 Modal verbs

With modal verbs, the continuous infinitive can have a different meaning from the simple infinitive.

They **might be staying** at the Sheraton Hotel. (= present possibility)

They **might stay** at the Sheraton Hotel. (= future possibility)

What a terrible noise! They **must be having** a party. (= logical conclusion)

We **must have** a party soon. (= personal obligation)

Exercises 5–6, page 115

Verbs which change meaning in continuous and simple forms

1 State verbs

- Verbs which describe states only occur in the simple form.

    Nick **seems** very friendly.

    I **didn't know** Claire's dad. He died before we met.

- The most common state verbs are:
    - be.
    - verbs of possession and unchangeable states (have, weigh, measure, fit).

        Oh, dear! This dress **doesn't fit** any more!
    - verbs to do with the senses (appear, see, look, smell, taste).

        The minister **appears** puzzled by the accusations against him.
    - verbs describing thoughts and processes (think, feel, expect).

        I **expect** he'll soon be here.

2 Verbs to describe states or actions

- If the verbs above are used in the continuous form, they become 'actions' of some sort.
- The verb be occurs in the continuous form when it refers to behaviour which is temporary and/or deliberate (i.e. a kind of 'action').

    Why **is** everybody so unhelpful? (= They are always like this – a state.)

    Why **is** everybody **being** so unhelpful? (= They are not normally like this.)

- Note that is being cannot be used when there is no volition (deliberate will) involved.

    The weather is very wet at the moment. [✓]

    The weather is being very hot at the moment. [X]

- Other verbs have a different meaning in their continuous and simple forms.

STATES	ACTIONS
It **looks**/**appears** to be OK. (= seems)	And the referee **is looking** at his watch … She**'s appearing** in public for the first time. (= performing)
I **see** a bright light. (= with my eyes)	I**'m seeing** Thomas tonight. (= meeting)
I **think** that's all. (= suppose/guess)	I**'m thinking** about what you said. (= considering)
I **expect** you're tired. (= imagine)	I**'m expecting** an important phone call. (= waiting for)
I have always **admired** Roosevelt. (= have had a good opinion of)	I **was** just **admiring** your new car. (= looking at it with appreciation)
I **have** a large family. (= possess)	She**'s having** a bath. (= taking)
It **weighs** 82 kg and **measures** 3 metres. (a fact)	The nurse **is weighing** and **measuring** the baby. (an activity)
My suit **doesn't fit** me any more. (= It's not the correct size.)	A man **is fitting** a new shower unit. (= installing)

NOTICE!

A few verbs which describe physical feelings (feel, hurt, ache) can be used in either the simple or continuous form to talk about the present moment. There is no difference in meaning.

'Why are you lying down?' 'My back **hurts**/**is hurting**.'

Are you feeling/**Do you feel** better today?

Exercises 7–8, page 115

CONTINUOUS VERB FORMS

1   Underline the continuous verb forms in the article. Explain why a continuous form is used in each case.

A TALL ORDER

I'm sitting in a café, waiting to meet Ray Close for our interview, when several people look up. In walks Ray and he's bending down to fit through the door. At just under seven feet (about two metres), he's unusually tall. 'People think that being a tall man makes it easy to meet women,' he says, 'but no one really wants to be with someone who towers over them. I was getting more depressed about it every day.' That's why he set up *Tallpals*, a dating website for tall people. Since he set up the website, he's been working really hard to promote it and now it seems to be paying off. He regularly receives emails from former clients who are now enjoying happy relationships.

Kyla Shayles was one of the first to sign up: 'Before I found out about *Tallpals*, I'd been going on dates through other dating websites. But I was always turning up on the date, only to be met with a shocked expression and then to have an uncomfortable evening, where the guy was constantly planning how to get out of the rest of the date,' she explains. 'I've been going on a few dates through *Tallpals* now and it's so much more relaxed, as we both know what to expect. At the end of last year I met a really nice guy and it's been going really well between us so far.'

2   Choose the correct answers.

1   A: Did you notice they seemed a bit quiet?
    B: Yes, I think they'd **argued / been arguing** again.
2   A: Do you think United will win the cup?
    B: No – they've **played / been playing** badly recently.
3   A: Do you want to come out with us after work?
    B: I can't – I haven't **finished / been finishing**.
4   A: What made you decide to move to China?
    B: I'd **thought / been thinking** about it for a long time, when I was offered a job there.
5   A: Why can't I watch the film tonight, Mum?
    B: Because you've **watched / been watching** TV all afternoon and you haven't **done / been doing** your homework yet.
6   A: Do you know what's going on with Stuart?
    B: No – I haven't **seen / been seeing** him for ages.
7   A: Why was Carol so annoyed with you?
    B: Because I'd **left / been leaving** a big pile of work for her to do.
8   A: What have you **done / been doing** recently?
    B: Mainly studying for my exam.

3   Complete the review with the correct form of the verbs in the box.

enjoy   follow   help   learn   put on   struggle   work

Something for everyone ☆☆☆☆

A whole cast of new autism-friendly shows are set to hit London's West End this summer, with *The Lion King* set to be the first. This show [1]_____ the recent trend on New York's Broadway, where several production companies [2]_____ similar events. *The Lion King* production staff [3]_____ hard for months to adapt the show so that people who have autism can [4]_____ it without stress.

Since May theatre staff [5]_____ the skills necessary to help people with autism, who often [6]_____ with the bright lights and loud noises in these shows. Autism charities in the UK [7]_____ to promote the productions at the moment and say they will make a great day out for people with autism and their families.

4   Change the sentences to make them true for you. Do not change the verb forms. Then work in pairs and compare your answers.

1   I'm trying to save money for a holiday.
    I'm trying to save money for a new mobile phone.
2   I'm spending too much time on social networking sites these days.
3   When I was a child, my parents were constantly telling me to clean my bedroom.
4   At about this time yesterday I was watching TV.
5   I think the economy in my country is improving.
6   I'm always forgetting to lock my front door.
7   I'm concentrating very hard on this exercise.
8   People in my country are definitely getting less healthy.

5 Match prompts 1–6 with responses a–f. Make sentences from the prompts using a continuous verb form. Then work in pairs and practise the conversations.

1 Jo's eyes / seem / get / worse
2 you / always / lose / mobile phone
3 you / come / work party?
4 I / hope / you / could / help / my homework
5 I / wonder / you / like / go / cinema
6 we / wonder / you / could / feed / cat / we / on holiday

a I can't – it's my mum's birthday and I promised to visit her.
b Sorry – I'm really bad at maths.
c Perhaps she needs new glasses.
d Yes, that would be great.
e Sure, no problem.
f I know! Can you call it for me so I can hear where it is?

6 Which infinitives (with or without *to*) are better in a continuous form?

1 I really must phone my parents.
2 Cassia's not in the office today – she must work from home.
3 You can't still get ready to go out after an hour!
4 Right now, I'd like to sit at home on the sofa with a good book.
5 Do you think Mario's likely to get home before eight?
6 You seem to spend a lot of time on the internet these days.
7 Gavin? He's bound to watch TV.
8 Where's Thomas? He's supposed to tidy his room.
9 I'd love to come out for lunch, but I've got too much work to do.
10 He seems to do well in this exam.

7 Match pairs 1–7 to endings a–n. Explain meanings i and ii of the verb in each pair.

1 i Those jeans look …
   ii I wasn't looking – …
2 i I really don't feel …
   ii I've got to sit down – I'm feeling …
3 i What time are we having …
   ii I don't have …
4 i Does this top fit?
   ii They've been fitting …
5 i Has the post arrived yet? I'm expecting …
   ii Sorry to hear your flight was delayed. I expect …
6 i I really admire …
   ii We were just admiring …
7 i I've been thinking …
   ii I think …

a dinner tonight?
b about changing my career.
c very unwell.
d very comfortable in these clothes.
e an important letter.
f people who do voluntary work.
g Or does it look too tight?
h who scored the goal?
i you're exhausted.
j you should get some advice before you make any decisions.
k new air-conditioning at the office – it's chaos!
l time to do that now – can someone else do it?
m this painting. It really lights up the room, doesn't it?
n great. You should wear them more often.

8 Complete the sentences with the correct form of the verbs in the box.

....
appear   look   measure   see   expect   feel   have   fit
....

1 I _____ through some old photos and I found one of Lucy when she was a baby.
2 Don't use the hot water! Mum _____ a shower upstairs.
3 Carla and her new boyfriend _____ a lot of each other at the moment.
4 How _____ about Dan's plans to move out?
5 I thought I heard the doorbell ring. _____ anyone?
6 'Why _____ that space?' 'It's for the new desk I've bought – I hope it _____ .'
7 Although the others looked nervous, Jamie _____ calm and relaxed.

PERFECT VERB FORMS

General

1 Perfect verb forms are used **to link two times**. The speaker is looking back from one point to **the time before that**:

- **the past and the present**
  Present perfect simple: *I've lived here for years.*

  Present perfect continuous: *Have you been waiting long?*

- **two points in the past**
  Past perfect simple: *When I got back, they'd all left.*

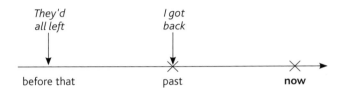

  Past perfect continuous: *We'd been driving for six hours when we ran out of petrol.*

- **two points in the future**
  Future perfect: *By this time tomorrow, I'll have finished all my exams!*

Present perfect simple and continuous

1 The Present perfect simple links the past and present in a number of different ways:

- when we are interested in the present result of a past action.
  Oh no! The computer's crashed again!
  (= It's not working now.)
  There has just been a bad accident on the M6.
  (= This is news, affecting people now.)

- when an action or state started in the past, but is incomplete or still in progress.
  I've been a Manchester United supporter for as long as I can remember.
  How long have you known each other?

- or when the period of time in which it takes place is incomplete.
  So far this year there have been a number of exciting new developments.
  His girlfriend's phoned about six times today.

> **NOTICE!**
> The Present perfect **cannot** be used with a time period that is finished.
>
> *Have you been out this morning?* ✓
>
> *Have you been out last night?* ✗

- when an action happened in the past, but is still current/relevant in the speaker's mind.
  This book has sold over a million copies. (= so it's very successful)
  I've been to Italy several times. (= so I know about Italy)

2 A number of time phrases are commonly used with the Present perfect simple. These include:

- present time periods: *today, this week, this year,* etc.
- adverbs whose meaning links the past and present: *for* and *since, already, just, recently, ever, never.*
- phrases like *twice, three times, several times,* etc. (see above for examples).

> **NOTICE!**
> We use the Present perfect simple in the pattern *the first/second/third time* + clause.
>
> *It's only the second time I've met Harry, but I feel as if we're already friends.*
>
> *Is this the first time you've eaten Korean food?*

3 The Present perfect continuous also links the past with the present. The continuous form stresses the duration of the action and so it is commonly found with *how long, for, since, a long time, all day, all week,* etc.
  We've been driving for three hours.
  I've been rushing around all day.
  I'm sorry. Have you been waiting a long time?
  When no time expression is used, the continuous form emphasises the recentness of the activity.
  I've played squash. (= This could have been at any time up to now.)
  I've been playing squash. (= and I'm out of breath now)

Exercises 1–2, page 118

Past perfect simple and continuous

1 The Past perfect is used to emphasise that one action happened before another action in the past, especially when the sequence is not completely clear from the context.

*When I got home, someone **had left** a message on the answerphone.*

*It was obvious from the state of the lock that someone **had tried** to break in.*

Because of this, it is common in reported speech and after verbs of thought and perception.

*Smith **told** the police he **had never met** the witness before that evening.*

*I **knew** at once that something **had happened**.*

*Miranda **wondered** where her mother **had hidden** the money.*

When the sequence of the actions is obvious, we generally stick to the Past simple.

*When I **got home**, I **checked** the answerphone for messages.*

2 The Past perfect simple is found with some of the same time phrases as the Present perfect, but they are used in a past context.

*When he met Christina, Jack **had already been** married.*

*It was **the first time I had ever spent** the night by myself in the house.*

*Rosa and Clara **had known** each other **since** their childhood.*

3 We also use the Past perfect continuous to describe an action which happened before a particular point in the past. With the continuous form, the speaker sees the action as being repeated or extended.

*We **had** only **been driving** for about 15 minutes when Jill asked me to stop the car.*

The relationship between the Past perfect continuous and the past is the same as the relationship between the Present perfect continuous and the present.

*I'**d been trying** to arrange an interview for months.* (= before she agreed)

*I'**ve been trying** to arrange an interview for months.* (= now)

REMEMBER!

The Past perfect (simple and continuous) is also often used to express the 'unreal' past after words like *if* and *wish*.

*If you **had been sitting** where I was, you would have had a much better view.*

*I wish **I had** never met **you**!*

Exercises 3–5, page 118

Other perfect forms

1 We use the Future perfect when we are thinking mainly about one point in the future and want to talk about the time before that. It is 'the past of the future'. (See Unit 9 Language summary, page 144.)

*When her boyfriend gets her letter, she'**ll have left**.* (a point in the future) (before that)

2 We can use a perfect *-ing* clause to mean *when*/*because* + subject.

***Having** (= When he had) **completed** his education, he started looking for a new job.*

***Having** (= Because I had) **studied** Latin for many years, I found Italian relatively easy.*

The subject of both clauses must be the same.

Because he had passed all his exams, his parents got him a car. ✓

Having passed all his exams, his parents got him a car. ✗

Exercise 6, page 119

3 In patterns which are followed by the infinitive form, the Perfect infinitive (*to*) *have done* emphasises that we are talking about a past action.

*I'd like **to meet** a famous person.* (= present/future)

*I'd like **to have met** John Lennon.* (= past)

*You should **be** more careful when you're overtaking.* (= generally)

*You should **have been** more careful when you overtook that car.* (= past)

The pattern *would* + perfect infinitive (without *to*) is often used to refer to an 'unreal' past action.

*Without your help, we **would** never **have got** this far.*

Exercises 7–9, page 119

02 GRAMMAR PRACTICE

PERFECT VERB FORMS

1 Decide if there is any difference in meaning between the sentences in each pair. Explain the differences.

1   **A:** Have you cleaned your flat?
    B: Have you been cleaning your flat?
2   **A:** Have you been out today?
    B: Did you go out today?
3   **A:** I've been visiting lots of countries.
    B: I've visited lots of countries.
4   **A:** I've worked here for over a year now.
    B: I've been working here for over a year now.

2 Cross out the options that are not possible.

1   Congratulations! We've *just / never / already* heard the good news!
2   Paul and Leonie have known each other *for ages / since they were little / recently*.
3   Have you been sending a lot of texts *lately / in the last few weeks / last week*?
4   I've been trying to call Ms Hymes *all day / several times / for hours*. Is she still busy?
5   I've read that book *three times / a long time / before*.
6   Shaun, this is the third time you've been late *for a week / so far this week / since Monday*!

3 Find and correct the mistakes in five of the sentences.

1   Callum! That's the third time I ask you to sit down!
2   I'm sorry I'm so late, but I've sat in a traffic jam.
3   She said she'd never seen him before in her life, but I know they've met several times.
4   It was really weird that Grandad phoned – we'd just talked about him!
5   I see from your CV that you've been working in three different companies in the last year.
6   Olly thought he'd remembered everything until he'd got to the church and realised the ring was at home.

4 Complete the stories with the Past simple, Present perfect simple/continuous or Past perfect simple/continuous form of the verbs in brackets. Then work in pairs. Cover the stories and try to remember as much as you can.

A

> When I ¹_____ (hear) that Owen ²_____ (leave) his new job after only a month, I ³_____ (not be) particularly surprised. This ⁴_____ (happen) several times before. But when he ⁵_____ (not answer) any of my phone messages, I ⁶_____ (phone) the company and ⁷_____ (find out) that he ⁸_____ (go) to prison for six months! Apparently, he ⁹_____ (steal) money from the company account! I was shocked – I ¹⁰_____ (know) Owen for years and he's one of the most honest people I ¹¹_____ (ever/meet). I'm sure the police ¹²_____ (make) a terrible mistake.

B

> Two brothers who ¹_____ (be) missing since Tuesday ²_____ (arrive) home safe and well last night. The two boys, who ³____ (leave) home after a family argument, ⁴____ (hide) in woods a few kilometres from their home.
> They ⁵_____ (not intend) to stay away for long, but they ⁶_____ (get) lost in the woods and ⁷_____ (decide) to wait until somebody came looking for them.
> Their mother Lily said she ⁸_____ (never/give up) hope of finding them alive.

5 Answer the questions. Then write new questions changing some of the words in bold.

1   How many **messages** have you **sent** today?
2   How long had you been **learning English** when you **started this course**?
3   How many **people** had you **spoken to** by eight o'clock last night?
4   How long have you **had** your **mobile phone**?
5   Is this the first time you've **studied** the **Past perfect continuous**?
6   Is there **anything** you wish you **hadn't said** this week?

6 Join four pairs of sentences starting with *having* + past participle. How can the other two sentences be joined?

1 I waited ages for a waiter to take my order. I decided to go somewhere else.
2 Amy's told so many lies in the past. Nobody will believe her this time.
3 We have looked at all the applications. We have decided to offer you the job.
4 I've been here lots of times before. The shop assistant knows me.
5 We saw the weather forecast. We decided not to play golf.
6 The doctor had never done an operation before. He was quite nervous.

7 Match sentences 1–8 to responses a–h. Then complete the responses with the correct form of the verbs in brackets.

1 I'm feeling really exhausted at the moment.
2 I haven't seen Mia online lately.
3 Jonas was really surprised when he realised we'd organised a party for him.
4 I've looked everywhere for the cat – he's not here!
5 I'm glad Liam didn't come shopping with us.
6 How did Lukas get into the show? I thought it was sold out.
7 Some people were badly injured in the accident.
8 Shall we sit in one of these seats here?

a I'd prefer _____ (sit) nearer the front if you don't mind.
b Yeah, but they're lucky _____ (survive).
c I know, she seems _____ (disappear).
d Well, maybe you should _____ (take) a few days off work.
e He pretended _____ (be) one of the cast!
f Don't worry, he can't _____ (go) very far.
g Oh, I'd love _____ (see) his face!
h Me too – he wouldn't _____ (enjoy) it.

8 Complete the second sentence so that it means the same as the first.

1 You started reading that book months ago!
You've _____ .
2 I bet Hannah's sorry she bought that games console.
I bet Hannah _____ .
3 I'd seen that film once before.
It _____ .
4 It's ages since we enjoyed ourselves so much.
We _____ .
5 Leonie was very nervous because she'd never spoken in public before.
Having _____ .
6 I'm glad I didn't live in the 18th century.
I wouldn't _____ .

9 Underline the perfect verb forms. Explain why a perfect form is used in each case.

1 A: Waiter, what soup is this?
B: It's bean soup, sir.
A: I don't care what it's been, what is it now?
2 A: I've changed my mind.
B: Oh good, does the new one work any better?
3 Q: Why did the plastic surgeon collapse?
A: Because he'd been sitting too near the fire.
4 A: Did you meet your son at the airport?
B: No, I've known him for years!
5 A: I've come to repair your doorbell.
B: You should have come earlier, I'm just going out.
A: But I've been standing on your doorstep all morning, ringing your bell.
6 Find the misprint: 'Foreign ministers today declared that their summit meeting had been a hug success.'

TIME AND TENSE

General

The different verb forms of English are often known as tenses. English has 12 verb forms (excluding passives). You have studied the usual ways in which these verb forms are used in Units 1 and 2. However, the relationship between tense and time in English is not always like this.

PRESENT	
Simple	*I live*
Continuous	*I am living*
Perfect	*I have lived*
Perfect continuous	*I have been living*
PAST	
Simple	*I lived*
Continuous	*I was living*
Perfect	*I had lived*
Perfect continuous	*I had been living*
FUTURE	
Simple	*I will live*
Continuous	*I will be living*
Perfect	*I will have lived*
Perfect continuous	*I will have been living*

Special uses of the Present simple

1 Present simple for past time

The Present simple is commonly used to talk about past situations:
- in newspaper headlines.
  *Anti-US protest **ends** in violence*
  *Minister **quits***
  *Strike **brings** city to a standstill*
- when we tell a joke or when we relate the story of a film, book or play.
  *A man **goes** to the psychiatrist and **says**, 'Doctor, I think I'm a pair of curtains.' The doctor **replies**, 'Pull yourself together.'*
  *Ingrid Bergman **plays** a rich woman in 19th-century Australia who **marries**, **becomes** an alcoholic and then **falls** in love with her cousin.*

> **Exercises 1–2, page 122**

2 Present simple to talk about now

We often learn that the Present continuous is used for talking about now, but sometimes the Present simple can be used.
- When we refer to an action which happens instantaneously at the moment of speaking, the Present simple is used. This usually occurs when the words carry a particular importance.
  *I **pronounce** you man and wife.*
  *I **beg** your pardon?*
  *I **name** this ship the Mary Rose.*
- When describing or commentating on a present action, the Present simple is used for an instantaneous action.
  *Owen **shoots** ... and it's a goal!*
- The Present continuous is used for a longer event.
  *And now I'**m slicing** the onions into little pieces and **putting** them into the saucepan.*

> **Exercise 3, page 122**

3 Present simple for future time

- The Present simple is commonly used to talk about future events which are programmed or timetabled.
  *A new production of Mozart's Don Giovanni **opens** at the Royal Opera House next week.*
- We often use the Present simple (and Present perfect) to refer to the future after time conjunctions such as *if*, *when*, *before*, *as soon as*, *until*, *once*, *while*, *by the time*, etc.
  *What'll happen **if we don't get** there in time?*
  *I'll phone you **as soon as we've checked in**.*
  *You can go home **as soon as you finish**.*
- We also use the present tenses after relative pronouns such as *who* and *where* and in subordinate clauses introduced by *as*, *than* and *whether*.
  *The first person **who phones in** with the correct answer will get the prize.*
  *I really don't mind **where we stop** as long as I get something to eat soon.*
  *You'll probably be on the same flight **as we are**.*
  *I'll enjoy the day **whether** the sun **is shining** or **whether it's pouring** with rain.*
- To describe future events which are officially organised or timetabled, we often use the present form of *be* + infinitive with *to*.
  *The Prime Minister **is to visit** India next year.*
  *The standard rate of tax **is to be raised** from next April.*
  *Is the archbishop **to retire** next year?*

> **Exercises 4–5, pages 122–123**

Past verb forms in unreal situations

1 Imaginary situations (general)

Past verb forms are used to describe imaginary situations which are contrary to known facts. However, they do not describe the past, but either the present or a general situation. They are commonly found:

* in clauses with *if*.

  *If men **had to** undergo pregnancy, there would be far fewer children in the world!*

  A variation on this form is the pattern *if + were + to*-infinitive.

  *If I **were to tell** you that you've just won $1 million, what would you say?*

NOTICE!

* In the 'unreal' past, *were* is traditionally used with *I* and *he/she*.

  *I'd listen to what he has to say if I **were** you.*

* Some people still consider this to be more correct, but either version is acceptable in modern British English.

  *If it **was** sunny, we could all go to the beach.*

---

* after *I wish*, *I'd rather/sooner*, *I suppose/imagine* and *it's time*. Again, these express ideas that are imaginable/desirable, but contrary to the actual facts.

  *I **wish I had** enough money to buy myself a new scooter.* (= But I don't.)

  Suppose you decided to sell your bike. How much would you want for it? (= You haven't decided to sell it yet.)

  I'd rather/sooner you didn't smoke. (= This is what I would like, rather than what I think will happen.)

  *You're nearly 28 years old. **It's time you went out** and **looked** for a real job.* (= But you aren't doing this at the moment.)

* when making requests more tentative and distant.

  *I just **wanted** to ask you something. Do you have a moment?*

  ***Was** there anything else, sir?*

  *I **was** just **wondering** if you **had** a few moments to discuss something important.*

Exercises 6–7, page 123

2 Imaginary situations in the past

We use the Past perfect to talk about an unreal situation in the past.

*If it **had been** up to me, I would never have chosen that colour for the living room.*

*I wish I **had** never **met** that hateful man.*

Exercise 8, page 123

Tense sequence

1 General rules

* The verb in a sub-clause is usually in the same tense as the verb in the main clause.

  *As soon as I **heard** my mother's voice (sub-clause), I **knew** something **was** wrong (main clause).*

* If the main clause is in the past, so are the verbs which follow it even if they are still true now.

  *From our very first meeting, I **knew** you **were** (NOT are) the right person for me.* (= You are still the right person now, but the fact is only important in relation to the past event.)

2 Reported speech

* The same general rule applies.

  *John **tells** me you **work** for a travel agency.*

  *Oh, hello! I **saw** James earlier on, and he **told** me you **were coming** (NOT are coming) to the party tonight.*

  *Claire **said** that she **would** (NOT will) probably be a bit late for the meeting this afternoon.*

* After a past tense reporting verb (*said*, *told*, etc.) the reported words are not in the same tense as the original (direct speech). In the example above, Claire actually said, 'I'**ll** probably be a bit late for the meeting this afternoon.'

* If the fact is still important now, we can use a present tense.

  *It was the scientist Sir William Harvey who first proved that blood **circulates** around the body.*

* With verbs like *say* and *tell* we tend to use the Past simple to report the exact words and the Past continuous to report the gist of what was said.

  *'I'm going to leave my job,' he **said**.*

  *John **was saying** how much he hates his job.*

Exercise 9, page 123

TIME AND TENSE

1 Rewrite sentences 1–6 as newspaper headlines. Use the number of words given in brackets.

1 The police have launched a crackdown on speeding motorists. (6)
Police launch crackdown on speeding motorists.

2 A footballer scored a hat trick, but his team was beaten. (6)

3 The President has hinted at changes in the privacy laws. (7)

4 The blues singer Leroy Morganfield collapsed on stage at the Newfield Stadium. (10)

5 A TV company has been fined after a three-year court case. (7)

6 A mother and daughter fell from a balcony, but both are OK. (9)

2 Complete the texts with the correct form of the verbs in the box.

bring	have (x2)	change	decide	arrive	find	be
order	meet (x2)	catch	reply	leave	shout	

A happing ending

Marilla, the protagonist, [1]_____ home after a huge fight with her mother and [2]_____ a train to London. When she [3]_____ in the big city, she [4]_____ all alone, until she [5]_____ Clifford.

A fishy business

A man [6]_____ some fish in a restaurant. When the waiter [7]_____ the food, he [8]_____ his hand on the fish. 'I don't believe it!' [9]_____ the man. 'Why is your hand on my fish?' The waiter [10]_____ , 'What, do you want it to fall on the floor again?'

Secrets and lies

When Ryan Miller [11]_____ a photo of an old school friend he hasn't seen for 20 years, he [12]_____ to look him up.

When they finally [13]_____ again, Ryan discovers his friend [14]_____ a secret that could [15]_____ his life for ever.

3 Decide who would say the following, and in what situation. Then choose the best answers to complete the sentences. (Both options are possible, but one is better.)

1 And so *I declare / I'm declaring* this museum open.

2 And *Dyson passes / Dyson's passing* to Serbatov and ... yes, *he shoots / he's shooting* ... goal!

3 *I chop / I'm chopping* the herbs finely before adding them to the sauce.

4 *I swear / I'm swearing* to tell the truth and nothing but the truth.

5 And now *we go / we're going* into the master bedroom, where the king and queen would sleep.

6 *I name / I'm naming* this ship *Titanic*.

7 *I suggest / I'm suggesting* that you think carefully about where you were at 10 p.m. on the night of the robbery, sir.

8 *The minister comes / The minister's coming* to the gates of the house, where dozens of reporters *jostle / are jostling* for position.

4 Match questions 1–8 with answers a–h.

1 Will you let us know if you hear from him?
2 When can I go out to play?
3 When do your English classes start?
4 What time does your train get in?
5 Will you give me a hand moving house on Sunday?
6 Who on earth will notice the mistake?
7 Where do we board the plane?
8 When are we going to see Auntie Claire again?

a Some time around 11:00.
b OK, if I'm not doing anything.
c Not until you've finished your lunch.
d At gate D34.
e Yes, the minute I get any news.
f The week after next.
g When she's feeling a bit better.
h Anyone who reads beyond the first paragraph.

5 Match the sentence halves and use the words in the box to join them.

what	whether	until	before
by the time	who	if	while

1 Do you think Marianne will agree to say
2 I'll have dinner ready
3 I'll buy another goldfish first thing tomorrow
4 I'll get in touch with the supplier
5 Ben's going to stay in and revise for his exam tonight
6 A reward will be available for anyone
7 Go through all those emails
8 What shall we do

a you find the one from Ms Donovan.
b he wants to or not.
c you get back.
d nobody's at home when we arrive?
e you're in the meeting.
f we ask her to?
g they notice the old one died.
h gives us information leading to the arrest of these men.

6 Rewrite the second sentence so that it means the same as the first. Use the word in brackets and an 'unreal' past form.

1 Jamie prefers us to meet at his house.
(sooner)
_____

2 I'm not in your position, so I'm not careful.
(if)
_____

3 Could I possibly ask you a huge favour?
(wondered)
_____

4 Abi is old enough now for her parents to let her go on holiday with her friends.
(time)
_____

5 I have to work until 8:00 this evening and I hate it.
(wish)
_____

6 They haven't offered me the job yet, so I'm not over the moon*.
(were)
_____

7 I don't want you to mention this to anyone.
(rather)
_____

* over the moon = absolutely delighted

7 Complete the questions in a logical way. Then work in pairs and ask and answer questions.

1 If you _____ English at all, how _____ ?
2 Suppose everyone _____ in another country for a year, where _____ ?
3 If you were to _____ a year off to travel, where _____ ?
4 Imagine you _____ back in time, where _____ ?
5 If you _____ a famous celebrity, who _____ ?

8 Write sentences using the correct form of the words in brackets to complete the interview.

A: So Brian, why did you decide to do this swim?
B: It was my daughter who persuaded me – ¹_____ (if / not / be / for her / I / never / do / it).
A: And what was the best moment of the swim for you?
B: Oh, getting to the end, definitely. ²_____ (I / not / miss / that for anything)
A: So, ³_____ (you / do / it / again)? Do you have any regrets?
B: Well, only that ⁴_____ (I wish / I / start / training earlier). Then ⁵_____ (I / be / better prepared).
A: ⁶_____ (there / be / one more thing / I / want / ask / you) Is it true that you had some problems with your producer?
B: Look, we'll have to stop the interview here, I'm afraid. ⁷_____ (it / time / I / get / to the studio)

9 Cross out the options that do not sound natural.

1 Phillippa just called – she *says / said* she's going to be a bit late.
2 When they told my sister she *hasn't got / hadn't got* the part, she was really upset.
3 It's OK. Lucy told me you *don't / didn't* like fish, so we're having chicken.
4 Ed *told / was telling* his boss he needed a pay rise and she was so shocked she didn't say anything!
5 Tomas says he *wants / wanted* to start looking for a new job next year.
6 Gina *told / was telling* me that the Sharpes' son *has been / had been* expelled from school!

ADJECTIVES AND ADVERBS

Word order

1   Adjectives normally come before nouns (attributive adjectives) or after verbs like *be, become, look, seem, get*, etc. (predicative adjectives).
    *We had a **fantastic** holiday.* (attributive)
    *Our holiday was **fantastic**.* (predicative)
    Most adjectives can be used in both ways.

*   Some adjectives are always attributive, so are only found before nouns.
    *the **chief** executive   the **only** solution*
    ***utter** chaos   the **entire/whole** performance*
    ***further** (= additional) information   **sheer** genius*
    *the **previous/former** president   the **main** difference*
    *the **western/southern** border   a **mere** detail*

*   Some adjectives are always predicative, so are only found after verbs.
    *I was still **awake** at 2:00 a.m.*
    *She got quite **upset** about her exam results.*
    *You two look **alike**.*

*   Sometimes, to express the same meaning, a different adjective is used in the two positions.
    *The children **were afraid** of the dark.* (predicative)
    *The **frightened children** ran out of the bedroom.* (attributive)
    *She **has been ill** for some time.* (predicative)
    *There were a lot of **sick people**.* (attributive)

*   Other adjectives change slightly according to whether they are attributive or predicative.

Attributive	Predicative
a **lone** gunman	The gunman was **alone**.
live animals	The animals were **alive**.
a **sleeping** baby	The baby was **asleep**.
a **drunken** argument	The men were **drunk**.
my **elder** sister	My sister is **older** than me.

Exercise 1, page 126

2   Other rules of word order:
*   general before specific
    *an **old Hungarian** folk tale*
*   opinion before description
    ***important domestic** issues*
*   *the first* and *the last* normally come before numbers.
    *We are on holiday **the first** week in May.*

Exercise 2, page 126

Compound adjectives

*   Compound adjectives consist of two or more words which are usually hyphenated. The second part of the compound adjective is often a present or past participle form.
    *a **mouth-watering** meal   a **well-known** brand*

*   Some compound adjectives are derived from phrasal or prepositional verbs.
    ***worn-out** shoes   the most **talked-about** play in London*

*   Compound adjectives are often found with numbers. The noun is in the singular form in these cases.
    *a **two-week** holiday   a **hundred-mile** journey*

*   We can also add another adjective after the noun, with a second hyphen.
    *a **25-year-old** man   a **three-mile-long** queue of cars*

*   We add *-like* (= similar to) and *-friendly* (= helpful to) to nouns to form compound adjectives.
    *a **child-friendly** environment   a **dream-like** state*

*   Many compound adjectives describing appearance are formed with noun + *-ed*.
    *a man with **dark hair** → a **dark-haired** man*
    *a dress with **short sleeves** → a **short-sleeved** dress*

Exercise 3, page 126

Prefixes and suffixes

1   We often use prefixes to modify the meaning of an adjective. Some of the most common prefixes are:

Prefix	Meaning	Examples
anti-	against	***anti**-war*, ***anti**-government*
bi-	two	***bi**annual*, ***bi**lingual*
dis-	the opposite of	***dis**honest*, ***dis**orderly*
in-	not	***in**complete*, ***in**competent*
inter-	between	***inter**active*, ***inter**continental*
mal-	badly	***mal**adjusted*, ***mal**odorous*
mis-	wrongly/badly	***mis**guided*, ***mis**informed*
mono-	one	***mono**lingual*, ***mono**syllabic*
multi-	many	***multi**-purpose*, ***multi**-cultural*
out-	beyond, outside	***out**dated*, ***out**lying*
over-	too much	***over**active*, ***over**worked*
post-	after	***post**-war*, ***post**-industrial*
pre-	before	***pre**-war*, ***pre**-industrial*
pro-	in favour of	***pro**-western*, ***pro**-European*
semi-	half	***semi**-precious*, ***semi**-professional*
sub-	under, below	***sub**tropical*, ***sub**conscious*
un-	not	***un**important*, ***un**grateful*
under-	not enough	***under**cooked*, ***under**paid*

There is no simple way of knowing whether prefixes require a hyphen. Check in a good learner's dictionary.

2 The following suffixes also help form adjectives:

Suffix	Meaning	Examples
-able	can be	adjust**able**, believ**able**, break**able**
-al		economic**al**, historic**al**, digit**al**
-ful	with	cheer**ful**, truth**ful**, hope**ful**
-ic		electr**ic**, symphon**ic**, atmospher**ic**
-ish	quite, not very	tall**ish**, redd**ish**, warm**ish**
-ive		impress**ive**, respons**ive**, invent**ive**
-less	without	cord**less**, stain**less**, fear**less**
-ous		humor**ous**, luxuri**ous**, harmoni**ous**
-y		mist**y**, hand**y**, price**y**

■ Exercises 4–6, pages 126–127

Gradable and ungradable adjectives

1 Ungradable adjectives have either a very strong meaning (e.g. *fantastic, appalling, unbelievable*) or an absolute meaning (e.g. *unique, right, wrong*). These 'absolute adjectives' do not normally have a comparative or superlative form.

2 Gradable adjectives can follow words like *very* and *quite* and have comparative and superlative forms, e.g. *very/quite/more/the most interesting*, etc.

Adverbs of degree

1 Highest degree

- **Absolutely** indicates the highest degree. Normally it is only used with ungradable adjectives.
  *We are **absolutely delighted** to welcome you all here.*
  *The weather was **absolutely awful** over the weekend.*
- Other adverbs which are used in a similar way: *completely, totally, utterly*.

2 High degree

- **Very** and **really** are used in British English to indicate high degree. Note that *really* can be used with both gradable and ungradable adjectives, but *very* can only be used with gradable adjectives. In American English, *real* is preferred to *really* in this case.
  *Thank you for a **really** (NOT very) wonderful evening.*
  *It was a **really** (NOT very) interesting experience for everyone involved.*
- We can add emphasis by repeating **very** (informal).
  *I'm just **very, very tired** – that's all.*
  or by adding *indeed* (more formal).
  *We were both **very tired indeed** by the time we drew up to the hotel.*

- Note that in British English *not very* + adjective with a positive meaning can be used instead of an adjective with a negative meaning.
  *'How was the film?' 'It was**n't very good**.'* (= It was bad.)
- Similarly, we can use *not that* + adjective to say it's not as much as you might expect.
  *She would never marry someone she's only just met: she's **not that stupid**.*

■ Exercise 7, page 127

3 Middle/low degree

- **Pretty**, **rather** and **quite** all indicate middle degree.
- **Pretty** is common in speech, particularly with positive adjectives.
  *We were **pretty happy** with the way we played.*
- **Rather** is more commonly used with negative adjectives.
  *Do you mind if I close the window? It's **rather cold** in here.*
  In British English, *rather* + positive adjective means 'more than was expected'.
  *I expected her to be absolutely furious at my suggestion, but in fact, she was **rather pleased**.*
- **Quite** also expresses middle degree with gradable adjectives.
  *It was **quite easy** to understand what their gestures meant.*
  With ungradable adjectives, *quite* has the meaning of 'completely'.
  *I'm afraid it's **quite impossible** (= completely impossible) for you to see Ms Hanson today.*
- **A bit**, **a little** and **slightly** are all used to indicate low degree. They are normally only used before adjectives with a negative meaning.
  *I'm just **a bit worried** you won't find your way. Shall I come and get you?*
  *On the way home, I began to feel **slightly** ill.*
- *A bit* is less formal than *a little* and *slightly*. However, we often use *a bit/a little/slightly* + comparative adjective with a positive meaning.
  *'How are you feeling today?' 'Oh, **a bit/slightly/a little** better, thanks.'*

■ Exercises 8–9, page 127

ADJECTIVES AND ADVERBS

1 **Rewrite the sentences. Use the adjectives in bold in the correct position and/or form. Make any other changes necessary.**

   1 She has a son from a marriage which was **previous**.
   _____

   2 The cinema was full of people who were **afraid** at the premiere of *Night Chills 2*.
   _____

   3 What reason seems to be **main** for his attitude, in your opinion?
   _____

   4 He tiptoed past the **asleep** dog and got himself a biscuit.
   _____

   5 Do you think that the difference is **only** between the two tablets?
   _____

   6 The doctor's waiting room was packed with people **who were ill**.
   _____

2 **Complete the sentences with the adjectives in brackets in a logical order. More than one answer may be possible.**

   1 The combination of _____ _____ actors and _____ _____ effects make this film a definite contender for an Oscar. (young, state-of-the-art, talented, spectacular)
   2 What was the _____ _____ spending of a(n) _____ _____ family in the 1980s? (American, average, typical, monthly)
   3 Type your postcode and click 'Find' to find out all about the _____ _____ concerts and a variety of _____ _____ events in your area. (musical, summer, outdoor, forthcoming)
   4 We recommend The Old Forge, a(n) _____ _____ house in beautiful surroundings, serving a(n) _____ _____ breakfast. (traditional, stone, charming, English)

3a **Match the text types in the box with texts 1–5.**

   a TV review   a holiday brochure   a clothes shop website
   a novel   an advertisement for accommodation

   1 This apartment with two bedrooms has a kitchen which is a good size and a balcony which faces south. (3)

   2 Abby smiled as her son, who was eight years old, tipped out the contents of his schoolbag: a birthday card which someone had made at home, an apple which he had eaten half of, a sandwich which was three days old and a pair of trainers which were covered in mud. (5)

   3 Wear this shirt which fits loosely and has long sleeves with your jeans which have straight legs and shoes with high heels. (4)

   4 Don't miss the first episode of the historical drama in three parts *Between the Wars*, a story which provokes thought featuring a cast who are all stars. (3)

   5 Discover the delights of Sicily on a tour which lasts five days. Stay in hotels which have four stars and are run by families, and sample food which is cooked at home and local wines. Representatives who speak English are always available to make your stay as easy as possible. (5)

 b **Rewrite the texts in exercise 3a using compound adjectives to make them sound more natural. Use the number of compound adjectives given in brackets.**

4a **Form compound adjectives using the prefixes in the box.**

   anti-   dis-   in-   mal-   mis-   over-   post-   un-

   1 __in__tolerant   5 ___crowded
   2 ___grateful   6 ___leading
   3 ___dated   7 ___nuclear
   4 ___connected   8 ___treated

 b **Complete the sentences with the compound adjectives in exercise 4a.**

   1 My grandparents used to have a rather *intolerant* attitude towards young people.
   2 She's raising money for a charity which rescues _____ animals.
   3 I thought the minister made some very _____ comments about taxes in the interview.
   4 There was a crowd of _____ protesters blocking the entrance to the site.
   5 This essay is nowhere near your usual standard – it's just a collection of _____ ideas.
   6 He let me give him a(n) _____ cheque for the rent.
   7 I had to go right out of my way to pick Adriana up and she didn't even say thank you – she's so _____ !
   8 I'm fed up with working in a(n) _____ office with no air-conditioning!

5 Form compound adjectives using the prefixes in the box to complete the questions. Then work in pairs and ask and answer the questions.

pre-	anti-	bi-	dis-	inter-
mono-	multi-	over-	sub-	under-

1 Have you ever been on a(n) ___continental flight?
2 Would you complain if you were ___satisfied with the food or service in a restaurant?
3 Would you ever buy ___owned clothes?
4 Who do you think is the most ___rated musician?
5 Have you ever felt ___dressed for an occasion?
6 What behaviour do you consider to be ___social?
7 Do you know anyone who is ___lingual?
8 Why is it good to use a(n) ___ lingual English dictionary?
9 How often do you have ___zero temperatures in your country?
10 What's your favourite ___purpose gadget?

6 Which objects in the box below can be:

1 cordless? _____   5 digital? _____
2 adjustable? _____   6 electric? _____
3 informative? _____   7 very pricey? _____
4 washable? _____   8 harmful? _____

tablet computer	soft toy	toothbrush	drill
washing machine	telephone	belt	

7 Cross out the options that are not possible. In some sentences both options are possible.

1 I was *very, very / very* relieved indeed when I arrived on time for my job interview.
2 Sean thinks Sadie's *absolutely / very* stunning, but I didn't think she was *that / very* attractive at first.
3 I'm *really / very* pleased that you can come and I know the children will be *really / very* delighted.
4 This is a *very / totally* unique picture and I am certain that it's *very / absolutely* valuable.
5 It may have been an interesting news article but it was also *completely / the most* false.

8 Tick the sentences where adverbs of degree are used correctly. Find and correct the mistakes in the other sentences, using *pretty, rather, quite, a bit, a little, slightly*.

1 I know it's a shabby old jacket, but it's actually slightly comfortable.
2 It's going to be pretty hot there – make sure you pack your shorts.
3 Although they look similar, if you look closely, you'll see they're actually slightly different.
4 Are you feeling pretty calmer now?
5 I'm a bit pleased with the amount of work I managed to get done today.
6 Mr Coulter is slightly concerned about your poor results recently.
7 It's quite ridiculous to expect teachers to accept the new education guidelines.
8 I'm rather sure that's the turning, coming up on the left.

9 Complete the app reviews with the words in the box. More than one answer may be possible.

hugely	unique	two-year-old	dissatisfied
asleep	lone	little-known	ingenious
impressive	absolutely	mind-blowing	attractive

This month's three best smartphone apps

Decor8 ✪ ✪ ✪ ✪

This is D-labs' first commercial app and we have to say it's really ¹_____ . It allows you to take photos of wallpaper, furniture, etc. when you're out, then shows you what they would look like in your home. The ²_____ developer is currently the ³_____ provider of this service and we wouldn't be surprised if this ⁴_____ little app becomes ⁵_____ successful.

Share Fair ✪ ✪

Social networking apps are nothing new and neither is this ⁶_____ app, but it's just been given a very ⁷_____ new design. With a sleek user interface, we think you'll agree that its new look is ⁸_____ stunning.

G-Control ✪ ✪ ✪

We can't stop playing with this app. When your phone is ⁹_____ , you click your fingers to wake it up. The app then uses the phone's proximity sensor to read the gestures you use to operate it. It has ¹⁰_____ potential, since it allows you to create ¹¹_____ personalised gestures to control your own phone. It's not cheap, but we don't think you'll be ¹²_____ with it once you've bought it.

MODALS

General

1 Modals are auxiliary verbs used to give a judgement or interpretation about an action or state. The following are often classified as full modal verbs: *can, could, may, might, must, will, would, shall, should.* They have the following features:
   - They do not have infinitive forms or the third person *-s.*
   - The negative is formed by adding *not/n't* to the verb.
   - The question is formed by inverting the modal and the pronoun.
   - They are followed by the infinitive without *to.*

2 The following are often referred to as 'semi-modals': *need, dare, have, ought to.* They follow some, but not all, of the above rules. (See Semi-modals, page 129.)

Possibility/Probability

1 *Could, might* and *may* refer to specific present/future possibilities.
   *Steve isn't here, but he **could**/**might**/**may*** (NOT ~~can~~) *be in the canteen.*
   *They say that it **could**/**may**/**might*** (NOT ~~can~~) *snow this year.*
   - We can make the probability greater by adding *well.*
   *This could/might/may **well** be McNally's last appearance at a world championship.*

2 *Can* is only used to refer to general (or 'theoretical') possibilities.
   *In summer the temperature here **can** reach 35°C.*
   *Lisa **can** be really moody sometimes.*

3 *Could/may/might have* + past participle can all be used to mean that something possibly happened.
   *Jay **may**/**could**/**might've phoned** while we were out.*
   - We also use the past form *could have* to say that it was possible for something to happen, but it didn't.
   *We **could have taken** a taxi, but we decided to walk home instead.* (= This didn't happen.)

4 We can also use *should* to talk about present or future probability. It shows that the speaker is fairly certain about something.
   *Have a look in my pockets – the car keys **should** be there.*
   *You **shouldn't** have to wait too long, Mr Carr.*

Exercise 1, page 130

Ability and willingness

1 *Can* and *be able to* express ability. The past forms are *could/was able to.*
   - We only use *could* as the past of *can* when we talk about general ability.
   *When I was younger, I **could** touch my nose with my feet.* (= This was something I could do if I wanted to.)
   - To talk about a specific event, we use **managed to** or **was able to**.
   *Although he was badly injured, he **managed**/**was able to** crawl his way to safety.* (= This was something he did.)
   - *Can* or *could* are often used with verbs of perception.
   *I **can** smell something burning.*
   *I **could** hear music coming from the upstairs room.*
   - There are a number of common fixed phrases with **can('t)**: *can('t) afford, can't stand* (= hate), *can('t) bear, I can imagine.*

2 *Will* is often used to express that you are willing to do something now or in the future.
   I'll do the washing-up. You sit down and have a rest.
   - The negative form *won't* expresses unwillingness or refusal to do something.
   *Mum, Holly **won't** play with me.*
   *I **won't** lower the price, and that's that.*
   - To talk about the past, *wouldn't* can mean 'refused to'.
   *We tried everything but he **wouldn't** cooperate.*
   - This can also be used with inanimate objects.
   *My car **wouldn't** start.*

Exercises 2–3, page 130

Permission and requests

1 *Can* and *could* are used for both permission and requests.
   Can/Could I get past, please?
   Can/Could you give me a hand to lift this?

2 *May* and *might* are only used for permission.
   May/Might I borrow your newspaper for a moment? ✓
   May you feed the cats while we're away? ✗

3 *Will* and *would* are only used for requests.
   Will/Would you just wait here for a minute, please? ✓
   Will I borrow your telephone to call home? ✗

4 *May, might, could* and *would* are more tentative, and therefore more polite than *can* and *will.* However, polite intonation is probably more important than the choice of modal.

Exercises 4–5, page 130

Obligation/necessity

1 Must

- *Have to* or *have got to* are more common in speech to talk about obligation than **must**, particularly when we talk about obligations which are externally imposed.
  *You **have (got) to** be 18 to vote.*

- *Must* is more often seen in written English, however.
  *Applicants **must** be over 18 years of age.* (= from an application form)

- The negative of *must* for this kind of obligation is *must not* and the past is *had to*.
  *Applicants **must not** be over 35 years of age.*
  *When I was young, you **had to** be 21 before you could go in nightclubs.*

- *Must* is often used for advice or recommendation because it expresses the speaker's sense that this is necessary or important. *Have to* is less common in this context.
  *It's an absolutely brilliant film. You **must** go to see it.*

- *Must* also expresses logical deduction.
  *That **must be** Isabel's sister, she looks so like her!*

- The negative of *must* here is *can't* and the past is *must have*.
  *That **can't be** your mother, she looks far too young.*
  *Laura **must have gone** home, she's not here.*

2 *Will* is also commonly used for logical necessity.
  *Is that the doorbell? It**'ll be** the pizza delivery.*
  *It's eight o'clock, he**'ll** probably **have left** the office by now.*

3 *Should* is used to talk about the right thing to do. The past is *should have/shouldn't have*.
  *These files **shouldn't be** in here – put them in Joel's office.*
  *You **should have listened** more carefully to what I said.*

Exercises 6–7, page 131

Semi-modals

1 *Have to/don't have to* are used to express obligation/lack of obligation. Note that we use auxiliaries to form questions and negatives.
  *What time **do we have to** be there?*
  *I've never **had to** work as hard as I'm doing at the moment.*

2 *Ought* has the same meaning as *should*. Unlike *should*, it is followed by the infinitive with *to*.
  *It's well after midnight. You **ought to be** in bed by now.*

- The past form is *ought to have*.
  *We really **ought to have booked** – there don't seem to be any tables.*

- The negative and question forms are *ought not to* and *ought (I) to,* but *Should* or *Do you think we ought to ...?* are preferred.
  *You **ought not to/shouldn't** shout – someone might hear you.*
  *Do you think we **ought to/Should we** ask for the bill?*

3 *Need* can be used as a normal verb, followed by an infinitive with *to*, a noun or *-ing* form. The past form is *needed*.
  *Do you **need to go** to the bathroom?*
  *My jacket **needs cleaning** – can you take it to the cleaner's?*

- However, the negative has a modal form *needn't*. Notice that the normal negative form *don't need to* has the same meaning.
  *You **needn't/don't need to** tell me if you don't want to.*

- The past form also has a modal form, *needn't have*. This expresses that something happened which wasn't necessary.
  *You **needn't have** brought milk – I've already got plenty in the fridge.* (= You did it but it was unnecessary.)

- This is different from *didn't need to*, which simply expresses that it wasn't necessary to do something.
  *Because it was Sunday, we **didn't need to** get up early.* (= It was unnecessary, so we probably didn't do it.)

- *Needn't/Need I*, etc. are also found in a few fixed phrases, such as:
  *You **needn't bother**.* (= often sarcastic, meaning it's not necessary to do something)
  Need I say more? (= Isn't it obvious?)

4 *Dare* is used in the negative and question forms to mean *have the courage to do something*.
  *I **daren't** tell him the truth in case he fires me.*

- The past is usually formed with the auxiliary verb *didn't*.
  *I **didn't dare** (to) ask her what had happened.*

- There are certain fixed expressions where the modal form of *dare* is used.
  *I **dare say** (= expect) you'll have a lot of questions.*
  How dare you suggest that I treated you dishonestly! (= I am very shocked/angry by ...)
  Don't you dare make fun of the way I speak! (= a strong warning not to do something)

Exercises 8–9, page 131

MODALS

1 **Decide if there is any difference in meaning between the sentences in each pair. Explain the differences.**

1 A: It may well be sunny at the weekend.
  B: It could well be sunny at the weekend.
2 A: He could have gone home early.
  B: He might have gone home early.
3 A: It can take up to three hours to get home.
  B: It could take up to three hours to get home.
4 A: We should win the league with this team.
  B: We could win the league with this team.
5 A: They could have got stuck in traffic.
  B: They may have got stuck in traffic.

2 **Rewrite the story replacing the phrases in bold with modal verbs.**

Benji's heavy meal

When her dog Benji **¹was not willing to eat** his food one evening, Rosie Duncan became worried. 'I called him, but **²he was not even able to get up** from his basket. I **³was able to see** that something was very wrong.' Vet Nigel Farr found that Benji had eaten nearly two kilos of small stones from the garden path. Nigel **⁴was successful in removing** all the stones in a two-hour operation, and now Benji is recovering after his strange meal. **⁵It was possible for Benji to die**,' said Nigel. Rosie has taken his words seriously and is replacing all the stones with bigger, less edible ones. **⁶Benji will probably be** safe in the garden now,' she smiles.

3 **Complete the sentences so they are true for you.**

1 At the moment I can hear _____ .
2 I sometimes dream about being able to
  _____ .
3 I can see _____ from my bedroom window.
4 I have never managed to learn _____ .
5 My parents annoy me when they won't
  _____ .
6 A few years ago I couldn't _____ , but now I can/and I still can't.
7 I can't stand it when _____ .
8 When I was a child, my parents wouldn't let me
  _____ .

4 **Cross out the options that are not possible. In some sentences more than one option is possible.**

1 Please **may / could / would** I be excused for a moment? I have to take this call.
2 Perhaps we **might / could / would** discuss this in private if you don't mind.
3 Hold this for me, **can / would / could** you?
4 **Will / May / Can** we have a look around if that's OK?
5 **Could / May / Can** you tell me where the nearest underground station is?
6 **Can / Could / Will** you turn the TV down, please?
7 **Could / Can / Will** I have the day off tomorrow, please?
8 Pass me my phone, **will / may / can** you?

5 **Read the responses and write questions asking for permission or making requests.**

1 A: _____
  B: Sorry, we only take cash.
2 A: _____
  B: If you've done all your homework, yes.
3 A: _____
  B: Yeah, all right – leave it in the sink and I'll do it later.
4 A: _____
  B: OK, as long as you put some petrol in it before you bring it back.
5 A: _____
  B: Do you have an appointment, madam?
6 A: _____
  B: Well ... how long for? She got very upset and started chewing the sofa last time.

6 Decide if the sentences below are written or spoken. Then complete them with modal verbs and the correct form of the verbs in brackets. Explain any differences in meaning.

1 Tickets _____ (present) at the entrance.
2 Warren's in a good mood – he _____ (see) the phone bill yet.
3 Passengers _____ (leave) luggage unattended.
4 Hurry up! Dad _____ (wait) for us.
5 You _____ (eat) that if you're serious about losing weight.
6 He's not in. Oh, I know, he _____ (go) to get the stuff for dinner.
7 I _____ (pay) someone to repair it – it's too difficult to do it myself.
8 All mobile phones _____ (switch off) in this area.

7 Rewrite the sentences using *must(n't)*, *will/won't*, *should(n't)*, or *have to*.

1 I strongly advise you not to miss the United game on Saturday.

_____

2 It is the management's obligation to act quickly to prevent bullying in the workplace.

_____

3 How long was it necessary for you to wait for your new passport?

_____

4 Is it necessary for you to carry an ID card in your country?

_____

5 Ring Alvaro later – it's unlikely that he's had time to unpack yet.

_____

6 It was wrong for you to invite Ali without asking me.

_____

7 I'm sure that's Zoe's book – she's just phoned up about it.

_____

8 I'm sure you drove like a maniac to get here so quickly!

_____

8 Complete the sentences with the correct form of *ought to*, *have to*, *dare* or *need*.

1 We'd love to stay longer, but Rachel _____ catch a train early in the morning.
2 I must do something about this room – it _____ completely reorganising.
3 Don't you _____ tell Yvette what she can and can't wear – it's not up to you.
4 We _____ left a bit earlier – we're going to hit the traffic now.
5 We _____ discuss it now if it's inconvenient.
6 You _____ do everything he says, do you?
7 I really hate _____ get up so early for work every day.
8 William _____ admit that he'd lost the pen drive with all the data on it.
9 You _____ got all dressed up – it's not really a formal dinner.
10 I know it was wrong to shout those rude words in class, but Ian _____ me to.

9 Match sentences 1–9 with responses a–i.

1 He definitely sent you the finished report last week.
2 Did you ask them to deliver it at the weekend?
3 Go on, have another slice of cake.
4 You sit down – I'll finish the washing-up.
5 I'm sure she didn't mean to upset you.
6 You have to invite your cousin to your party.
7 Come on, keep going. It's not much further.
8 Clara was in the shop for ages, deciding which top to buy.
9 I got you these to say thanks for everything.

a I shouldn't really.
b You don't have to.
c I can't!
d He can't have!
e Oh, you shouldn't have!
f I dare say.
g Yes, but they wouldn't.
h Must I?
i I can imagine.

PASSIVE FORMS

Passive forms with *be*

1   Unlike active sentences, in passive sentences, the subject of the sentences is not the doer of the verb (the agent).
    Someone stole my purse. (active)
    (subject)
    My purse was stolen. (passive)
    (subject)

2   Normally the agent is not included in a passive sentence because it is unimportant or obvious who the agent is, or because we want to avoid saying who is responsible.
    *A man **is being interviewed** in connection with the attack.*
    *Several people **were injured** in the explosion.*
    *The relevant documents **have been lost**.*
    *   But if the agent is of particular interest, we use **by**.
        *Paper money was invented **by the Chinese**.*

3   Note the passive of *-ing* forms.
    *Don't you ever worry about **being attacked**?*
    *He was upset at **having been omitted** from the final list.*

4   The passive infinitive form (without *to*) is often used after modal verbs.
    *There is no limit to what **can be achieved**.*
    *I very much doubt whether he **will be allowed** to continue.*
    *I really think he **should be given** another opportunity.*

5   Some verbs are not usually used in the passive form. Some of the most important are:
    *   intransitive verbs such as *arrive, happen, come, fall, crash*.
        He arrived late. (NOT ~~was arrived~~)
    *   state verbs such as *consist, belong, have, seem, be, depend, exist*.
        The Baltic States consist of Latvia, Lithuania and Estonia. (NOT ~~are consisted of~~)

6   Some verbs are most often found in common passive phrases.
    *Children **aren't allowed to** smoke in school.*
    *Some pupils in the school **are involved** in crime.*
    *We**'re supposed to** hand in our projects today.*
    *I**'m not used to** late nights any more.*

Exercise 1, page 134

Using passive forms

1   Normally, the beginning of a sentence tells us what the topic is and new information is added at the end. When the topic of the sentence is not the agent, the passive is used.
    *The Guggenheim Museum in New York **was designed** by Frank Lloyd Wright. It is currently situated in 5th Avenue, but there are plans to move it to Wall Street.*
    (The topic is the Guggenheim Museum.)
    *Frank Lloyd Wright **designed** several well-known buildings, including the Imperial Hotel in Tokyo and the Guggenheim Museum in New York. He died In 1959.*
    (The topic is Frank Lloyd Wright.)

Exercise 2, page 134

2   We often use the passive when we want a style that is impersonal and objective. For this reason, the passive is common in academic writing and newspaper reports.
    *Water **is released** from the reservoir to the turbine.* (scientific text)
    *Italian singer Martina Barrotti **has been cleared** of tax evasion in an Italian court.* (newspaper article)
    *   The passive is often avoided in less formal contexts (see below).

3   The passive is often used with reporting verbs like *believe* and *think*. These constructions are common in formal writing.
    People believe that Bill Gates is the richest man in the US. (active)
    *Bill Gates **is believed to be** the richest man in the US.* (passive)
    ***It is believed** that Bill Gates is the richest man in the US.* (passive)
    *   Other verbs commonly used in this way are:
        allege, assume, consider, expect, intend, rumour, know, report, suppose, think, understand.
        *It **is rumoured** that the President is about to resign.*
        *The multi-millionaire businessman **was alleged** to have committed fraud.*
        *It **is not** yet **known** whether there are any survivors of the attack.*

Exercise 3, page 134

Passive forms without *be*

1   *Be* is often omitted in newspaper headlines.
    England ~~is~~ beaten at football
    Hundreds ~~are~~ made homeless by floods

2   In relative clauses using passive constructions, the relative pronoun and verb *to be* can be omitted. This is known as a 'reduced relative clause'.
    the people (who were) chosen to appear on the show
    (= the people chosen to appear on the show)
    the best play (which has ever been) written
    (= the best play ever written)

3   Passives are often used as adjectives at the beginning of a sentence. This is a fairly formal usage, and is more common in writing.
    Locked away in his prison cell room, he gradually fell into despair.
    Released in two days' time, The South is probably Manuel García's most ambitious film so far.

> Exercises 4–5, pages 134–135

Verbs with two objects

1   Some verbs have two objects, indirect and direct.
    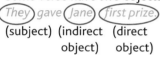
    (subject) (indirect   (direct
                object)   object)
    •   In the passive form the indirect or direct object can become the subject of the sentence.

    (subject)   (direct object)

    First prize was given to *Jane.*
    (subject)   (direct object)

2   Some other verbs which follow this pattern are: *ask, give, hand, lend, offer, pay, promise, show, teach, tell.*

> Exercise 6, page 135

Passive forms with *get* and *have*

1   We often use *have* + past participle to talk about services which we arrange and which are paid for or for things you experience which may be unpleasant.
    *It's really cheap to **have your ears pierced** in this shop.*
    *I **had** my bag **stolen** while I was on the Underground.*

2   We can use *get* + past participle for actions which are accidental or unexpected.
    *Unfortunately, I fell asleep in the sun and my shoulders **got burned**.*
    *It's inevitable that some things **get broken** when you move house.*

3   We can also use *get* + past participle when the process is in some way difficult.
    *It's taken a long time, but Christopher finally **got** his novel **published**.*

4   There are also a large number of idiomatic expressions where *get* + past participle is used to mean 'yourself', such as *get dressed* (= dress yourself), *get undressed*, *get changed*, *get engaged*, *get lost*, *get started*. Passives with *get* are generally more colloquial than passives with *be*.
    *The couple **were** married in Rome.* (= more formal)
    *The couple **got** married in Rome.* (= more informal)

> Exercises 7–8, page 135

Avoiding the passive

In conversation and other informal contexts, people often avoid the passive, because it sounds more formal. Active verbs with 'impersonal' pronouns like *you*, *we* and *they* are preferred. Compare the examples:
They arrested him this morning. (colloquial style; they = the authorities)
He was arrested this morning. (more formal style)
They say he's a multi-millionaire. (usual in conversation; we also use *people* as the subject here)
He is said to be a multi-millionaire. (formal contexts only)
We use the passive less in conversation. (less formal)
The passive is used less in conversation. (more formal)
You should replace the cartridge every three months. (verbal instructions)
The cartridge should be replaced every three months. (written instructions)

NOTICE!

The pronoun *one* also exists in English, but is considered excessively formal by most younger speakers and is therefore avoided.

*~~One has~~ **You** have to be careful here after dark.*

PASSIVE FORMS

1 Find and correct the mistakes in the sentences. Look at the words in bold.

1 I was terrified – we **could be killed**!
2 The cat **was disappeared** one morning and we haven't seen him since.
3 I used to **love been given** presents on my birthday. Now it just reminds me how old I am.
4 My computer **was crashed** at the weekend, and so I couldn't do my homework.
5 Do you think Finlay **should be tell** about his mother's accident?
6 He must get tired **of calling** the wrong name all the time.
7 You're late. What **was happened**?
8 That contract isn't worth the paper **it's write** on.

2 Rewrite the encyclopaedia entries so that the topic is at the beginning of each sentence. Change some active forms to passive and some passive forms to active.

1

Audrey Hepburn was a British actress and humanitarian. People know her best as a film actor, and several awards were received by her for her roles. From the mid-1960s more and more of her time was devoted by her to working with disadvantaged people through UNICEF, right up until her death in 1993.

2

Bali is a province of Indonesia, which covers the island of Bali and a few small neighbouring islands. People nickname it 'the Island of the Gods'. It is very popular with tourists and people know it for its highly developed arts. Java and Lombok border it to the west and east.

3

George R. R. Martin is an American fantasy author and screenwriter. People know him best for *A Song of Ice and Fire*, adapted for TV as *Game of Thrones*. More than 20 books have been written by him, as well as a number of screenplays.

4

The Eiffel Tower is a huge iron tower situated on the Champ de Mars in Paris. Engineers working for Gustave Eiffel's engineering company designed it. They erected it in 1889 as the entrance to the World's Fair. It has had many uses since then, and during World War I the French military used the tower to communicate with ships in the Atlantic Ocean. Nowadays the tower is a popular tourist attraction, and seven million people visit it every year.

3 Rewrite the sentences in two ways, as in the example.

Everyone knows that the fugitives are in Spain.
  a *It is known that the fugitives are in Spain.*
  b *The fugitives are known to be in Spain.*

1 We understand that the Princess is expecting her first baby.
  a _____
  b _____
2 Organisers expect over 5,000 people to attend the music festival this weekend.
  a _____
  b _____
3 Experts think that Napoleon's recently discovered war diaries are fake.
  a _____
  b _____
4 Some people allege that the CEO embezzled funds in excess of $900,000.
  a _____
  b _____
5 We have reports that an anonymous telephone buyer paid over $20 million for the Dalí.
  a _____
  b _____
6 There are rumours that Johnny Depp is among the guests at the film festival.
  a _____
  b _____

4 Complete the headlines with past participles from the box to make them passive in meaning.

fine   ~~release~~   arrest   find   name   leave   deliver

1 **Prisoner _released_ by accident**
2 **Birthday card _____ ten years late**
3 **Finger _____ in bag of popcorn**
4 **Robber's address _____ at crime scene**
5 **Criminal _____ while reporting stolen car at police station**
6 **Woman _____ $500 for speeding on her bicycle**
7 **Baby _____ after internet address**

5 Match the headlines 1–7 in exercise 4 with sentences a–g. Then join the pairs of sentences using reduced relative clauses.

a A prisoner was released accidentally 12 days ago. He has been recaptured.

   1–sA prisoner released accidentally 12 days ago has been recaptured.

b A baby was born yesterday. It has been named Junior. com!

   _____

c A man was wanted for armed robbery. He was arrested when he went to a police station to report his car being stolen.

   _____

d A woman was fined $500 for riding her bicycle too fast. She has described the amount as unbelievable.

   _____

e A birthday card was posted ten years ago. It has just arrived at its destination.

   _____

f A finger was found in a bag of popcorn. Laboratory tests have confirmed that it was human.

   _____

g A piece of paper was left at the scene of a crime. It had the robber's name and address on it.

   _____

6 Rewrite the sentences in the passive.

1 Oh, sorry – someone told me that Oscar Lopez worked here.

   _____

2 She shouldn't have given that customer a full refund.

   _____

3 Did anyone pay you for all that extra work on the website you did?

   _____

4 I wish they had taught me how to drive when I was at school.

   _____

5 Although they offered me a better deal, I still decided to change phone company.

   _____

6 They sent the wrong email to hundreds of people because of a computer error.

   _____

7 In the event of a delay, we will give passengers a voucher for a free snack and drink.

   _____

8 What kind of questions did they ask you at the interview?

   _____

7 Decide if there is any difference in meaning between the sentences in each pair. Explain the differences.

1 **A:** The suspect's girlfriend got arrested.
  B: The suspect got his girlfriend arrested.

2 **A:** After years of the same, I decided to restyle my hair.
  B: After years of the same, I decided to have my hair restyled.

3 **A:** I've got my leg stuck in the chair!
  B: My leg's got stuck in the chair!

4 **A:** Did you finish the report in time?
  B: Did you get your report finished in time?

5 **A:** During the protests, our windows were smashed.
  B: During the protests, our windows got smashed.

6 **A:** Our house was broken into last night.
  B: We had our house broken into last night.

8 Complete the article with the correct form of the verbs in brackets.

Kopi Luwak ^{1}_____ (know) among coffee experts as the most expensive coffee in the world. It ^{2}_____ (mainly/produce) in Indonesia, where it ^{3}_____ (farm) since the colonial era. So what ^{4}_____ (make) Kopi Luwak so special and therefore so expensive? The secret ^{5}_____ (lie) in its production process and depends on a small mammal native to the area, called the Asian palm civet. Only the ripest coffee cherries ^{6}_____ (select) by the civet, which then eats them, digesting the fruity pulp and secreting the coffee beans in its faeces. These ^{7}_____ (then/collect) by coffee farmers and cleaned and packaged. In some parts of the world they will ^{8}_____ (sell) by specialist traders for up to $700 a kilo.

ADVERBS

Types of adverb

1 Adverbs are an important way of adding information to a sentence and of modifying the information that is there. There are different types:
   - adverbs of place (e.g. *over there, away, at home*)
   - adverbs of time (e.g. *nowadays, at that time*)
   - adverbs of manner (e.g. *beautifully, hard*)
   - adverbs of frequency (e.g. *always, once in a while*)
   - adverbs of probability (e.g. *certainly, possibly*)
   - 'focus' adverbs (e.g. *only, even, especially*)
   - adverbs of degree (e.g. *very, quite, enormously*)

2 Adverbs can be single words or phrases. Adverbs formed from adjectives often end in *-ly*, but there are many adverbs that do not end in *-ly*.

The position of adverbs

1 **Adverbs of place and time** most often go at the end of the clause or sentence.
   *I wasn't aware of any problem **at the time**.*
   *I had an odd experience **on the way home**.*

   - But they are often put at the beginning for emphasis.
   ***On the way home** I had an odd experience.*
   ***This season** United have played very well at home.*

> **NOTICE!**
>
> - ***Already*** usually occurs in the mid position, but it can be found at the beginning or end of a clause.
>
>   *Their daughter is only three, but **already** she can write her own name.*
>
>   *Their daughter is only three, but she can **already** write her own name.*
>
>   *Their daughter is only three, but she can write her own name **already**.*
>
> - ***Still*** usually occurs in the mid position.
>
>   *My mother's **still** being prescribed antibiotics.*
>
> - At the beginning of a sentence, *still* is often used as a discourse marker to indicate a contrast with what has gone before.
>
>   *He's a miserable old guy. **Still**, you've got to admire him.*
>
> - With questions and negatives, ***yet*** usually occurs at the end of the sentence/clause.
>
>   *Johnny **hasn't** arrived **yet**. Would you mind waiting for a few moments?*
>
> - We can use the pattern *yet + infinitive with to* in a more formal context in affirmative sentences.
>
>   *We have **yet to see** the full effects of the changes.*

Exercise 1, page 138

2 **Adverbs of manner** are often found next to the word they describe.
   *I **understand perfectly** what you mean.*
   *Many people regard her as being **emotionally unstable**.*

   - Sometimes changing the position of an adverb can subtly change meaning.
   *He was **perfectly aware** that we could see him.*
   *He was aware that we could **see him perfectly**.*

> **NOTICE!**
>
> Where there are several adverbs at the end of the sentence/clause, the order is: manner, place, time.
>
> *Dad sat **happily in his armchair**.*
>   (manner)   (place)
>
> *Are you going to stay **at home all evening**?*
>   (place)   (time)
>
> *United have played **very well at home this season**.*
>   (manner)   (place)   (time)

3 **Adverbs of frequency and probability** typically go before the main verb and after the first auxiliary or the verb *be*.
   *The old man **hardly ever** left his home.*
   *Your father was **almost certainly** right.*
   *Members of our staff have **frequently** been attacked for no reason.*

   - They can also go at the beginning or end of the sentence, but only in sentences which emphasise the frequency/probability.
   ***Almost certainly**, your father was right.* ✓
   ***Frequently**, members of our staff have been attacked for no reason.* ✓
   *The old man left his home **hardly ever**.* ✗

   - Longer adverbial phrases describing frequency normally go at the end of the sentence.
   *I visit my grandmother **as often as I can**.*
   *I try to go to the gym **once or twice a week**.*

   - **Adverbs of probability** are often used in conversation as single-word answers.
   *Will the election result be close? **Undoubtedly**.*

- If the adverb refers to what will *not* happen, it goes before the negative auxiliary.

  *My mother **still doesn't** believe me.*

  *They **probably won't** have got your letter yet.*

- Generally, we do not put an adverb between a verb and its direct object.

  *He took the puppy **gently** out of the basket.* ✓

  *He took **gently** the puppy out of the basket.* ✗

Exercises 2–4, page 138

Adverbs of manner with and without -ly

1 Although many adverbs of manner end in -ly (e.g. *easily*, *slowly*, *clearly*), many do not.
  *We went **straight** home when the film finished.*
  *Do you have to drive so **fast**?*

2 We do not form adverbs from adjectives which end in -ly (e.g. *lively*, *friendly*). We use *in a …-ly way* instead.
  *He was looking at us **in a** very **unfriendly way**.*
  *She always tries to explain grammar rules **in a lively way**.*

Exercise 5, page 138

3 Some pairs of adverbs have a different meaning with and without -ly.

- *deep/deeply*
  Deep is an adverb of manner meaning 'going far down or in'. *Deeply* is often used of emotions, and means 'intensely'.
  *The submarine is travelling **deep** below the surface of the water.*
  *People in this part of the country feel very **deeply** about this issue.*

- *free/freely*
  These are both adverbs of manner, but *free* means 'without paying' and *freely* means 'without restriction'.
  *Railway employees travel **free**.* (= without paying)
  *Everyone can talk **freely**.* (= without restriction)

- *hard/hardly*
  Hard is an adverb of manner. *Hardly* occurs in the mid-position and means 'almost not'.
  *She works **hard**.* (= she works a lot)
  *She **hardly** works.* (= she does almost no work)

- *late/lately*
  Late is an adverb of manner. *Lately* is an adverb of time meaning 'recently'.
  *Do you often go out **late**?*
  *Have you been going out a lot **lately**?* (= recently)

- *right/rightly, wrong/wrongly*
  Right means 'in the correct way'. *Rightly* is a comment adverb, expressing the speaker's idea that someone was entitled to do or feel something. *Wrong/wrongly* work in the same way.
  *I'm sure I'll get it **right** (**wrong**) next time.*
  *Quite **rightly** (**wrongly**) in my view, they have decided to appeal against the decision.*

Exercise 6, page 139

4 Many **adverb + adjective** and **adverb + verb** combinations are commonly found together and can be seen as set phrases.
  *It is one of the most **technologically advanced** societies on earth.*
  *It's **highly unlikely** that this project will succeed.*
  *The doctors **tried desperately** to save his leg.*

Exercise 7, page 139

5 Verbs such as *feel*, *look*, *seem*, *sound*, *taste* and *smell* usually take an adjective, not an adverb.
  That smells nice! NOT ~~That smells nicely.~~

Focusing adverbs

Focusing adverbs are used to focus attention on particular words.

1 *Even*
  Even is used to emphasise that the following words or information is extreme or surprising.
  *I did everything I could to get money. I **even** asked strangers to lend me a few pence.*

2 *Only*
  Only has a 'limiting' effect. It usually comes immediately before the word it qualifies.
  ***Only** you know what really happened that night.* (= you and nobody else)
  *I could **only** answer one of the questions.* (= I could answer one question and no more than that)

3 *Especially*
  Especially emphasises that the information is 'more than the others'.
  *I like all kinds of sport, **especially** basketball.*
  Note: *particularly* works in the same way.

Exercise 8, page 139

ADVERBS

1 Complete the sentences with *still*, *already* or *yet*.

1 I've got to go back home tomorrow. _____ , I've had a great holiday.

2 Is it eight o'clock _____ ? We really should finish work now and go home!

3 We've been through this so many times _____ – you're too young to go away with your friends.

4 Are you _____ trying to fix that computer? Why not just take it back to the shop?

5 I don't think they've finished filming the new series _____ .

6 We've _____ been past that shop once – are you sure you know the way?

7 I _____ haven't decided what I want to do for my birthday.

8 The Presidential candidate has admitted that he has _____ to file his income tax returns for this year.

2 Put the words in brackets in the correct order. Start with the underlined word. More than one answer may be possible.

1 We've had a wonderful time. (to / we / here / soon / back / hope / very / come)
_____

2 (phone / read / text message / carefully / James / his / quickly / the / down / then / put)
_____

3 I haven't seen you for ages. (all / sometime / coffee / for / get / let's / together)
_____

4 (possibly / this / shopping / you / with / give / a / could / hand / me / ?)
_____

5 (all / played / well / Briggs / really / yesterday / afternoon) He deserved to win the match.
_____

6 (automatically / every / in / the / on / all / six o'clock / rooms / air conditioning / at / the / morning / comes)
_____

7 (just / you / in / now / see / did / car park / anyone / the / ?) My car's been stolen!
_____

3 Complete the sentences so they are true for you.

1 In my country, we hardly ever _____ .

2 I _____ a couple of times a year.

3 I think people should _____ once in a while.

4 I would never ever _____ unless _____ .

5 I like to _____ most evenings.

6 Every now and then, it's nice to _____ .

4 Complete the responses with the adverbs in the box. Then work in pairs and ask and answer the questions.

possibly	maybe	conceivably
hopefully	(almost) certainly	most likely
no doubt	definitely (not)	probably (not)

1 A: Do you think you'll go out much this weekend?
  B: _____ .

2 A: Are you planning to have a meal out in the next couple of days?
  B: _____ .

3 A: Do you think your teacher will be in a good mood tomorrow?
  B: _____ .

4 A: Would you live in another country if you had the chance to?
  B: _____ .

5 A: Are you going to travel abroad next year?
  B: _____ .

6 A: Do you think you'll still be studying English in a year's time?
  B: _____ .

7 A: Are you likely to take an exam in the next six months?
  B: _____ .

8 A: Would you ever tell a lie to someone close to you?
  B: _____ .

5 Put the words in brackets in the correct place in the recipe instructions. Use the adjective or adverb form of the words.

A RECIPE

1 This little pasta dish is quick and easy to prepare, but the ingredients complement each other so that you'll love every bite! (simple, perfect)

2 Bring a pan of water to the boil, then cook half a kilo of pasta for about three minutes, or until it floats. Drain and set aside. (heavy, fresh)

3 Chop half an onion and crush two cloves of garlic, and fry them in a little olive oil until soft and brown. (rough, slight)

4 Meanwhile, slice a courgette and add that to the onion and garlic, and cook for another five minutes, stirring. (fine, continuous)

5 Turn the heat off and add the pasta and 150g parmesan cheese, th_ mix everything together before the cheese melts too much. (quick_

6 Slice two lemons and squeeze the juice over the pasta, then mix everything together. (generous)

7 Season with a little salt and ground black pepper. (fresh)

8 Tastes with ciabatta and a white wine. (great, dry)

6 Choose the correct answers to complete the sentences.

1 We found the whole situation *deep* / *deeply* embarrassing.
2 I had *hard* / *hardly* finished what I was saying when Gina interrupted me.
3 I can't understand why we did so badly. What are we doing *wrong* / *wrongly*?
4 Entrance to the museum usually costs £20, but students and teachers get in *free* / *freely*.
5 How *late* / *lately* did you stay at the party?
6 These holidaymakers are *right* / *rightly* appalled at the state of the facilities in this hotel.

7 Complete the sentences with the correct form of a verb from box A and an adverb from box B.

A

| sell | try | feel | understand | go |
| complain | club | eat | apologise | react |

B

| smoothly | bitterly | well | desperately | strongly |
| perfectly | sensibly | badly | together | profusely |

1 Carol will have been working here for 25 years in March. Let's _____ and get her a nice present.
2 The firefighters _____ to control the wildfires, but it was several days before they could bring them under control.
3 I _____ what you mean, madam, and I can assure you that it won't happen again.
4 A lot of people _____ about this issue, so be careful what you say at the meeting.
5 The government has started a campaign to stress the importance of _____ and exercising regularly.
6 People _____ about the new tax, which was felt to be unfairly hard on the poor.
7 I _____ for not handing my essay in on time.
8 I'm pleased to report that our new range of educational software _____ very _____ last year.
9 It's difficult to make suggestions to Chris. He always _____ so _____ to criticism and opposite points of view.
10 I thought the press conference _____ very _____ yesterday, didn't you?

8 Put the adverbs in bold in the correct place in the quotes. Which are focusing adverbs?

1 'Friends are made by many acts – and lost by one.' (*Anon*) **only**
2 'It is the intellectually lost who ever argue.' (*Oscar Wilde*) **only**
3 'Nothing is hard if you divide it into small jobs.' (*Henry Ford*) **particularly**
4 'It takes good manners to put up with bad ones.' (*Anon*) **especially**
5 'It is easier to forgive an enemy than to forgive a friend.' (*William Blake*) **even**
6 'If a wife laughs at her husband's jokes, is he funny or is she smart?' (*Anon*) **always**
7 'A brilliant man knows whether the applause for his words is politeness or appreciation.' (*Anon*) **only**
8 'Silence is misinterpreted, but misquoted.' (*Anon*) **often**, **never**
9 'Answer a letter while you are angry.' (*Chinese proverb*) **never**
10 'I don't know anything about music. In my line, you don't have to.' (*Elvis Presley*) **even**

9 Find and correct the mistakes in the sentences.

1 What's that you're cooking? It smells nicely.
2 Georgiana's exhausted. She's been working really hardly.
3 Despite their promises, we have already to see the government introduce the changes.
4 Considering how expensive it is, it's greatly unlikely the new product will sell very well.
5 Is that a new top? It looks really well on you.
6 The party was a bit of a disaster. Even a few people turned up.
7 The protests showed that the people felt very deep about the government's plans.
8 The teacher didn't look very happy when Vinnie arrived lately for class again.
9 We, on the way home, stopped off at a little café for lunch.
10 I try to do as often exercise as I can.

139

INFINITIVES AND *-ING* FORMS

General

1 Every sentence must have a main verb. In addition, many sentences have infinitives (with or without *to*) and gerunds/present participles (the *-ing* form).

2 These occur in a number of different positions in the sentence, but they are not the main verb (except if they are part of a modal verb – see below).
   - as the subject: *Parking around here has become more and more difficult.*
   - after the main verb: *I never expected to win!*
   - after an adjective: *The result of the election is impossible to predict.*
   - after a noun: *We didn't have any trouble finding our way here.*
   - after a preposition: *Without seeing all the evidence, I don't want to comment.*
   - as a clause: *Marina stared out of the window, not even trying to concentrate.*

3 *-ing* forms can be gerunds or present participles. If the *-ing* form functions as a noun it is a gerund. If it functions as a verb, it is a participle.
   Walking is one of the best forms of exercise. (= gerund)
   Who's that man walking towards us? (= participle)

4 Infinitives and *-ing* forms can be found in both the affirmative and negative forms.

Infinitive	*-ing* form
Try to hurry!	*Telling him was silly.*
Try not to drop it.	*Not telling him was silly.*
He seems to be doing well.	
He seems to have done well.	*Without having done it, I ...*
He seems to have been doing well.	
I want to be told the truth.	*I prefer being told the truth.*
I would like to have been told earlier.	*She's angry about having been deceived.*

Infinitives and *-ing* forms after adjectives

1 Adjectives are normally followed by an infinitive.
   The situation is likely to get worse before it gets better.
   It's extremely difficult to understand why people do this.

2 *Busy* and *worth* are exceptions because they are always followed by the *-ing* form.
   Jiang was busy doing his homework when I phoned.
   We believe that it's a risk worth taking.

3 Some adjectives can be followed by an infinitive, or a preposition + *-ing* form. The infinitive tends to refer to a particular occasion/situation, the *-ing* form to a more general feeling. Compare:
   The old lady was afraid to cross the busy road, so she asked a man to help her. (= unwilling to do something particular, because of fear)
   My granny is afraid of being robbed, so she always keeps her money in a money belt. (= a general fear)

4 There can be other differences in meaning too.
   I was so anxious (= worried) *about making a mistake that I could hardly say a word.*
   We are very anxious (= keen) *to come to an agreement as soon as possible.*
   It's good (= pleasant) *to see you again.*
   I was never good at (= clever at) *remembering names.*
   I'm sorry to interrupt, but would you mind explaining again? (= regret about something we are doing or are about to do)
   Sorry for losing my temper last night. (= to apologise for an earlier action)

> Exercise 1, page 142

Nouns with infinitives and *-ing* forms

1 Many nouns are commonly followed by an infinitive.
   There are no plans to replace the existing Town Hall.
   It's time to take a long, hard look at our financial situation.

2 Other nouns are followed by an *-ing* form or preposition + *-ing* form.
   There's no hope of finding any more survivors now.
   We had no problems finding accommodation.

> Exercise 2, page 142

Verbs with infinitives and *-ing* forms

1 **Verb + *to*-infinitive**
   - Many verbs are followed by a *to*-infinitive.
     The police attempted to break up the demonstration.
     The economic situation appears to be improving.
   - Some verbs can have an object before the infinitive. Verbs like this include: *want, ask, beg, expect, help, need, would like.*
     I want to go home. / I want you to go home.
   - Other verbs must have an object. Verbs like this include: *advise, order, remind, allow, forbid, invite, encourage, permit, teach, force, persuade, tell.*
     Politicians are urging people to vote.
     The police have warned people to be careful.

> Exercise 3, page 142

2 Verb + bare infinitive

- A small number of important verbs take a bare infinitive (an infinitive without *to*). Most important are modals and semi-modals. (See Unit 5 Language summary, page 128.)
- We also use the bare infinitive after *let*, *make*, *would rather*, *had/'d better*:

  *I think we **had better leave** before we cause any more trouble.*
  *Please don't **let him upset** you.*

- The bare infinitive can also be used with verbs of perception (*see*, *watch*, *hear*, *feel*). Notice the difference in meaning between the infinitive and *-ing* form.

  *We heard the children **sing** the national anthem.* (= the whole song)
  *We heard the children **singing** the national anthem.* (= part of the song – in progress)

Exercise 4, page 142

3 Verb + *-ing* form

- Some verbs are usually followed by an *-ing* form or a preposition + *-ing* form.

  *It's time to **stop worrying** and **start living**!*
  *I'd like to **apologise for causing** so much trouble.*

- A number of verbs take an object + preposition +*-ing* form. Verbs like these include: *accuse/suspect* sb *of*, *condemn*, *blame/criticise/forgive/punish/thank* sb *for*; *discourage/prevent/stop* sb *from*, *congratulate* sb *on*.

  *The police **suspect** Atkins **of dealing** in illegal arms.*
  *I don't **blame** you **for being** angry.*

- In the passive form, the preposition comes directly after the verb. This is common in newspaper reports.

  *Atkins **is suspected of dealing** in illegal arms.*

Exercise 5, page 143

4 Verb + *to* -infinitive or *-ing* form

- A small number of verbs can take both an infinitive and an *-ing* form. For some verbs the infinitive is used to look forward, the *-ing* form to look backwards.

  *I remembered **to book** the tickets.* (= I didn't forget.)
  *I remember **meeting** him.* (= I have a memory of it.)
  *We must stop **to get** some petrol.* (= stop for a purpose)
  *Dad's stopped **smoking**.* (= He doesn't do it now.)
  *I regret **to tell** you that the performance has been cancelled.* (= I regret something I am about to tell you.)
  *I regret **leaving** her.* (= I regret something in the past.)

- With *like*, *love* and *hate*, the *-ing* form is normally used in British English, but the infinitive is also common in American English. After *would like*, the infinitive is always used.

  *I love **dancing**.* (Br/US)   *I love **to dance**.* (US)

- The verbs *start* and *begin* can be used with either without any change of meaning.

  *I **started/began learning/to learn** English for work.*

Exercise 6, page 143

Other uses of *-ing* forms

1. *-ing* forms are often the subject of the sentence.
   ***Blaming** other people isn't going to help.*
2. Prepositions are always followed by *-ing* forms.
   *Losing your home is **like losing** an old friend.*
3. We often use the pattern *by* + *-ing* to describe the method we use in order to do something.
   *You can stop a door from squeaking **by putting** a little oil onto the hinges.*

- Remember that *to* is a preposition in the patterns below, and so takes the *-ing* form.

  *I'm not used **to living** alone.*
  *We look forward **to seeing** you in July.*

Exercise 7, page 143

Participle clauses

1. Participle clauses are similar to reduced relative clauses.
   *The woman **who is standing** by the door is my ex-wife.*
   *The woman **standing** by the door is my ex-wife.*
2. We use a similar type of clause with verbs of perception like *see*, *hear*, *remember*.
   *I **saw him**. He was **carrying** a heavy bag.*
   *I **saw him carrying** a heavy bag.*
3. We can also use a participle clause to join two sentences together when they have the same subject.
   *Elizabeth sat quietly in the corner. **She was smiling**.*
   *Elizabeth sat quietly in the corner, **smiling**.*

Exercises 8–9, page 143

INFINITIVES AND -ING FORMS

1 Complete the sentences with the adjectives in the box, a preposition and the infinitive or -ing form of the verbs in brackets. More than one answer may be possible.

afraid	determined	anxious	possible
delighted	wrong	advisable	keen

1 Would it be _____ (send) me a copy of the report?
2 Harry's _____ (make) an early start in the morning, so we'd better get to bed soon.
3 I know you're _____ (meet) the President, but I'm sure everything will be fine.
4 I'm _____ (see) so many familiar faces here tonight.
5 My mother hasn't travelled abroad very much in her life as she's _____ (fly).
6 It isn't _____ (you/take) this medicine while you're pregnant.
7 In the end I think Priscilla realised she was _____ (be) so difficult about the meal.
8 Jo was _____ (not let) us see how upset she was.

2 Join the pairs of sentences using the nouns in bold. Use a dictionary if necessary.

1 We have tried to resolve the conflict peacefully. We have failed. **attempts**
   All _____ .
2 After the performance you will be able to meet the actors. **opportunity**
   You _____ .
3 The government is planning to build 250,000 new homes. How will that affect property prices? **plans**
   How _____ .
4 The company has decided to hire a new manager from outside. What do you think of that? **decision**
   What _____ ?
5 Kelly refused to sign the contract. Did that surprise you? **refusal**
   Did _____ ?
6 You are moving abroad next month. Does that worry you? **thought**
   Does _____ ?
7 It wasn't necessary to be so rude to the waiter. **need**
   There _____ ?
8 You found a job after graduating. Was it difficult? **difficulty**
   Did _____ ?

3 Complete the sentences so they are true for you.

1 I have arranged _____ this weekend.
2 I would never agree _____ .
3 I have sometimes been tempted _____ .
4 My teacher always encourages me _____ .
5 I aim _____ by the end of this year.
6 It's quite easy to persuade me _____ .
7 I hate being forced _____ .
8 I often need to be reminded _____ .

4 Match the sentence halves and use the correct form of the verbs in the box to join them.

go	disagree	be	stay	open
slam	bother	tidy up	tell	discuss

1 My first boss was such a tyrant that nobody dared
2 You needn't
3 This letter looks like it might be important. Hadn't you better
4 By the looks on their faces, we could all
5 Tom's angry because I wouldn't let him
6 Because she'd been naughty, the teacher made Kate
7 Those books you ordered should
8 Would you rather
9 What on earth happened in the meeting this morning? I heard Jamie
10 Did you see the fireworks

a it and see what it says?
b the door as he went out.
c out after midnight.
d arriving any time now.
e the classroom before she left.
f with him.
g that something was wrong.
h this in private?
i about the report now – it's late.
j off over the river last night?

5 Put the prepositions in the box in the correct place in the sentences.

for	from	with	of	on

1 When you see April, make sure you congratulate her getting married.
2 Extremist political parties were prevented gaining too much power.
3 The gang have been charged kidnap and extorting money.
4 I wasn't accusing you cheating. I was just surprised that you knew all the answers.
5 I don't think I'll ever forgive Tony forgetting my 30th birthday.
6 The government has been criticised collecting people's personal data.
7 I don't blame you ignoring her after the way she spoke to you.
8 What can I do to discourage my son spending too much time playing video games?

6 Choose the correct answers to complete the sentences.

1 Did you remember *leave* / *to leave* / *leaving* the spare key with Sally?
2 I can't *face* / *stand* / *help* wondering if we would have been better going by train.
3 Can you imagine never *having to* / *have to* / *having* work again?
4 Adam, can you please stop *tap* / *to tap* / *tapping* your fingers on the desk?
5 She *objects* / *doesn't like* / *doesn't approve of* couples living together before they're married.
6 I'm afraid I must insist *on you paying* / *on paying* / *you paying* your bill today, sir.
7 He just couldn't *like* / *face* / *succeed* telling his wife that he'd lost his job.

7 Complete the sentences using your own ideas. Use *-ing* forms.

1 _____ is a good way of saving money.
2 _____ is a good way of doing regular exercise.
3 _____ is a good way of losing weight.
4 _____ is a good way of remembering new vocabulary.
5 _____ is a good way of relaxing.
6 _____ is a good way of meeting new people.

8 Join the pairs of sentences using participle clauses.

1 The DJ kept us dancing all night. She was playing our favourite music.
2 The old man went off down the road. He was muttering to himself.
3 We were taking a short cut through the back streets. We found a lovely little café.
4 Vanessa was thinking about what Mike had said. Vanessa sat on the bus.
5 Can you hear that strange noise? It's coming from downstairs.
6 I heard the boy next door. He was practising his trombone for hours.

9 Complete the blog with one word in each gap.

The future of our city

I was [1]_____ to hear about the Mayor's [2]_____ to 'redevelop' one of our city's beautiful parks by building a shopping centre there. I would like him to [3]_____ how he can [4]_____ funding the project, especially when he claims he cannot [5]_____ to maintain green areas in other parts of the city.

I realise the development plans will bring new jobs and better infrastructure to the city, but do we really want to [6]_____ one of the few green spaces we have left in this sprawling metropolis? Moreover, the ugly design of the proposed shopping centre [7]_____ even the oldest factories in the city [8]_____ attractive!

Perhaps the worst problem caused by [9]_____ in our park will be the pollution. Not only will we be drastically reducing the amount of clear air in the city, but the noise from the added traffic will make [10]_____ nearby unbearable.

I think these plans are a disgrace, and that the mayor needs to [11]_____ the reality that people don't want new buildings in their parks. If we care about the future of our city, we should all be [12]_____ our very best to make sure this plan doesn't become a reality.

FUTURE FORMS

General

Many forms are used to talk about the future in English. In many cases, a number of different forms are possible, depending on how we see the event.

1 will/shall

The contracted form *'ll* is most common in speech. We use *will/shall* to talk about:

- predictions based on our feelings and expectations, rather than evidence in the present. This use is common in academic writing. Adverbs of probability are often used here. (See Unit 7 Language summary, page 136.)

  I believe that, by the end of the 21st century, the world will be at peace.

  A new form of energy **will almost certainly** emerge.

- things we see as 'facts in the future'.

  The meeting will finish at 1:00 and then lunch will be served.

- decisions made at the moment of speaking.

  There's someone at the door ... I'll ring you back later, OK?

- willingness or refusal to do something.

  I'll sing at the party if you like, but I won't wear a silly costume.

> **NOTICE!**
>
> In the question form of the first person *shall* is commonly used to make offers and suggestions.
>
> **Shall I** carry that for you?
>
> **Shall we** move on to the next question?

2 going to

We use *going to* to talk about:

- our intentions for the future.

  I'm not going to borrow any more money from now on.

- a prediction based on some present evidence.

  From what I've seen so far, it's going to be a difficult game.

  In practice, *will* and *going to* are often interchangeable.

3 Present modals

Present modals can have a future meaning. (See Unit 3 Language summary, page 120.)

The economic picture may/might/could look very different in ten years' time.

4 Present continuous

We use the Present continuous to talk about definite arrangements for the future, where a specific future time is stated or understood.

What are your plans for the weekend? Are you doing anything special?

5 Present simple

We use the Present simple:

- to talk about timetabled future events or events which are 100% certain.

  The conference begins on Tuesday and ends on Friday. Tomorrow's Monday.

- in subordinate clauses, following words like *if*, *unless*, *in case*, *before*, *after*, *when*, etc.

  I'll pass on the message as soon as she gets back. We will only succeed if we all work together.

- in clauses following *what/who/which* and *whatever/wherever*, etc.

  I don't care what happens next year. Don't forget to email me, wherever you are.

  It is important to note that in all of these cases the context makes it clear that the future is intended. (See Unit 5 Language summary, page 128.)

6 Future continuous

We use the Future continuous:

- to talk about an action in progress at a specific time in the future.

  This time next week, I'll be doing my exams. In a hundred years' time, we'll probably all be working when we are 80.

- to talk about something which will happen as part of the normal course of events.

  I'll be seeing Anne later this afternoon – I'll pass on your message to her then. I can easily give you a lift, I'll be passing your house.

- to ask tentatively/politely about future plans.

  Will you be using the computer later on? Will you be needing anything else?

7 Future perfect

- Like other perfect forms, the Future perfect is used to talk about an action which will be completed before a point of time, in this case a point in the future. Compare:

  I'll finish my report on Friday night. (= I will finish it at that time.)

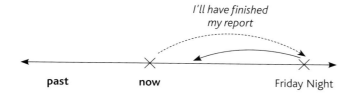

I'll have finished my report

past   now   Friday Night

I'll have finished the report by Friday night. (= I will finish it before that time.)

- The Future perfect continuous form can be used to talk about the duration of activities before a point of time in the future, often with *for* or *since*.
  I'll have been working in this same building for ten years next month!
- Note that the Future perfect and especially the Future perfect continuous are not very common forms.

Exercises 1–4, page 146

Future time phrases

We often use phrases with a future meaning to talk about the future, rather than a future verb form.

1 *about to/on the point of/on the verge of*

- We use *about to* to talk about something that is going to happen very soon.
  It's not a good time to talk. I'm about to go into a meeting.
- *On the point of + -ing* can be used with the same meaning.
  Beckham is on the point of signing a new contract with Manchester United.
- *On the verge of* is used in a similar way.
  Jo is on the verge of giving up her university course, because she really hates it.

2 *is/are to*

We use this form to talk about actions which are officially arranged. This is a common form in news reports.
  The Prime Minister is to visit Pakistan early next year.

3 *(un)likely to*

This is very common for making predictions.
  Mass space travel is unlikely to become a reality.

4 *due to*

We use *due to* in more formal speech or writing to say that something is planned to happen at a particular time.
The game is due to start at 20:00.

5 *set to*

We use *set to* when something is likely to happen. This form is common in news reports.
  The government is set to introduce the reforms early next year.

6 *bound to*

You use this if you are sure something will happen:
  Carrie's bound to be late – she always is.

Exercises 5–6, page 147

Future in the past

A number of the forms above have a past form which describes the 'future in the past'.

1. If we talk about plans or intentions in the past, we use the Past continuous or *was going to*.
  When I was little, I was going to be the world's greatest ballerina.
  We had to go to bed early, as we were all getting up at 6:00 the following morning.

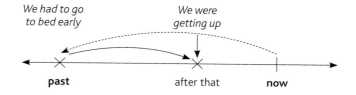

We had to go to bed early   *We were getting up*

past   after that   now

2. We often talk about things which were planned in the past but did not take place.
  We were going to invite Henry to the party, but we couldn't find his phone number.
  I was on the point of going out when the phone rang.
  I was about to say that when you interrupted me.
  Oh no! I was supposed to phone my mother last night.

3. We can use *would* or *was to* to talk about an action which did take place, but was still in the future and not anticipated at the time.
  Bogart met Bacall, who would later become his fourth wife, in 1944.
  Who would have believed that this unknown teenager was to become one of the world's greatest movie stars.

Exercises 7–8, page 147

FUTURE FORMS

1 Which sentences do not refer to the future? Explain why.

1 Which hotel are you going to stay in?
2 It's only 10:30, so Jane will still be in the meeting.
3 I'll be thinking of you while you're having your interview.
4 The car won't start. We'll have to get a taxi.
5 As soon as you get there, give me a call, OK?
6 What time are we leaving for the airport?
7 I'll often have a coffee and a biscuit during my morning break.
8 The north of the country will have thunderstorms.
9 Where shall I sit?

2 Choose the correct answers to complete the sentences.

1 A: Did I tell you? I*'m leaving* / *leave* the company next month.
   B: Oh, that's a shame. Where are you going?
2 A: Can you give the dog her medicine?
   B: Sorry. She *won't take* / *isn't going to take* it from me.
3 A: I'm sure we'll enjoy whichever play *we'll see* / *we see*.
   B: Yes. You're right.
4 A: My birthday *is* / *will be* on a Monday, so I don't expect anyone will feel like coming out.
   B: Of course they will!
5 A: This data is all wrong – the presentation *will be* / *is going to be* a disaster!
   B: Don't worry. You'll be fine.
6 A: *Are we going to get* / *Shall we get* a bus to the party?
   B: OK, good idea.
7 A: I'm *losing* / *going to lose* five kilos by the summer.
   B: Good for you!
8 A: Oh no, it's broken!
   B: Don't worry. *I'll buy* / *I'm going to buy* you a new one.

3 Complete the sentences with *will*, the Future perfect or Future perfect continuous form of the verbs in brackets.

1 At the end of this month, Manisha _____ (live) here for just over ten years.
2 By the time you've finished speaking to your mum on the phone, it _____ (be) too late to go to the cinema.
3 Abdul will most likely be exhausted when he arrives – he _____ (drive) for about eight hours.
4 All the best seats _____ (go) if you don't buy the tickets soon.
5 Ask me again next week – I _____ (choose) which design I want by then.
6 You _____ (never/find) somewhere open at this time of night.

4a Complete the predictions for the year 2030. Use the correct active or passive form of the verbs in the box.

own allocate work live commit implant read

1 Scannable microchips containing important personal data will _____ at birth.
2 Lifelong email addresses will _____ at birth.
3 People will _____ e-books rather than paper books.
4 Many people will _____ alone.
5 Fifty percent of the workforce will _____ as freelancers.
6 More crime will _____ by online criminals than by hand-to-hand criminals.
7 People will _____ virtual pets rather than real ones.

b How likely do you think each prediction in exercise 4a is? Add an adverb of probability.

5 Rewrite the second sentence so that it means the same as the first using the words in bold.

1 Arrangements have been made for Ryan Lewington to sign a £5 million contract to play for United. **is**
Ryan Lewington _____ .

2 A new manager probably won't be announced until after the summer. **unlikely**
A new manager _____ .

3 We've set up a meeting with the client for 9:00 a.m. tomorrow. **due**
We _____ .

4 After today's guilty verdict O'Reilly is likely to receive a life sentence. **set**
O'Reilly _____ .

5 The film's going to start soon – come on! **about**
The _____ .

6 I think Brazil are certain to win the World Cup this year. **bound**
Brazil _____ .

6 Match headlines a–f to news stories 1–6. Then complete the news stories with *is to*, *is set to* or *is due to* and an appropriate verb.

a Arsenal set to do the double this weekend
b Laptops for kids
c Rumours of new gadget launch
d Star student to get special award
e Li may lose role
f High-speed rail link to open

1 US actor Vicki Li, who _____ the main role in the upcoming thriller *Offside*, may have to drop out after she was diagnosed with cancer.
2 Computer company Cryono _____ the launch of a new gadget at a special event on 12th June, according to rumours in the industry.
3 Schoolchildren in Chile _____ with free laptops to use in school.
4 Having won the FA Cup earlier in the season, Arsenal _____ the double if they win the league this Saturday.
5 Michael Carty, a 21-year-old student from Birmingham, _____ a special award for his work in developing special software for blind people.
6 The high-speed rail link between Leeds and London _____ at 8:00 a.m. on Saturday.

7 Match sentence halves 1–10 to a–j. Then explain the 'future in the past' idea in each sentence.

1 I was on the point of phoning the police
2 Rachel had to go home early because
3 It was at that conference that Pete met Matthew,
4 I was about to ask Mum if you could stay for dinner
5 When we were 18, we were going to be
6 When he was young, his parents decided to move to Australia, a decision
7 We were going to buy tickets on the way here
8 Mike didn't blame Lia for being annoyed – living in such close proximity to the in-laws
9 Although he was optimistic at the time, Harry
10 James bought the new car on an impulse,

a which would change his life forever.
b would regret his choice of business partner in the years to come.
c when she turned up safe and sound.
d which he was to regret more and more as time went on.
e was always going to be difficult.
f she was leaving for France early in the morning.
g who was later to become his boss.
h rich by the time we were 30!
i but she was angry with me for not tidying up.
j but the queue was too long.

8 Complete the sentences with a name – your name, the name of a classmate, a friend, a family member or a famous person – to make them true.

1 _____ is about to finish something they're working on.
2 _____ will have moved house this time next year.
3 _____ will be cooking a meal in a couple of hours' time.
4 _____ will never change.
5 _____ is going on holiday soon.
6 _____ is on the point of leaving their job.
7 _____ is going to eat out this weekend.
8 _____ is having friends to stay this weekend.
9 _____ will have made some important decisions by the end of the year.

ELLIPSIS AND SUBSTITUTION

Ellipsis

1   'Ellipsis' means leaving out one or more words when they are obvious from the context. In informal speech, it is common to miss out the beginnings of certain phrases when it is clear *who* or *what* is being referred to. This often happens with:
    - imperative *be*. *(Be) careful! (Be) quiet!*
    - pronouns. *(I) don't think so. (I) don't know.*
    - pronouns + *be*. *(It's) nice to meet you. (I'm) sorry.*
    - pronouns + *be* + articles. *(It's a) nice day. (It's a) pity. (It's a) good thing you were here to help.*
    - auxiliary verbs + pronouns. *(Have you) got the time? (Are you) coming? (Have you) finished?*

2   Words are often missed out after an auxiliary verb to avoid repetition.
    If you're not prepared to lend me the money, then I'm sure Jeffrey is (prepared to lend me the money).

3   If a verb is followed by an infinitive with *to*, we include the *to* but omit the verb.
    *There's no need to stay if you don't want **to** (stay).*

4   If something has already been mentioned earlier in the conversation, then it is often missed out:
    'Would you like a glass of juice?'
    'Yes, please.'
    'Apple ~~juice~~ or orange ~~juice~~?' 'Orange ~~juice~~, please.'

▌ Exercise 1, page 150

Reduced relative clauses

- In more formal speech and writing, we often miss out words in relative clauses.
- The relative pronoun and verb *be* can be omitted.
  *Students (who are) **taking** the exam need to register before the 12th May.*
  *The songs (which were) **written** by Clyde tend to have more frequent chord changes.*
- Note that where the main verb is an *-ing* form, this is an active form. When the verb is a past participle, this is a passive form.
- An *-ing* form can sometimes be used with state verbs in the active voice:
  Please return all equipment ~~which belongs~~ to the club.
  *Please return all equipment **belonging** to the club.*
- If the relative clause contains an adjective, then in a reduced relative clause the adjective moves back to attributive position:
  Employees who are experienced do not need training.
  ~~Employees experienced do not need training.~~ ✗
  Experienced employees do not need training. ✓

▌ Exercise 2, page 150

Substitution

Substitution is when a single word is used to replace a word or phrase, often to avoid repetition.
- *One* is used to substitute a single, countable noun.
  *I'd love to have a dog, but Mum won't let me have **one**.*
- *Ones* is used to substitute plural, countable nouns.
  *Which shoes look better, the brown **ones** or the black **ones**?*
- *Some* is used to substitute uncountable nouns.
  *This ice cream is gorgeous! Would you like **some**?*
- *Do/does* substitutes a verb + object.
  *I don't like football, but my wife **does**.*
  'I have to get up really early tomorrow.' 'I don't!'
- *So* substitutes a clause.
  *'Does this bus go to the station?' 'I think **so**.'*
  NOT '~~I think this bus goes to the station.~~'
- *So/Neither/Nor* + auxiliary + subject substitutes a whole clause.
  *'We're going to Spain for our holidays.' '**So** are we!'*
  *'I'm not taking a holiday this year.' '**Neither/Nor** am I.'*

▌ Exercise 3, page 150

1   **Personal pronouns**
    - If a pronoun is used in isolation, we always use the object pronoun form.
      'Who would like to start?' 'Me!' NOT '~~I.~~'
      Similarly, in modern English we use object pronouns as the complement of a phrase.
      'Who left the door open?' 'It was me.' NOT ~~It was I.~~
    - When the sex of a person is not clear or unimportant, we can use:
      either *he/she* or *his/her* depending on the likelihood of the person being male or female.
      *One of the teacher's main responsibilities is to make sure **her** students are learning.*
      the plural pronoun *they* or *them*.
      *'There's **someone** waiting to see you.' 'What do **they** want? Can you ask **them** to wait for a moment?'*
    - *You* is often used to mean 'people in general'.
      ***You** never know what **you**'re going to find.*
    - The pronoun *one* is used in more formal contexts with the meaning of 'people in general'.
      *As **one** walks through the city, **one** is constantly reminded of its turbulent history.*
      If the speaker is not stated, *they* is used.
      ***They**'re building a new sports centre opposite the station.*
    - *It* and *there* can be used as the subject of a sentence.
      ***There** are plenty of reasons why.*
      *'Who's that?' '**It**'s Maria.'* NOT ~~I am/She's Maria.~~
      It can also be used to refer to 'the situation'.
      *I've already made **it** quite clear that I'm not interested.*

▌ Exercise 4, page 150

2   Reciprocal pronouns

- We use reciprocal pronouns (*each other*, *one another*) when an action involves two or more people or things doing the same thing to each other.
  *The important thing is to try to understand **each other**.*
- Some verbs take a preposition (*with* or *to*).
  *My two cousins haven't spoken **to each other** for years.*
- *One another* is a little more formal and old-fashioned.
  *Do you promise to love **one another** for ever?*

3   Reflexive pronouns

- Reflexive pronouns emphasise that a person is doing the action to him/herself, not to another person or thing.
  *Here are some extra towels for you to dry **yourself**.*
- We can also use reflexive pronouns to emphasise who the pronoun refers to.
  *He didn't write the speech **himself**: one of his PR men did it.*

Exercise 5, page 151

4   *this/that*, etc.

- When we refer forward to something we are going to say, or something that is going to happen we use *this*.
  *I hate to tell you **this**, but …*
- When we refer back to something we said, or something that has already happened we use *that*.
  *Sorry about **that**. It won't happen again.*
- On the telephone in British English, the speaker uses *this* to refer to him/herself; we refer to the other person as *that*.
  *Hello, **this** is Alan here. Is **that** you, Richard?*

Exercise 6, page 151

5   Referring to other parts of a written text

- In written texts, pronouns are often used to refer to things in the text mentioned previously, later and outside the text.
- Pronouns are often used to refer to things previously mentioned in the text, in order to avoid repetition. This is called **anaphoric reference**.

  Every year the Andersons went on holiday to the same town in Spain.
  They never seemed to get bored with it.
  The Andersons *never seemed to get bored with* the same town in Spain.

- Sometimes the reference can be ambiguous or misunderstood.
  Tia took her phone off the table and smashed it into pieces.
- In the example above, *it* could refer to the phone or the table. In this case we would avoid using a pronoun in order to make the meaning clear.
- Pronouns can also refer to things mentioned later in the text. This is known as **cataphoric reference**. This is often used as a literary device, to encourage the reader to continue reading the text.
  When she got home, Catherine sank into the chair and fell asleep.

Exercises 7–8, page 151

10 GRAMMAR PRACTICE

ELLIPSIS AND SUBSTITUTION

1 Match sentences 1–8 to responses a–h. Then cross out words/phrases that can be left out.

1 You need to tidy your room.
2 Here you are, sir, two bottles of water.
3 It's tipping it down* outside.
4 It was lovely to see Sally again, wasn't it?
5 Have you sent Judy the templates yet?
6 Excuse me, is Briggs Street near here?
7 Could you give me a lift?
8 How many times have I told you not to leave the back door open?

a No, I'm just going to send Judy the templates.
b Yeah, it's a good thing I brought an umbrella.
c No, we only ordered one bottle of water.
d I have no idea, I'm sorry.
e I'm sorry, I don't drive.
f I already have tidied my room.
g I didn't leave the back door open, it was Shelly.
h Yeah, it's a pity she couldn't stay longer.

*tipping it down = raining heavily

2 Rewrite the sentences using a reduced relative clause.

1 They watched the street performers who were dancing energetically at the traffic lights.
   _____

2 The woman who was found guilty of the murder was sentenced to life imprisonment.
   _____

3 Of all the films that were directed by Shane Meadows, this is my favourite.
   _____

4 Despite jumping off the train which was moving, the stunt man was uninjured.
   _____

5 All new members receive a welcome pack which contains a badge and a handbook.
   _____

6 Do you see that woman who is wearing the black dress? That's Paula.
   _____

7 Dogs that are small don't need so much space to run around in.
   _____

8 The information which was sent out in the email was wrong.
   _____

9 I've never heard of the woman who is giving the talk today.
   _____

3 Replace any repetitive words/phrases in the conversations with the words in the box.

....
so (x3)   do   did (x2)   does   one   ones   nor
....

1 A: My friend Mark works in the same building as you.
   B: I know he works in the same building as me – I met him in the lift the other day.
2 A: I'll probably go to the supermarket.
   B: If you go to the supermarket, could you buy milk?
3 A: That man who just went by was the lead singer of *The Octagons*.
   B: I thought he was the lead singer from *The Octagons* – his face looked familiar.
4 A: We didn't understand a word of what he said.
   B: I didn't understand a word. Nobody told me he only speaks Russian.
5 A: We saw that new comedy at the cinema.
   B: Really? We saw that new comedy at the cinema on Sunday! Where were you sitting?
6 A: Great. I didn't expect them to provide me with lunch, but they provided me with lunch.
   B: And what was on the menu?
7 A: Do these shoes look OK?'
   B: I think the blue shoes would look better with those jeans.
8 A: Was it this necklace you wanted to look at?
   B: No, it was the necklace with the diamonds.
9 A: I hope Daniel passes his driving test this time.
   B: I hope Daniel passes his driving test this time, too.

4 Rewrite the sentences, making any changes necessary to make them true for the place where you live.

1 You're always bumping into people you know.
2 If someone new moves in, the neighbours make an effort to get to know them.
3 There has been a big increase in crime.
4 People are finding it difficult to get work at the moment.
5 It's quite easy to find your way around.
6 You can always find somewhere interesting to go out.
7 They've pulled down a lot of old buildings recently.
8 There are quite a lot of people living on the streets.

5 Put the words in the correct order. Then think of a context for each.

1 for / stick / need / up / more / yourself / you / to
   _____

2 at / just / other / looked / they / each
   _____

3 to / to / trying / other / nice / we're / be / each
   _____

4 any / we / each / more / don't / other / love
   _____

5 the / ones / I / black / myself / prefer
   _____

6 really / by / you / it / do / did / yourself / ?
   _____

7 herself / happened / what / blames / she / for
   _____

8 together / on / pull / come / yourself
   _____

6 Complete the sentences with *this* or *that*.

1 I shouldn't have said _____ . I'm really sorry.
2 Hi, is _____ Carla? _____ is Yasmin.
3 You might not agree with _____ , but I think we need to trust Kevin a bit more.
4 Good afternoon, _____ is New Telecom and we'd like to offer you savings on your phone bill.
5 You're not going to believe _____ , but we won!
6 I can't believe Marta said _____ to the teacher! How rude!

7 Find and correct the mistakes in the sentences.

1 You don't have to go if you don't.
2 Someone wants to speak to you. It said it's important.
3 I'm glad you said you don't trust her. So don't I!
4 It wasn't me who ate the last biscuit, Dad – it was she!
5 If you've never seen him perform live, then I'd recommend seeing *The Greentones*.
6 We make our own cheese here at Gopledown farm. Would you like to try ones?
7 Sue and Fiona haven't spoken to each another for years.
8 'Are Keith and Val going to give us a lift?' 'I think do.'
9 Did you do this all by himself? What a good boy!
10 I'm Pete. Nice meet you.

8 What do the pronouns in bold in the text refer to?

The legend of Prambanan temple

If you've never seen [1]**it**, then Candi Prambanan (Prambanan Temple) is well worth a visit. [2]**It** stands on a site about 20 km east of the Javanese city of Yogyakarta and is one of the largest Hindu temples in south-east Asia. Historians have several theories about when it was built, but none of [3]**them** are as interesting as the legend of the slender virgin. Legend has it that after [4]**her** father was killed in battle, Princess Rara Jonggrang was required to marry Prince Bandung, who had won the battle and killed her father. [5]**She** reluctantly agreed, but only if [6]**he** built a temple with 1,000 statues before dawn. Prince Bandung asked the spirits for help and when [7]**they** had built 999 statues, the princess lit a huge fire to the east of the site. Because [8]**they** thought it was the sun rising, the spirits flew away and the prince failed to build all 1,000 statues. The prince was furious and turned [9]**her** into stone in revenge, and she became the last of the statues – some say the most beautiful of

1 *Candi Prambanan* _____
2 _____
3 _____
4 _____
5 _____
6 _____
7 _____
8 _____
9 _____
10 _____

GLOBALISATION

1 Replace the phrases in bold with words/phrases in the box.

Americanised	brain drain	clash of cultures
global brand	local produce	sweatshops
way of life	multinational corporations	

1 Over the last 30 years, our culture has become more **American in character**.
2 The company has been criticised for its **factories where people work hard in bad conditions** in developing countries.
3 The economic crisis is threatening the traditional **behaviour, habits and customs** of the local people.
4 From humble beginnings, the company has become a **name which is recognised all over the world**.
5 The recession has resulted in a **movement of highly skilled people to another country**.
6 I always try to buy **food grown in my country** where possible.
7 The move from a rural to an industrial economy is often marked by a **conflict arising between people with different cultural values**.
8 A number of **large companies with offices in many countries** dominate the market.

URBANISATION

2 Choose the correct answers to complete the sentences.

1 Houses located near *high-rise buildings / green belt land* are very expensive.
2 There are several *no-go areas / residential areas*, but generally living here is safe.
3 By using *reclaimed land / infrastructure*, the planners were able to widen the coastal road.
4 They are demolishing the *green belt land / slums* in preparation for the Olympics.
5 Before the children were rescued, they had been living in *overcrowding / squalor* for years.
6 Since the mayor introduced bus lanes, *congestion / sprawl* on the roads has improved.

OTHER WORDS AND PHRASES

bold not afraid of taking risks: *It was a bold concept, certain to create controversy.*

brand new completely new, not yet used: *a brand new car*

scale (of change) the size, level or amount of sth: *In recent years the scale of change in climate patterns has been worrying.*

side effect an unexpected or unplanned result of a situation or event: *These policy changes could have beneficial side effects for the whole economy.*

to build sth from scratch to start sth without using anything that existed or was prepared before: *He built the business up from scratch.*

to draw up [T] to prepare a written document, such as a list or contract: *The government has drawn up a list of all its spending plans for the next year.*

to drive prices sky-high to force prices to go to extremely high levels: *The recent housing shortage has driven house prices sky-high.*

to head upwards to increase to a higher level: *The rate of inflation is heading ever upwards.*

to keep up with [T] to increase at the same speed and by the same amount as sth else: *Food production is not keeping up with growing demand.*

to mass-produce [T] to produce in large numbers using machinery, so that each object is the same and can be sold cheaply: *Henry Ford was the first person to mass-produce cars.*

to use sth as a template to use sth as a model in order to build sth similar: *The first smart city was used as a template for building others in different areas.*

3 Complete the sentences with words/phrases from the box above in the correct form.

1 Oh no! I've spilt wine all over my _____ dress!
2 The government is selling green belt land to developers in order to _____ demand for housing.
3 Since the 1990s the _____ of change in the mobile phone industry has been unprecedented.
4 Plumbing systems designed by the Romans are still _____ for modern systems today.
5 A(n) _____ of urban living is an increase in emotional disorders.
6 My grandfather built our house _____ .
7 The new art gallery, with its _____ design, was opened today.
8 During the meeting, we _____ our budget plans for the year.

FEELINGS

1 Choose the correct answers to complete the sentences.

1 The CEO should be *ashamed / sorry*, accepting a huge bonus in these difficult times.

2 Jake was feeling a bit *scared stiff / apprehensive* about his new job, as it was the first time he'd ever done anything like this.

3 When they asked me if I was on a pension, I was absolutely *indifferent / mortified*. I'm only 45!

4 Don't take what Jeanette said too seriously. She's *helpless / under a lot of pressure* at work at the moment.

5 When I realised the burglars had been through all my personal things, I felt completely *disgusted / wound up*.

6 When the kids heard you were coming to stay, they were *overjoyed / envious*.

7 I know you're really busy, but I'm *desperate / insecure* – I literally don't have anyone else to ask.

8 When your parents see the mess you've made, they're going to be really *relieved / cross*.

IDIOMS WITH *LAUGH*, *CRY* AND *TEARS*

2 Find and correct the mistakes in the sentences.

1 What have you said to Alicia? She's in rivers of tears.

2 Whatever you do, don't ask Tom about his job – we'll all be boring to tears.

3 Remembering a joke she'd heard, Dominique burst off laughing.

4 We were really upset when we couldn't get tickets, but we had the last tears when the concert was cancelled!

5 The actor gave such an emotional acceptance speech that the audience was close to cry by the end.

6 You may think it's funny now, but it'll be no laughing thing when it happens to you.

OTHER WORDS AND PHRASES

aspiration a strong desire to have or achieve sth: *The young politicians had aspirations of becoming Prime Minister one day.*

peer group a group of people who are the same age, social class, etc. as yourself: *This TV show is popular with my peer group.*

to backfire to have the opposite effect to the one intended: *The company's new policy backfired when a number of employees threatened to quit.*

to be heavily regulated to have strict rules controlling an activity or process: *The construction industry is heavily regulated in order to ensure safety.*

to be left out to not be included in sth: *Despite playing well all season, Gribbs was left out of the team for the final.*

to fit in to be accepted by the other people in a group: *Being so much younger than the others, Kate found it hard to fit in with her sister's friends.*

to flatter [T] to praise sb in order to please them or get sth from them, even though you do not mean it: *Scott would always flatter Maria by praising her cooking.*

to pamper yourself [T] to give yourself the things that you want and make yourself feel warm and comfortable: *Pamper yourself with a stay in one of our luxury hotels.*

to set out to do sth to start doing sth or making plans to do sth in order to achieve a particular result: *They set out to become the number one team in the league.*

to set sth up to make the arrangements that are necessary for sth to happen: *There was a lot of work involved in setting up the discussion group.*

to turn people off [informal] to make sth/sb unattractive to people: *Women who smoke really turn me off.*

3 Complete the sentences with words/phrases from the box above in the correct form.

1 I had a lovely day at the spa. It was a great chance to _____ myself.

2 I'm not sure we should paint the café walls bright yellow. It might _____ people _____ .

3 A lot of young actors have _____ to star in a Hollywood film one day.

4 I never _____ in at school – I had different interests from everyone else.

5 It can be difficult to develop a new medicine, as the market is so _____ .

6 Many thanks to Rachel for _____ this new reading group.

7 Jake's plan to impress Carla _____ when he played a song that reminded her of her ex.

8 In the beginning we only _____ write a few articles, but it's grown into a substantial book.

MONEY AND ENTERPRISE

1 Cross out the options that are not possible.

1 Can you lend me £20? I'm really *hard up* / *loaded* / *skint* at the moment.
2 Steve's business became yet another sign of these difficult times when it *went bust* / *went bankrupt* / *broke even*.
3 You can't sell that painting – it's *pricey* / *priceless* / *worthless*.
4 Patti had to take on a part-time job to make up for her meagre *pension* / *ransom* / *alimony*.
5 Despite the global recession, some countries have actually experienced *high unemployment* / *economic expansion* / *an increase in GDP*.
6 We'll have to pay a generous *advance* / *fee* / *tip* if we want to secure his services.
7 Don't be so *flashy* / *stingy* / *tight*. You always disappear when the bill comes!

WORTH

2 Choose the best response, a or b.

1 Shall we get a bus there?
   a It's not worth it – the taxis are so cheap.
   b It's worthless – the taxis are so cheap.
2 I can't decide what to buy Karina for her birthday.
   a Have you tried giftz.com? It's worth a fortune.
   b Have you tried giftz.com? It's worth a quick look.
3 Sometimes I feel like I'm not getting anywhere.
   a You need to worth your while before people will take your ideas seriously.
   b You need to prove your worth before people will take your ideas seriously.
4 How much change do you need?
   a Ten pounds' worth.
   b A worthwhile amount.
5 Do you want these documents?
   a No, we've finished so they're not worthy.
   b No, we've finished so they're not worth keeping.
6 How was your holiday?
   a Amazing! Visiting the outback is definitely a worthwhile experience.
   b Amazing! Visiting the outback is definitely a for what it's worth experience.

OTHER WORDS AND PHRASES

collaborative involving people working together to achieve sth: *We hope this website will become a collaborative project, with everybody contributing ideas.*

entrepreneurial willing to take risks in business: *It was his entrepreneurial spirit which was the driving force behind his success.*

favourable publicity good reports and reviews of sth in the media: *The success of the project was largely due to the favourable publicity it received.*

innovative an idea or way of doing sth that is new, different from and better than those that existed before: *This project is an innovative way of dealing with climate change.*

non-profit-making established for some other reason than to make money: *The Education Standards Council is a non-profit-making organisation which aims to raise national standards in teaching.*

quirky unusual, especially in an interesting way: *I like his quirky sense of humour.*

self-funded paying for itself: *This is a partly self-funded project as we will pay our own expenses.*

to get off to a flying start to begin very well or successfully: *The charity campaign got off to a flying start, raising over £5,000 in the first month.*

to pledge money to make a formal, public promise to give money: *The government pledged £50 million to support victims of the tsunami.*

3 Complete the conversations with words/phrases from the box above in the correct form.

1 A: What's this you're watching?
   B: It's a programme where people test their _____ skills by competing to see who can make the most money in a week.
2 A: Brisa's new business seems to be doing very well.
   B: Yes, it's really _____ start.
3 A: I can't believe the tickets for the event are so expensive!
   B: Well, they're a(n) _____ organisation, so all the money's going to a good cause.
4 A: Do you think our new logo is too strange?
   B: No, I love it, but it's true, it is a(n) _____ design.
5 A: And now on to your new film – I understand it's been very successful so far.
   B: Yes, fortunately, it's received a lot of _____ in the media.
6 A: Did you know Maria has a community garden on the roof of her building?
   B: Yes, it's a(n) _____ project and everyone living in her block is involved.

SELF-IMPROVEMENT

1 Find and correct the mistakes in the sentences.

1 After extensive research, they found that the so-called 'wonder drug' actually did more bad than good.
2 Doing yoga regularly has been shown to improve your mental good-being.
3 I like doing exercise, but I find it difficult to stay it up regularly.
4 Elena had to reduce the amount of voluntary work she was doing, as she was starting to feel underwhelmed.
5 Running a marathon really examines your endurance.
6 We strongly believe that long-distance travel lengthens your horizons.
7 Did you find that having counselling improved your me-esteem?
8 My husband swears by homeopathy, but I think the benefits are purely psychiatric.

BODY IDIOMS

2 Complete the sentences with the words in the box.

eye   face   hands   head   heart   leg   nose   stomach

1 Judy had butterflies in her _____ before she gave the speech to the national convention.
2 The government has been criticised for turning a blind _____ to corruption in the senate.
3 Grace Rose's autobiography is a truly _____-rending story of how she came from nothing to become a successful singer.
4 Joel was finding it really difficult to get his _____ round the new guidelines.
5 When Phil came in wearing that stupid outfit, we all found it hard to keep a straight _____ .
6 Penny's so rude! I spent hours making that meal and she just turned her _____ up at it.
7 Don't worry, it's not that dangerous. Nick was only pulling your _____ .
8 With a final score of 52–16, the women's basketball team won _____ down.

OTHER WORDS AND PHRASES

demotivated feeling unenthusiastic or unwilling to do sth: *After working hard for years and not getting promoted, Christian felt demotivated in his job.*

manageable target a goal which it is possible to achieve: *If you want to successfully lose weight, you need to set yourself manageable targets.*

metabolic rate the speed at which food is processed into energy in your body: *Exercise can increase your metabolic rate.*

nutritional information information on food packaging which tells you about the properties of the food: *I always check the nutritional information of food before I buy it, in order to find out how many calories it has.*

rigorous severe or strict: *Olympic athletes have to undergo a rigorous training programme before they are ready to compete.*

to bore sb to death to make sb feel extremely tired or impatient because they have no interest in the subject: *The teacher bored the students to death with stories about her youth.*

to do sth religiously to be careful always to do sth: *He exercises religiously every morning.*

to drop off [T] to take sb by car to a place and leave them there: *We usually drop the kids off at school on our way to work.*

to let sb down to not do sth that sb trusts or expects you to do: *When they lost the game, the team felt as if they had let the fans down.*

to steadily put on weight to become fatter or heavier at a regular rate: *Since he stopped doing regular exercise, he's been steadily putting on weight.*

to tone up (your muscles) to improve strength and firmness: *He began to use weights in order to tone up his muscles.*

trim slim and in good shape: *Years of working as a personal trainer meant Joe was always trim.*

3 Complete the sentences with words/phrases from the box above in the correct form.

1 Most fish have a high _____ . They can digest their food quickly.
2 Dean has a lot of potential, but his behaviour often _____ him _____ .
3 If you want to become a soldier, you have to go through _____ physical and mental tests.
4 The film went on for too long and by the end we were _____ .
5 Don't try to do too much at once – set yourself _____ every week.
6 When she was young, Pilar studied English _____ every night, and now she's fluent!
7 Wow, you're looking _____ ! Have you been going to the gym?
8 This cereal bar has no _____ on the side, so I can't check how much saturated fat it contains .

POLITE SOCIAL BEHAVIOUR

1 Complete the sentences with the correct form of the words/phrases in the box.

gentlemanly	awkward	impression	cough
over the top	familiar	drop in	pushy
row	sneeze	yawn	

1 The assistants are far too _____ ; it just puts me off shopping there.
2 Jon had a terrible cold – he was _____ and _____ all over the place.
3 Miles has such _____ manners. He always treats people with respect.
4 You need to arrive on time for the meeting with the clients, in order to create a good _____ .
5 I hope Anne didn't think I was rude. It's just that I didn't sleep well last night and couldn't stop _____ .
6 Carole didn't like the way Ed kept touching her while they were talking – she felt he was being overly _____ .
7 We hope you don't mind us turning up unannounced, it's just that we were in the area and thought we'd _____ .
8 Some people like Andrea's energy and enthusiasm, but I find it a bit _____ .
9 Geoff's not an elegant dancer. His movements are rather _____ .
10 My parents are so embarrassing! They're always _____ in public.

COMMUNICATION

2a Match verbs 1–12 to phrases a–l.

1	circulate	a	questions and make the other people feel at ease
2	gabble		
3	dry up	b	other people and dominate the conversation
4	ask		
5	stumble	c	from time to time
6	crack	d	nervously about whatever comes into your head
7	look		
8	talk over	e	lots of jokes
9	giggle	f	and make small talk
10	make	g	nervously
11	listen	h	over your words
12	pause	i	carefully to what other people say
		j	because you can't think of anything to say
		k	eye contact
		l	stiff and uncomfortable

b Decide if the phrases in exercise 2a are positive (+) or negative (–).

OTHER WORDS AND PHRASES

patronising talking in a way that implies you are more intelligent or important than the other person: *He's so enthusiastic when he praises people that sometimes they think he's being patronising.*

supportive giving help or encouragement, especially to sb who is in a difficult situation: *My husband was very supportive when I decided to change my career.*

tactful behaving in a way not likely to embarrass or upset other people: *Ryan tactfully explained that Simon needed to do something about his personal hygiene.*

to close up to refuse to talk about sth: *Every time I ask him about his relationship, he just closes up and changes the subject.*

to drop hints to suggest sth to sb, without telling them directly: *Olly's been dropping hints about his birthday all week.*

to face facts to accept that a difficult situation exists: *It's time you faced facts. You can't survive on a salary that low.*

to get defensive to act as if sb is criticising you when they're not: *When I make a suggestion, she gets defensive and doesn't listen.*

to mind your own business to not ask questions about sth which doesn't concern you: *'How much do you earn?' 'Mind your own business!'*

to pull yourself together to force yourself to stop behaving in a nervous, frightened or uncontrolled way: *With an effort, Damian pulled himself together and finished the race.*

to resent [T] to feel angry or upset about a situation or about sth that sb has done, especially because you think that it is not fair: *Craig resented the fact that his girlfriend didn't trust him.*

3 Complete the conversations with words/phrases from the box above in the correct form.

1 **A:** Sorry, I'm just not very good with computers!
   B: OK, there's no need to _____ . I was only making a suggestion.
2 **A:** I just can't bear it if I never see her again.
   B: But, you have to _____ . She doesn't love you.
3 **A:** I don't think I'm ever going to find a job.
   B: Oh come on! _____ and start looking properly.
4 **A:** I'm so proud of you for winning that award!
   B: I couldn't have done it without you. I mean it – you've been really _____ .
5 **A:** I'm not stupid, you know!
   B: I wasn't being _____ . You did a good job!
6 **A:** I don't want to talk about it.
   B: You can't just _____ every time I mention it!

EDUCATION

1 Complete the second sentence so that it means the same as the first. Use the words in the box.

postgraduate	retake	workshops	assessment
assignments	truancy	numeracy	scholarship

1 We need to improve children's ability to do basic mathematics.
   We need to improve children's _____ .
2 On this course we calculate final grades based on work done during the course.
   On this course we use continuous _____ to calculate final grades.
3 Do students deliberately stay away from school without permission at your school?
   Is _____ a problem at your school?
4 Keith decided to stay on at university and study after completing a first degree.
   Keith decided to stay on at university and do a _____ degree.
5 Sandy had to take the exam again after failing it.
   Sandy had to _____ the exam after failing it.
6 There is an amount of money to help pay for a course available for applicants who show exceptional ability.
   There is a(n) _____ available for applicants who show exceptional ability.
7 This semester you have to complete six written pieces of work.
   This semester you have to complete six written _____ .
8 Attendance at the practical skills class is not compulsory, but is highly recommended.
   Attendance at the _____ is not compulsory, but is highly recommended.

LEARNING

2 Choose the correct answers.

1 I hate algebra. No matter how hard I try, it just doesn't *create* / *make* sense to me!
2 I know it seems hard now, but it'll be worth it in the *long-time* / *long-run*.
3 Fiona was a bit overwhelmed on her first day, but it didn't take her long to get the *hang* / *right* of it.
4 Giving your child lots of praise may not necessarily *build* / *grow* their self-esteem.
5 If you want to do well on the course, you'll need to *do up* / *put in* a bit more effort.
6 Too much work can have a negative *disadvantage* / *impact* on your health.
7 The first look at his busy timetable *shattered* / *broke* Dave's illusions about university life.

OTHER WORDS AND PHRASES

to speak out to publicly speak in protest about sth, especially when protesting could be dangerous: *The students who had spoken out against the government were arrested.*

to hang around to wait or spend time somewhere, doing nothing: *When we were kids we used to spend hours hanging around the park.*

to die down if sth dies down, it becomes less strong, active or violent: *Jill waited for the children's excitement to die down before getting them ready for bed.*

to move away to go to live in a different area: *My best friend moved away when I was ten, and I never saw him again.*

to saunter off to walk away in a slow relaxed way, especially so that you look confident or proud: *Trying to show he didn't care, he sauntered off with his hands in his pockets.*

to see sb off [T] to go to an airport, train station, etc. to say goodbye to sb: *They've gone to the airport to see their son off.*

to chat away to talk in a friendly informal way for a long time, especially about things that are not important: *John and I sat up until the early hours chatting away happily.*

to eat up [T] to eat all of sth: *Come on, eat up, there's a good girl.*

to be around to be present in a situation or place for a while: *My father wasn't around much when I was young.*

3 Complete the sentences with words/phrases from the box above in the correct form.

1 I don't believe it! I told Jake he was being rude and he just calmly _____ , ignoring me!
2 If you _____ at the weekend, you should come out with us on Saturday.
3 The presenter waited for the applause to _____ before introducing the contestants.
4 You don't need to go to the airport on your own, I'll come and _____ you _____ .
5 Someone needs to be brave enough to _____ about what's going on in this company.
6 You can't have any ice cream until you've _____ your vegetables.

DESCRIPTIVE ADJECTIVES

1 **Match the adjectives in the box with the words in bold in the sentences.**

frumpy	garish	scruffy	sleek
stark	tacky	twee	vulgar

1 For the school fair, Laura made pretty little wooden **animals** in cute colours. _____
2 In the dawn light, the **landscape** looked plain and without colour. _____
3 That dress really shows off her slim and attractive **figure**. _____
4 Tony painted the front of his **house** in very bright, unpleasant colours. _____
5 Katerina is quite good-looking, but she wears old-fashioned, boring **clothes**. _____
6 I knew I shouldn't have let you buy the **decorations**. They just look cheap and badly made! _____
7 Anna bought a very ugly bright purple **sofa**. _____
8 I was surprised to see Lee wearing a suit. Usually **he** looks so dirty and untidy. _____

LOOK, SOUND AND *FEEL*

2 **Complete the conversations with the correct form of** *look, sound* **or** *feel.*

1 **A:** What was the film like?
   B: Terrible. But at least the _____ track was good.
2 **A:** What do you think of the changes the management are bringing in?
   B: I've got mixed _____ . We do need to modernise, but a lot of people are going to lose their jobs.
3 **A:** What's wrong with Judy?
   B: I've no idea. I asked her how Carl was and she gave me a dirty _____ and walked off!
4 **A:** Who do you most admire?
   B: I really _____ up to my grandfather because of what he's had to deal with in life.
5 **A:** How was the meeting?
   B: Really boring! We had to listen to Mike _____ off about the working hours policy.
6 **A:** How's the diet working out?
   B: Fantastic! I'm eating healthily and exercising regularly. I _____ on top of the world!

OTHER WORDS AND PHRASES

the benefit of hindsight the advantage of being able to understand a situation because it has already happened: *With the benefit of hindsight, we can see we should have got there earlier.*

there's no accounting for taste used humorously to say that you do not understand why sb has chosen sth: *Why did she marry someone like that? There's no accounting for taste!*

to be ahead of one's time to be very advanced or new, and not understood or accepted: *The band was, in many ways, ahead of its time, and it was only later on they got the recognition they deserved.*

to be an instant hit to become very popular very quickly: *Their new album was only released last week but has already become an instant hit.*

to be heartbroken to be extremely sad because of sth that has happened: *When Gavin told Vicki their relationship was over, she was heartbroken.*

to catch up with [T] to improve and reach the same standard as others: *At the moment our technology is more advanced, but other countries are catching up with us.*

to conform to expectations to be similar to what people expect or think is usual: *James doesn't conform to the usual expectations of what a police officer should be like.*

to go down well to get a good reaction from sb: *The film went down well in the US.*

to live the dream to live your life in the way you've always dreamed of: *Since he became a professional footballer, Gary has been living the dream.*

to snap up a bargain to buy sth immediately, because it is very good value: *I managed to snap up a bargain with this cheap computer in the January sales.*

3 **Complete the text with words/phrases from the box above in the correct form.**

Keeping up with The Jones

Fans of 90s rock group The Jones who didn't get the chance to see them when they were first famous will now have the chance to see them after they announced they are getting back together for a reunion tour this summer. The Jones first rose to fame with their debut album *Tiger Stone*, which was a(n) [1]_____ on its release in 1992. They followed up with a second in 1993, *Cloudland*, which also [2]_____ well with fans, before they shocked the world by splitting up in 1994. 'Life was great, and we were [3]_____ ,' explains drummer Ned Jones. 'But I realise now, with [4]_____ , that it was too much, too soon and we couldn't handle it.' Fans were [5]_____ at the time, but yesterday's announcement will make a lot of older people happy.

CHARACTERISTICS AND BEHAVIOUR

1 Replace the phrases in bold with the correct form of the words/phrases in the box.

highly strung	hyperactive	irritable	laid-back
mess around	neat freak	fussy	sulk
overbearing	keep herself to herself		

1 Carlos has been **quietly angry and refusing to discuss what's wrong** for days now.
2 I hate sharing a desk with Eva – she's such a **person who has to keep everything clean and tidy**.
3 Don't have another coffee. You know you'll be **unable to keep still and have too much energy** all evening.
4 Stop **spending your time badly** and do your homework!
5 Jim's wife can be a bit **bossy and controlling**.
6 Kate's got a rather artistic temperament; she's so **nervous and easily upset**.
7 Sorry for being **quick to get angry** recently. I've been under a lot of pressure.
8 I don't know how you can be so **relaxed and not worried about anything** at a time like this.
9 Don't be **concerned about unimportant details**. We're only staying here for one night.
10 After she retired from the music business, she **lived a quiet life on her own**.

JUST

2a Put the words in the correct order to complete the sentences.

1 The politician was arrested _____ (the government / had / after / a / announced / just) crackdown on corruption.
2 _____ (the colour / just / I / to / that's / wanted) paint our living room.
3 We had to complain about the food – _____ (it / awful / just / was)!
4 _____ (just / sit / I / you / could / to / ask) over here?
5 This app is great _____ (just / and / 99 cents / it's).

b Match sentences 1–5 in exercise 2a with the meanings of *just* a–e.

a only
b exactly
c a short time
d for emphasis
e with polite phrases

OTHER WORDS AND PHRASES

that's asking too much used when sb demands too much of sb else: *They want us to work longer hours for less pay? That's asking too much.*

to be a sucker for sth [informal] to like sb or sth so much that you cannot refuse or resist them: *I'm a total sucker for Mexican food.*

to be conscience-stricken to feel very guilty about sth that you have done wrong: *I hurried home, conscience-stricken at leaving my mother alone.*

to be thick-skinned to not be easily offended by criticism or insults: *To be a traffic warden, you need to be pretty thick-skinned.*

to exchange confidences to share secrets with sb: *When I was a teenager I used to exchange confidences with my best friend.*

to have it all to have everything you've always wanted: *By the age of 30, Hans had it all: a fast car, a huge house and a beautiful wife.*

to make a snap decision to make a judgement or decision quickly, without careful thought or discussion: *Jill regretted her snap decision to buy a new phone when she got her credit card bill at the end of the month.*

window-shopping looking at goods in shop windows without intending to buy any of them: *I had an hour to spare, so I went into town just window-shopping.*

3 Complete the sentences with words/phrases from the box above in the correct form.

1 When I was little, I stole some chocolate from a shop, but I was so _____ that I went back and told them!
2 I don't mind helping you with your homework, but I'm not going to do it for you. That's _____ .
3 You need to choose what to study at university carefully – you can't just _____ .
4 Stacey and Ryan got to know each other well and often _____ .
5 Do you really not care what they say about you? You can't be that _____ .
6 When I lived in, Rio de Janeiro, I _____ : beaches, mountains and amazing nightlife.

DESCRIBING FUTURE DEVELOPMENTS

1 Complete the sentences with the correct form of the words/phrases in the box.

become a reality	catch on	pave the way
fulfil (your) potential	meet with	sustainable
massive boom	underway	

1 This is only a temporary measure. We need to find a more _____ solution in the long term.
2 The lower import tax will _____ for greater foreign investment.
3 Despite being popular at first, the idea never really _____ .
4 Plans to build a new shopping centre _____ a lot of resistance from local residents.
5 Do you think intelligent robots will ever _____ ?
6 There has been a(n) _____ in air travel as tickets have become cheaper.
7 Hanna's really talented, but she'll need to work really hard if she wants to _____ her _____ .
8 Construction of the new airport is _____ and should be completed in 2023.

WAY

2 Find and correct the mistakes in the sentences.

1 Many people see the use of technology in education as way forward.
2 Your essay is too way long at the moment. You need to reduce it by about 200 words.
3 Don't leave without me! I'm in the way and will be there in five minutes.
4 Can I go to the party with you? I'm afraid I don't know a way.
5 Please don't stand there – you'll only get on the way.
6 I think you've put that picture the wrong way down.
7 Not way will we win the World Cup with this team.
8 Don't let her have the own way or she'll never leave you alone.

OTHER WORDS AND PHRASES

non-invasive surgery medical treatment which doesn't involve cutting into the body: *Modern laser treatments are non-invasive.*

to be yet to happen to be expected to happen but not having happened yet: *The government are yet to lower taxes as they promised before the election.*

to come to pass [literary] to happen after a period of time: *And so it came to pass, they had two children and lived happily ever after.*

to outstrip [T] to do sth better or more successfully or in greater quantity than sb else: *The use of smartphones has outstripped the use of more basic mobile phones over the last year.*

to pinpoint the cause of sth to discover or explain the real reason for a problem: *Investigators are working to pinpoint the cause of the accident.*

to run sb's life to organise and manage what another person does every day: *In the future we may use computers to completely run our lives.*

to surpass [T] to be even better or greater than sb or sth else: *This season, Gardner is set to surpass Jones's record of ten gold medals.*

tricky sth that is difficult to deal with or do because it is complicated and full of problems: *I can get you tickets for the game but it'll be tricky.*

3 Complete the second sentence so that it means the same as the first. Use words/phrases from the box above in the correct form.

1 a We're still waiting for the corrected documents to arrive.
   b The corrected documents _____ arrive.
2 a We won't have to open you up with this surgery; we use tiny cameras instead.
   b This surgery is_____ ; we use tiny cameras instead.
3 a Normally you'd be welcome, but it's not very easy at the moment as my parents are staying.
   b Normally you'd be welcome, but it's a bit _____ at the moment as my parents are staying.
4 a It's difficult to know exactly why this model didn't sell well.
   b It's difficult to _____ of this model's poor sales.
5 a Eventually, peace returned to the two war-torn countries.
   b And so _____ that peace returned to the two war-torn countries.
6 a A lot more tablets than computers have been sold this year.
   b Sales of tablets have _____ those of computers this year.

10 VOCABULARY PRACTICE

TRUTH AND LIES

1 Choose the correct answers to complete the sentences.

1 Since there were no witnesses, the attacker *got away with it* / *passed it off*.
2 Michiko's behaving very badly. It's time you told her a few *white lies* / *home truths*.
3 Accusations of *plagiarism* / *making an excuse* severely damaged the professor's reputation.
4 A lot of newspapers are more concerned with *telling fibs* / *spreading malicious gossip* about celebrities than reporting the news.
5 Marco was devastated when he found out his wife had been *cheating on him* / *testifying under oath*.
6 There were only about 100 people there, not 1,000 – you're *committing perjury* / *exaggerating*.

2 Match each of the descriptions (1–5) with two phrases from the box.

committing forgery	exaggerating	plagiarism
committing perjury	telling a fib	telling tales
embellishing the facts	telling a white lie	
telling a few home truths	testifying under oath	

1 They involve copying someone's work or ideas.
2 They happen in court.
3 They involve making something sound more important than it is.
4 They are things children do.
5 They are both told for good reasons.

WELL

3 Add *well* in the correct place in responses a–f. Then match them with sentences 1–6.

1 I'm really sorry I wasn't there yesterday.
2 What's the matter? You look awful!
3 I'm afraid this level of service just isn't acceptable.
4 How was your presentation this morning?
5 What's Greg like to work with?
6 What time did you get home last night?

a I really don't feel. I think it was something I ate.
b It went, fortunately, and the boss looked pleased.
c He's great. As as being clever, he's a really nice guy.
d You could have called to say you weren't coming!
e I'm not sure, but it was after midnight.
f Said! It's about time someone complained.

OTHER WORDS AND PHRASES

activist sb who works hard doing practical things to achieve social or political change: *He was an animal rights activist.*

to be estranged to be no longer seeing, talking to or living with a husband/wife or relative: *Though they're still married, they have become estranged and live in different cities now.*

to be set up by sb [informal] to be the victim of a dishonest plan that is intended to trick sb: *She was set up to look like the person responsible, while the real criminal escaped.*

to drop charges to stop accusing sb of a crime: *The police dropped the charges against him because they didn't have enough evidence.*

to have a conviction overturned to have a guilty verdict changed so that it becomes the opposite of what it was before: *His conviction was overturned by the court of appeal.*

to infiltrate [T] to secretly join an organisation or enter a place in order to find out information about it or harm it: *Police attempts to infiltrate radical environmental groups were largely unsuccessful.*

to protect sb's identity to make sure nobody else finds out who sb is: *After he became a witness, the police decided to protect his identity in order to prevent him being attacked.*

to provide intelligence to give secret information to sb about a foreign government, military or criminal plans: *He had been providing intelligence to other countries for years.*

to reconcile (two things) [T] to find a way in which two ideas, situations or facts can both be true or acceptable: *The possibility remains that the two theories may be reconciled.*

undercover working secretly in order to catch criminals or find out information: *While working as an undercover detective, he managed to arrest three well-known drug dealers.*

4 Complete the sentences with words/phrases from the box above in the correct form.

1 I can confirm that we now have a reliable source on the other side who is _____ us with accurate _____ .
2 When the real thief was arrested, the police _____ the _____ against Phil immediately.
3 The plans have met with strong opposition from environmental _____ .
4 Let's sit down and talk about this. I'm sure we can find a way to _____ our differences.
5 The terrorist was finally caught after agents managed to successfully _____ the group.
6 Even though I've _____ my _____ overturned today, the court's original decision has ruined my life.

Audio script

UNIT 1 RECORDING 1

1   I, I think the idea of globalisation is, is, is a, is a great thing, I like the sense that the world is a smaller place and that things are accessible. And I guess what I think really stands out for me is the, um, the sort of sharing of ideas, really. Um, you know, maybe we can inspire each other, learn from each other. Um, and um, yeah, I think yeah, create a, a of sense of tolerance, um, for each other.

2   Well, globalisation's become a bit of a swearword for a lot of people. Um, there are good aspects to it, I suppose, but one of the things that gets on my nerves is, you go to any town in England and the high streets are all – or almost all – identical. It's the same shops, the same franchises and there seems to be so little individuality. There's no room for individuality and I think that's a great shame because we're missing out on the qualities you would get from local areas that specialise in whatever. But there's no chance for that to flourish because of the big chains that are global. And, uh, it's a bit too bland for me.

3   Living in London you, you just see globalisation all the time and I think this city is a fantastic example of, of the positive side of globalisation, really, because people are so tolerant on the whole. Uh, if you go into particularly the city of London, say, you've got people from all different countries who come to work here in the financial sector. Um, then you go into the café next door and there's all different accents and, and it's so usual now that people don't really comment on it or notice it. And, um, it's only when you leave London and go to perhaps somewhere more rural that you, you realise that it's not the same everywhere else. And, um, although that brings some tension sometimes I think, on the whole, it's a just a brilliant, brilliant thing.

4   Do you know what I really love, is being able to see a movie that I really want to see, and if I'm not in my own country, even if I'm abroad, I can still see it. But the only problem is that when everybody's got the same movies available and you go to America, or you go to Australia, and you can see the same movies roughly at the same time. The only problem is that the, the local stuff, the independent movies, the small kind of cooler movies don't seem to figure as much, it's just globalisation, I suppose, tends to favour the, the movie-makers with more money. And so, you know, some of that, um, some of that low-budget stuff is really exciting and really interesting, and that doesn't surface quite as much. But, you know, the plus is that if you're abroad and, and you think, 'Oh I really want to see that movie,' you can.

5   Well, I think globalisation is a good thing, actually. Um, a few years ago my friend and I went on a graduation trip, uh, to Japan, for two weeks. And we were really excited because we were always really into Japanese culture and food and everything. And when we got there, at first, it was amazing to eat authentic Japanese food all the time. But after a week I just really wanted something from home and very simple and not with fish in it. So, um, we ended up going to McDonald's and that kind of became my everyday thing because I just couldn't stand having fish every morning for breakfast. Um, so yeah, I'm definitely for globalisation.

6   Yeah, I must say, I think, in general, it's a really good thing. Uh, you know, with my life here it suits me, the kind of globalisation thing. But I must say, I recently visited Cuba and it, it seems that a place like that, that hasn't really been affected by globalisation, you know, has very little internet and, uh, there's no American multinational companies and fast foods and things like that, and no advertising. It's just great to be there because you don't feel bombarded by all the kind of global brands that we all have to live with all the time. And, as I say, although I actually like globalisation in general, while I'm there, I'm just delighted that it hasn't affected the place. So it's a shame, really, there are not a few more countries that haven't kept their identity as much as Cuba has.

UNIT 1 RECORDING 2

I = Interviewer   JJ = Jennifer Jenkins

I: I've come to Kings College, London, to talk to Dr Jennifer Jenkins, who's a Senior Lecturer in Applied Linguistics. Now, Jennifer, you're quite interested in the teaching and learning of International English; can you explain in general terms what this is?

JJ: It's based on the fact that nowadays the majority of people who speak English around the world are non-native speakers of English – they, they've learnt it as a second or subsequent language, they use it to speak with each other and therefore, they're not really learning what's always been called English as a foreign language – English to speak to native speakers of English. They're learning it for more international communication and that has all sorts of implications for the sorts of things that they need to be able to do.

I: So what would be the main differences between the kind of English that's widely taught around the world today and perhaps what you describe as a more international form?

JJ: Well, there'd be various differences. There'd be differences in what they need to be able to do when they're pronouncing English, there would be some differences in the grammar, there'd be some differences in, er, use, or not, of idioms.

I: Is there anything that's widely taught when teaching English that would be missed out in International English?

JJ: Yes, I think, for example, that there doesn't seem to be much point in teaching learners to say the T H, the /θ/ and /ð/ sounds. Um, because most of the world's learners of English, speakers of English who are non-native speakers don't pronounce the /θ/.

I: And what is the thinking behind the idea of International English?

JJ: Well, there are two things. One is that the more different groups of people round the world speak English, the more important it becomes to make sure that they have enough in common so that they can understand each other, that they're intelligible to each other and here pronunciation is very important because their pronunciation is the thing that will vary most, um, among different speakers of English. Um, and the second thing would be that now that English is spoken as an international language, nobody owns it any more. The native speakers of English don't own it and so don't have the right to expect everybody else around the world, when they speak English, to conform to 'native-speaker' ways of speaking, that everybody has the right to develop their own ways of speaking English.

I: So what would you say are the advantages for students and teachers of this form of English?

JJ: Well, one, one advantage would be that they actually have rather less to do, rather less to learn, because instead of trying to learn the entire, um, way of speaking of a native speaker, which is incredibly complicated and most learners never do achieve this in any case, so they've got less to do, but they're also allowed to, um, keep something of themselves in their English. They're speaking English as, say, a Japanese speaker of English or, um, an Arabic speaker of English, a Spanish speaker of English, um, and therefore they are allowed to be themselves in English.

I: Right. And how do you see English being learnt and spoken in, say, 30 years' time? How do you feel it will have changed?

JJ: Well, the English that's being spoken internationally, I think, for example, will have no longer, um, say, British-based or American-based idiomatic language because this is not useful for international communication, so that will have gone. I think that, um, quite probably, the nouns that we call uncountable nouns, like 'information' and so on, will have become countable nouns for international use. I expect, in Britain, we'll carry on talking about, um, 'information' as a 'piece of information', but quite possibly, the rest of the world will be saying 'three informations' without treating it as an uncountable noun. I think, quite likely, the third-person-singular '-s' in the Present simple tense will have gone for international use. Um, I think, in pronunciation, I think the /θ/ sound will have gone and possibly the /ð/ sound as well. Most learners will say, instead of /θ/, will say a /s/ or a /t/, as most of them do anyway at the moment, um, but it will just be legitimate then.

I: There must, on the other hand, be students who, who will want to speak English the way that they perceive it to be spoken in Britain or America. So what would you say to them?

JJ: Well, I'd say, first of all, I'd want to explain the facts to them, the fact that they are the majority – that the non-native speakers of English are the majority. And having explained that and also the fact that they're much more able to express themselves – who they really are, their identity – in English, if they keep something of their background, of their mother tongue, I would then say that we can't patronise learners, that if learners still want to learn to speak as closely as possible to a native speaker – say, a British or American English – it's their choice, and the important thing is to give learners choices so that they can make up their own mind what it is they want to do.

I: Well, Dr Jenkins, thank you for talking to me about that. It'll be interesting to see how far things change.

UNIT 1 RECORDING 4

1 This maybe isn't the most original way, but, uh, I think I really improved my English when I watched films and TV programmes with the subtitles on. Um, the subtitles help you to, of course, understand better, but you don't feel like you're really studying a language, you just feel like you're enjoying a film with, uh, drama or romance or murder. And it's, it's, it's just like enjoying yourself and it's not like you're learning anything.

2 I'll tell you what I'd say, actually, and this is something I've done myself. Um, I went to learn Spanish in Argentina and, uh, I found the thing that helped more than anything was doing a class in tango – uh, guitar, I play guitar. Um, and you know, you go in the class and you're not thinking about learning the language, you're thinking about the instrument or, you know, whatever the class is you decide to take.
And somehow it seems to sink in a bit more, the language actually sinks in rather than if you're focusing on grammar or whatever. And just, you know, playing the chords and learning the vocabulary of music, uh, I found that was absolutely fantastic and I'd recommend that to anyone.

3 This sounds a bit weird but a friend of mine told me that the best way she found to learn English or to improve her English, I should say, was to try and think in English whenever she could. So when she was by herself, walking down the street or on a bus or whatever, she'd, she'd look around and try and describe in her head what she could see.
Um, then she used to also imagine conversations she might have with people in the future or imagine a conversation with a friend or something in her head. And I think sometimes, when she was by herself, she used to talk out, talk out loud to herself, even. So she had a whole, she was doing all this practice, all the time, just by herself in her free time. It sounds pretty clever to me.

4 Um, when I was 19, I think, I went to England to become an au pair and learn English. And, um, the best thing about this was, uh, if I was ironing or hoovering the house for example, I will put uh the radio on or YouTube or something like that and listen in the background, so I have, all the time, the English language going into my brain without really thinking about it. I think it's best if you don't concentrate, if it, if it goes on, you know, in the background, is really helpful.

5 Well, I've always believed that, uh, learning a foreign language, you have to communicate constantly in that language. So I would always say, you know, get yourself a girlfriend from the country of the language you wish to learn.

6 Well, when I lived in Poland, uh, I was never very extroverted as a person, but when I first came to England, um, I realised that the only way that I would get better in English was to just talk to everybody. Um, so I made myself, uh, have conversations with, with old people I met on the street or, um, at a bus stop or, or shopkeepers, um, even people in the cafés. Uh, some people, they weren't always very friendly, but, uh, but lots of people actually are and they're very polite, uh, especially the older people.

7 You know what I do, uh, to keep up my Spanish, is I just go online regularly and read the news websites, all in Spanish, of course. And, um I, I choose to read about something I really am interested in anyway. Um, I just find that's, that's more helpful. So I may be reading about, in my case, I love football, so I'd been reading about football or maybe business – and something I'm interested in, anyway. And, um, it's just so much easier to read in a foreign language if you're interested in what you're reading about. And it's great for your vocab and it sort of just reminds you about what you already know.

UNIT 1 RECORDING 5

1 The main news today is, of course, the weather, as Hurricane Georgina approaches the east coast, forcing tens of thousands of people to evacuate the area. Businesses along the projected path of the hurricane have closed early, windows have been boarded up and all flights into and out of the area have been suspended. The storm has also caused a sharp drop in share prices across the world as markets respond to the fear of substantial damage to the US economy and disruption to trading. Analysts fear that the clean-up operation could cost over $15 billion, although this is still much less than the $100 billion in clean-up costs and damages that Hurricane Katrina cost in 2005.

2 Japanese firm Toyota has announced that it is to create 200 new jobs at its factory in Derbyshire. The factory has been manufacturing cars for over 25 years and the cars produced there are sold all over Europe. Local people have welcomed the news, with MP Rita Perkins calling it a vote of confidence in Derbyshire and its people. On the same day as this news, however, local firm Mulkins, which manufactures cutting tools, announced that it was to close with the loss of 150 jobs. Mulkins has struggled to export its goods to foreign markets in the face of strong competition from abroad.

3 A new report into the attitudes of Australians towards climate change suggests that while the vast majority of people think climate change is happening, there is a lack of agreement about the causes. Many still refuse to accept that climate change is the result of human activity, with a third of the people questioned believing that it is part of a natural process. The other two-thirds believe big-polluting nations such as the US and China are mostly responsible. Together, those two countries produce over 12,000 million tonnes of greenhouse gases a year.

4 Over the past few days queues of people have been forming outside an old colonial building in south Mumbai. They have been queuing, believe it or not, for a coffee! Last Friday, Starbucks opened its first coffee house in India in Mumbai's historic Elphinstone Building. Two more coffee houses in the chain are scheduled to open this week. Starbucks already has around 20,000 branches in more than 60 countries, so in some ways the only surprise is that it's taken them so long. Not everyone, however, is happy at the prospect of western brands entering the Indian market and independent retailers have been holding rallies against ...

UNIT 2 RECORDING 2

P = Presenter   A = Andrew

P: And now for Inside Track, the slot where we get to ask an industry insider about some of the secrets of their trade. Today we are talking to advertising insider Andrew Troullides about how adverts appeal to our emotions. Welcome to the programme, Andrew. Tell me, do you think most adverts appeal to our emotions?

A: Not necessarily. Actually, I think a lot of advertising is rational.

P: Define what you mean by 'rational advertising'.

A: Well, if the ad points out certain features and benefits that are superior to the competitors', then that's a rational appeal. The most obvious rational appeal is price, so if the advert says, 'Our supermarket or our brand is better value for money than the other ones,' then that's a rational appeal; or, you know, 'This washing powder cleans better,' or 'This car uses less fuel,' – those are all appealing to our logic.

P: So how does that contrast with an advert that appeals to our emotions, then?

A: Well, say, if the washing powder advert shows a mother wrapping her baby in a soft towel or happy children running around in the garden getting dirty while their mother smiles and washes their clothes; that's an emotional appeal because the advert is saying, 'If you use this washing powder, it shows that you love your children – it shows you're a good mother.'

P: Um, but, surely, what most people prefer is straightforward facts and information? Why do advertisers feel the need to make an emotional appeal?

A: One problem is that facts and information can be very boring. I mean, talking about the mileage and fuel consumption of a car, for example, is pretty dull. And if you take cars, small cars, say – to be honest, these days most of them are pretty much the same under the bonnet – there aren't really many differentiating factors in terms of quality. So the ad tries to bring in a sense of excitement – maybe suggest a sense of the adventures that you might have in your new car – or in some other way appeal to people's aspirations. Maybe it makes them feel that other people will look up to them if they buy this particular car. It's interesting that a lot of advertising for expensive luxury cars – like, say, a BMW – is aimed at people who will never be able to afford that car. But the idea is that the people who do buy the BMW, they feel that other people will envy them for having that car. It gives them kudos, increases their credibility, makes them feel ahead of the game.

P: So ads try to make us feel superior to other people?

A: Um, not always. Other ads might be about fitting in with your peer group, being one of the gang. This is true of a lot of advertising for fashion or music, for gadgets like, say, phones or iPods; the message is that if you haven't got one of these, then you're left out, you're not part of the group.

P: So, basically, they are trying to make us feel good about ourselves one way or another?

Audio script

A: One way or another, yes. You know, going back to that supermarket or food brand, some adverts basically say, 'We're not the cheapest; we're a luxury, but you deserve a luxury, you deserve to pamper yourself,' so you see someone sitting with their feet up enjoying the chocolate or lying by the pool of a luxury hotel eating the ice cream. There was one brand of beer a few years ago whose slogan was 'Reassuringly expensive'; and the message there is, 'Treat yourself – you're worth the best.'

P: And this obviously means the company can charge more for the product?

A: Yes, that's how you create a valuable brand; people feel they are paying for a particular benefit – whether it's a particular brand of T-shirt that makes them feel cool or whatever.

P: Do ads ever appeal to negative emotions? Do they ever try to upset people or deliberately annoy them?

A: They would never deliberately set out to annoy people, but some ads definitely set out to shock people, especially, um, things like public health campaigns. The anti-smoking campaigns we've had in this country are probably the best example of that. It's often charity ads which appeal to 'negative' emotions, funnily enough; you know, shock people or make them feel guilty – and that's just a numbers game, really; with a certain percentage of people, that will work and they will donate to the charity.

P: Does that sort of thing ever backfire?

A: Yes, it can backfire if you use the wrong tone of voice. People don't like being shouted or lectured at in ads, so if charities or health campaigns do that, they can really turn people off.

P: But, surely, advertisers must test their ads to check they have the right effect?

A: Oh absolutely. All ads are pre-tested with focus groups to monitor people's emotional responses and make sure they have the kind of effect that's intended. You know, how did that particular word make you feel? How do you feel when you see that image? That kind of thing. These days advertising companies often set up discussion groups online and check responses in different countries. Something like the Nike slogan 'Just do it' – that will have been tested all over the world to check that is has the right emotional effect on people in different places.

P: And are there any restrictions on the kind of appeal you can make to people's emotions? Do the government have any rules about this sort of thing – for products that might be considered bad for people, for example?

A: Oh yes! In most countries, things like beer advertisements, for example, are very heavily regulated. So you can't show people under 25 in them, for example, but you also can't appeal to certain emotions. You can't show too much enjoyment, sexual achievement, etc. etc. You can't make the ad too funny; it can be a bit funny, but not too funny.

P: Interesting. That's something we haven't really talked about. Lots of ads seem to appeal to our sense of humour – how does that work?

A: Well, I think it's often the case that the advertisers simply feel they should entertain people, you know, if they are taking up their time in the breaks between TV programmes. But there can be a bit more to it than that. It's interesting that a lot of ads for online gaming and betting use humour. The message there is basically, 'OK, we all know that betting is a bit silly and not very good for you, but, hey, it's fun; and you're the kind of person who likes a bit of fun!'

P: So, once again, in a sense, it's subtly flattering people's self-image?

A: Pretty much, yeah.

P: Well, we've run out of time, sadly, Andrew, but thanks very much – that was fascinating! And now the news …

UNIT 2 RECORDING 4

A: This story is called *The Tell-Tale Heart* and it's a short story written by the American writer Edgar Allan Poe in the 1840s – so, a long time ago – but it's quite a famous story in American literature and there have been a couple of films based on it, too. It's a very short, quite simple story in a way, and it's told in the first person. The narrator starts by claiming that he is not in the slightest bit insane even though he has murdered someone, which, of course, is instantly disturbing, so right from the beginning you have a strong sense of unease.

The narrator tells us that he has murdered an old man, not because he hated him or because he wanted his money, but because he couldn't bear the old man's 'evil blue eye'. You never really find out what his relationship is with the old man, but you get the impression that he lives with him,

maybe as a servant or something like that. Again, he insists that he is not insane and as evidence of that, he describes the calm, cold-blooded way in which he planned the murder. He describes how every day for seven days he put his head round the old man's bedroom door during the night and stood with a covered lantern, and then shone a thin beam of light into the man's eye at midnight. However, every night the man's eye is closed, so he leaves the man unharmed, holding an unlit lantern in silence while the old man is sleeping.

Then, on the eighth night, the old man hears him as he enters the room and wakes up, terrified. For a whole hour the narrator – the murderer – stands in the darkness in the old man's bedroom in silence, not moving a muscle. And even though there isn't a single sound, you know that the old man knows that someone is there and that he has a strong sense of foreboding. And the tension builds up and builds up … The narrator can hear the old man's heart beating louder and faster, and at that point he finally shines the light into the man's eye, which this time is wide open. The old man screams because he knows his life is about to end. And at this point, the narrator moves quickly and murders him – smothers him, presumably – it's a bit ambiguous in the story. And all the time the narrator is reassuring the reader that he is completely sane and, as 'proof', he describes how cleverly he hid the body: how he lifted up the floorboards and hid the body under there, then nailed them back down and cleared away all the mess.

But, anyway, someone has heard the old man's scream because the police come round to interview the narrator and he takes them into the room where the old man died and they sit in chairs, just above where the body is hidden, and the police interview him, but he tells them that the old man has gone away to stay in the country for a while; and according to him – the narrator – he is so calm and pleasant that the policemen don't suspect him at all. Except that, as the conversation goes on, the narrator starts to hear a sound; and the sound gets louder and louder, and he is convinced that it is the sound of the old man's heart beating, coming up from beneath the floorboards, and it's getting more and more deafening and he can't understand why the policemen can't hear it, too.

Anyway, I won't give away the ending, but it's a very, very chilling story – not one that you would want to read when you are alone late at night!

B: One of my favourite stories is *Les Misérables*. I've seen the film and the musical several times and I'm always in floods of tears by the end because it's so tragic and so moving. It's based on the book by the French writer Victor Hugo, which, I must admit, I haven't actually read because it's extremely long!

Anyway, it's set in France at the beginning of the 19th century and it concerns the situation of the poor, and particularly the way the criminal justice system treats them. It's a very long story, with several sub-plots which are too complicated to go into, but the main thread of the plot concerns an ex-convict called Valjean and the story opens as he is released from prison after serving 19 years for stealing a loaf of bread. In prison, he has been mistreated by a law enforcement officer called Javert, who appears and reappears throughout the story, pursuing him wherever he goes.

Valjean is taken in by a kindly local bishop and despite the fact that Valjean steals from him, the bishop treats him with trust, gives him some silver and makes him promise to reform. Thanks to this kindness, Valjean rises to become a factory owner and the mayor of a local town. However, he changes his identity in order to hide his criminal past.

Meanwhile, a 'fallen woman' called Fantine comes to work at Valjean's factory. She has an illegitimate daughter called Cosette, who she can't afford to look after and has to send away to live with a family who treat the little girl like a slave. To make matters worse, Fantine loses her job at the factory and when she defends herself against a man who attacks her, she's arrested by the law enforcement officer, Javert. Eventually, she dies, heartbroken. Javert also recognises Valjean, who he wants to arrest for assuming a false identity, but Valjean escapes and goes off to rescue Fantine's daughter, Cosette. So, Valjean adopts Cosette as his daughter and they move to Paris. There, the now grown-up Cosette falls in love with a wealthy law student called Marius, who is part of a radical group campaigning for democracy and justice for the poor. There are many more complicated sub-plots and Javert continues to pursue Valjean, but, anyway, the story culminates in an uprising against the government, which ends in failure and in the death of many brave young men who have been fighting for justice. In the course of all this, Valjean saves Javert's life. However, Javert, in turmoil over his failure to capture Valjean and Valjean's compassion towards him, commits suicide. During the uprising, Valjean also saves Marius, who, once recovered, marries Cosette. However, all is not well, as Valjean, after admitting his criminal past to Marius, goes into hiding from the law, leaving Cosette in distress. Eventually, Marius realises that Valjean saved his life, so he takes Cosette to see the dying Valjean and they are finally reunited on his death bed, where the story ends.

The whole story just fills you with this huge sense of injustice and despair at the way poor people just cannot escape their past or fight the system, which is completely against them. Certain moments in the story, like Fantine's death, are just heartbreaking. But at the same time, certain parts of it are very uplifting – like when the bishop helps Valjean at the beginning or the idealism of the students in the uprising. The songs in the musical and film are also amazing – and the story never fails to move me!

UNIT 3 RECORDING 1

1 The answer, strangely, is *priceless*. The idea is that it's so valuable that you cannot put a price on it. *Pricey* means 'rather expensive for what it's really worth' and worthless means 'it's worth nothing'. *Worthwhile* is not related to money – it means 'worth spending your time on'.

2 *Tight* – or *tight-fisted* – *penny-pinching* and *stingy* are colloquial phrases used to describe someone who doesn't like spending money. *Flashy* – or *flash* – means more or less the opposite: it describes someone or something that is expensive but vulgar, in bad taste.

3 If you give someone in authority some money to do you a favour, this is called a *bribe* – and is, of course, illegal! An *advance* is when you get given some of your salary money before payday. It is also used in publishing – authors often receive advances before their books are published. A *deposit* is money you pay to someone to reserve or set aside for you something you want to buy, before you pay the final amount – for example, you might pay a deposit when you book your holiday, then pay the final amount a few weeks before you go. A *fee* is the money that you pay to any professional person for their services – to a doctor, lawyer, etc.

4 The words that describe someone who has little or no money are *skint*, *broke* and *hard up*. If you are *loaded,* it means that you are rich or have a lot of money at the moment. All these words are colloquial.

5 The correct order from most to least positive is: 1 *make a large profit*, 2 *be in the black*, 3 *break even*, 4 *be in the red* and 5 *go bankrupt*, which means that your business has to shut down.

6 A waiter, hairdresser, taxi driver, etc. receives a tip from a satisfied customer. People who have retired receive a pension, either from their company or from the government. Children receive pocket money, usually from their parents. A kidnapper asks for or receives a ransom, normally from the family of their victim, and an ex-spouse receives alimony or maintenance – typically an ex-wife from her ex-husband.

7 High unemployment, a large government deficit, businesses going bust and government spending cuts are normally associated with an economic recession. High share prices, high property prices, high salaries, an increase in GDP – Gross Domestic Product – and economic expansion are all associated with an economic boom.

UNIT 3 RECORDING 2

The story of Stella Liebeck is often quoted as a symbol of what has come to be known as 'compensation culture' in the USA today. Listen to the facts and make up your own mind.

One morning in February 1992, Stella Liebeck, a 79-year-old woman from Santa Fe, New Mexico, drove 60 miles with her son, Jim, and her grandson, Chris, to Albuquerque airport in order for Jim to catch an early flight. After she dropped Jim off, she and her grandson stopped at a burger restaurant for breakfast. Her grandson, who was driving the car, parked so that Stella could add cream and sugar to her coffee. She put the cup between her knees and tried to pull the lid off. As she tugged at the lid, the cup tipped over and scalding coffee poured onto her lap. She screamed and a horrified Chris rushed to help her.

Stella received burns over 16 percent of her body and was hospitalised for eight days. Her daughter stayed home for three weeks to look after Stella following her release from hospital. Treatment for her burns, including skin grafts, lasted for more than two years. Eventually, Mrs Liebeck wrote to the burger company asking if they would consider selling their coffee at a lower temperature and to refund her medical expenses – about $2,000 – plus the lost wages of her daughter who stayed home to care for her. The company offered her just $800.

Only then did Stella consult a lawyer, who advised her to sue the company. The jury awarded her $160,000 in actual damages and an extra $2.7 million in punitive damages against the fast-food restaurant in question. The sum was eventually reduced to $640,000, but not before there was a huge outcry in the US media, and Stella Liebeck had unwillingly become a national celebrity.

UNIT 3 RECORDING 3

D = David   B = Becky

D: OK, so what's your, what's your take on this Stella Liebeck thing then?

B: Well, I think she was entitled to some compensation.

D: What do you mean 'some compensation'? What do you mean by 'some compensation'?

B: Well, I mean, lets, let's be blunt about this: she burned herself, she had to undergo medical treatment, her family member had to take time off of work …

D: What I find really interesting is when you just said that she burned herself. Now, not once did she admit that it was her fault. You've just said she burned herself, and that's exactly what I think: she burned herself, so she shouldn't get any compensation from them.

B: Yeah, but David, the coffee was absolutely ridiculously hot. It's one thing for a company to serve hot coffee, but it was 180 to 190 degrees.

D: Companies would not serve coffee that hot if the public didn't demand in the first place that they got really hot coffee. You do it the other way round, you'd probably get people suing them for having cold coffee and their tooth fell out or, I mean, you know, ridiculous!

B: But the coffee that you have at home isn't that hot and people say, 'Oh, coffee's great!' and that's the temperature they want it – it's 135 to 140. I mean, that's a significant difference …

D: You have to ask yourself …

B: … in temperature …

D: You do have to ask yourself why they have it that kind of temperature. I mean, presumably, they have it that kind of temperature because people want it that kind of temperature.

B: Well, OK. I think people want it hot, but I, you do have to realise as well that there've been approximately 700 cases of people being burned by scalded – scalding coffee, so …

D: Well, …

B: … I mean, obviously, restaurants and, and take-out food places have got to take this on board …

D: There …

B: … they just can't sell it that hot.

D: There may well have been 700 cases of people being burned by scalding coffee, but, but they didn't all sue, did they? I mean, she's the only one, the only one who's sued – as far as I know, anyway.

B: No, she's, she's the most famous one because she got most money out of it.

D: I'm sorry, I'm sorry, no way should she have give-, been given that money. No way!

B: Look, the fast-food chain makes 1.3 million dollars a day selling coffee. They could afford this.

D: It is ridiculous, it is ridiculous to claim that just because a company makes a lot of money and they can afford to pay people compensation, they good, they, they, they should! It's, the thing is, nowadays what happens is that we, we have to blame someone and the person to blame is never yourself, never ever yourself; it's always somebody else's fault; always!

UNIT 3 RECORDING 5

1 That's it, I've had enough of Vijay! Not only does he never clean up, but he also expects me to make him food when he's hungry!

2 That's easy – it was the day I graduated from university. Never before had I felt so proud. All my family were there to cheer me on.

3 It's funny how everything changes when you have children. I've always loved my parents, but only now can I really appreciate what they did for me.

4 No way will I have finished my research degree by the end of the year. I've

Audio script

still got so much data to analyse before I can do anything useful with it.

5 Under no circumstances should you go into that part of town on your own, especially at night. It's just too dangerous.

UNIT 3 RECORDING 6

1 Write down the name of something you own that is worth quite a lot.
2 Write down the name of something you own that is probably worthless.
3 Write down something difficult you have done that wasn't worth the effort.
4 Write down the name of a job that you consider to be really worthwhile.
5 Write down the name of a tourist attraction in your area that is worth a visit.
6 Write down the name of a tourist attraction in your area that isn't really worth seeing.
7 Write down approximately how much an hour's worth of parking costs in your city centre.
8 Write down the name of a gadget you own that has proved its worth.
9 Write down the name of a celebrity you know who is worthy of the public attention they have received.
10 Write down the name of something from your childhood that is worth keeping.

UNIT 4 RECORDING 2

Hannah

S = Sam   H = Hannah

S: So how are your New Year's Resolutions going then, Hannah?
H: Mm ... well, quite positive. I've started working with a personal trainer!
S: Wow! What made you decide to do that?
H: I just suddenly decided. I'm always starting going to the gym and then not keeping it up, so I decided I needed to try something new. My husband was going to buy me this fancy new phone for Christmas, but then I asked him to pay for some sessions with a personal trainer instead.
S: But you're not overweight – I don't know why you're so worried.
H: Yeah, but I'm totally unfit. I mean, I can't even run for the bus and I kind of need to tone up my muscles and stuff.
S: And is it good?
H: Well, I've only been three times so far, but, yes, it's better than I expected, actually. The trainer, Adam, is really nice and he looks at your overall fitness and tells you where you need to develop strength before you can build up your fitness more. So, um, for example, I stand on my feet in a bit of a funny way and so I have to do special ankle-strengthening exercises to improve the way I stand; and that will help me to be able to move better and get fitter.
S: Sounds cool getting that kind of personalised advice. But the trainer must be super-fit himself. Don't you feel a bit inferior – you know, not being very fit yourself?
H: Not really. He's very, very encouraging and the targets he sets are quite manageable, so you don't get demotivated. And it's fun, actually. The gym normally bores me to death, but the time passes really quickly because the exercises are really varied and you have to do them quickly one after another, moving really quickly from one machine to the other, and you're chatting a lot of the time. So, yeah, it's really good.
S: Oh well, good for you! Let me know how it goes.

Ted

S = Sarah   T = Ted

S: You're looking trim, Ted!
T: Thank you very much – I've lost eight kilos, actually.
S: That's quite a lot!
T: Yeah, well, I'd been steadily putting on weight ever since I started this job and got stuck in an office all day. I used to play football quite a lot and then I just stopped doing any kind of exercise.
S: Mm, well, you've certainly lost it now! What's your secret? I feel quite envious!
T: I got this app on my phone called FitnessFriend and I've been using it for about a year. It's really cool, actually. You put in your weight and age, and how active your lifestyle is and then it calculates your metabolic rate and works out how many calories you need to eat to lose, gain or maintain your weight – whatever your aims are.
S: Uh huh.

T: Then you put into it what you've eaten and all the activities you've done and it works out for you whether you've eaten the right amount to achieve your aims.
S: Sounds a bit complicated to me.
T: No, it's not, really – you soon get into it. That's what I really like about it, actually; it's really scientific, based on calculations – you know how that sort of thing appeals to me. And you can set it to do things like remind you to go to the gym.
S: Really?
T: Yeah, or it can work out how far you've run or walked or whatever, and how fast you went compared to your last run, so you're kind of competing with yourself. Yeah, I really like all the calculations it can do. Let me show you this – I think this is the best thing about the app. It's really cool! Give me that packet of biscuits. Look: you can scan the barcode of whatever you are eating and it tells you all the nutritional information, like how much sugar and fat and how many carbohydrates and so on. So you just enter how many biscuits you ate or how many grams, etc. and it works out how many calories you had!
S: Ha! Amazing! Don't you ever feel tempted to cheat?
T: Well, yeah, that's the only problem: it's easy to cheat. But I guess you're only cheating yourself at the end of the day.
S: I guess so. Well, I have to say I'm very impressed, but I'm not sure it would work for me. Perhaps I'm just not that scientific!
T: Oh well!

Nicola

M = Mina   N = Nicola

M: You ran a marathon a few years ago, didn't you, Nicola? That must have been amazing!
N: Yeah, I did it with my friend Julie. We were raising money for cancer research. My dad had died of cancer the year before and her sister had also had it, so that was kind of what got us started.
M: Oh, sorry to hear that. But you used to run before that, didn't you? I mean, you didn't start running from scratch?
N: No, we'd both done a bit of running, but not that seriously; and we just got talking about it one day when we were dropping our kids off at nursery. We'd both been thinking separately about having a go at the marathon and the more we talked about it, the more enthusiastic we got!
M: So how did you go about training? I mean, I wouldn't even know where to start!
N: We found a training programme in a running magazine and, basically, we just followed it rigorously – religiously – for about six months. You had to run five times a week and it started short – about 20 kilometres a week – and gradually, you built up to about 75 to 100 kilometres a week.
M: That must have been incredibly gruelling!
N: It was horrible, completely horrible! Some days I really didn't want to get out of bed and do it, but we just stuck to it come rain or shine. I even ran 20 kilometres once with a bad stomach bug – I can still remember it now ... ugh!
M: And did doing it with someone else make a big difference?
N: Oh yeah, it made all the difference in the world. On the days when you really didn't want to get up and do it you just felt you had to, to be there for the other person. There's nothing worse than letting the other person down. And, of course, it was someone to talk to – long runs can be pretty boring. We just chatted for hours and hours; we got to know each other really well! But yeah, more than anything, I suppose, it was just that you feel obliged to keep the other person motivated and that keeps you motivated, too.
M: That and the thought of all the money you were raising!
N: Yeah, the charity we signed up with was really helpful, too. They had support meetings and they had a physiotherapist you could consult and all that sort of thing.
M: So, I guess you felt you couldn't let them down either?
N: Exactly. And once we had done it, it was amazing. We were even in the newspaper! When I look back on it, it really feels like one of the achievements of my lifetime.
M: Yeah, you must feel so proud! And you must have got so fit!
N: Yeah, I was incredibly fit. To be honest, I've never quite managed to keep up that level of fitness since, but I'm still definitely miles fitter than I was before. And I still run four or five times a week – and still with Julie.
M: Wow, good for you! I don't think I could ever do that, but I'm full of admiration ...

UNIT 4 RECORDING 4

A Child psychologist Camila Batmanghelidjh, whose family came to Britain from Iran in the 1970s, had had a dream ever since her own difficult childhood – to open a drop-in centre where underprivileged children from troubled homes could take refuge when they were not at school. When she finally found the premises that she had been looking for, she was warned that the centre would be overrun by local teenage gangs, many of whom carried knives and even guns. Rather than trying to keep these wild teenagers out, Camila made a highly courageous decision: to open her doors to them, too. But experience convinced her that they would never respond to the authority of middle-class social workers, so again, she made a very unusual decision: to recruit as care workers young men who were themselves ex-gangsters and drug dealers, to whom these youngsters would be better able to relate. 'No child is born a criminal,' believes Camila. Thirteen years later, Camila's charity, Kids Company, looks after 17,000 vulnerable young people in London and feeds 2,000 children who are starving because, for one reason or other, their parents are unable to feed them.

B Fourteen-year-old Jack Slater was still wearing his school uniform when he leapt in to help security guards who were being attacked by a group of men in his local shopping mall. The fight had broken out after the group of four men were asked by the security guards to leave the shopping centre because they were causing trouble. Jack, whose bravery was captured on CCTV, had gone to the shopping centre with a friend after school. Dozens of adults gathered to watch the fight, but only Jack moved in to help. He saw one of the security guards being pinned to the ground and jumped on the back of his assailant and pulled him away. The police later arrived and arrested all four of the men. Jack was tracked down from the CCTV footage and presented with a £50 shopping voucher by the shopping mall to thank him for his actions.

C On 27th May, Lucy Gale, a taxi driver from West Yorkshire, came across a collision on a level crossing between two cars. When she arrived at the scene, both vehicles were on the line. An elderly woman driver was lying across the steering wheel of one car and the other driver was frantically trying to get out of his vehicle. Lucy looked round and saw that a train was approaching. She crossed the line on foot, dragged the woman from the vehicle and took her to a place of safety. Having made sure the woman was safe, Lucy went back to the car and, after a struggle with the seat, managed to drive it off the crossing just as the train passed. She then went to the other car and forced the other driver's damaged door open in order to let him out. Her actions stopped the train from derailing and, in all probability, prevented a serious rail accident.

D He received burn injuries on his face, back and arms, is still recuperating and lost one year of school. But ask him: would he put his life in danger once again if caught in a similar situation? 'Every time,' Om Prakash says. The boy, the son of an Uttar Pradesh farmer, pulled several of his friends alive out of a burning van, caring little about his own safety. On 4th September Om Prakash was going to school along with other students in a Maruti van. But all of a sudden, the van caught fire because of a short circuit. The driver immediately opened his door and fled. But Om Prakash broke open the van door and pulled out the others, ignoring the flames that had spread to his face, back and arms. He rescued eight children.

E When Martine Wright lost both her legs in a bomb attack in London, it seemed as if her life had come to an end. She lost 80 percent of the blood in her body and spent ten days in a coma. However, Martine was determined to fight her way back. She had to learn to walk again and as part of her rehabilitation, she started playing wheelchair tennis and then switched to sitting volleyball. Since then she has managed to gain a place in the British Paralympic sitting volleyball team and competed in the London Paralympic Games. Martine, who has also got married, had a child and done a parachute jump since she lost her legs, says that her experiences have made her determined to grab every opportunity that comes her way.

UNIT 5 RECORDING 1

1 So something that really annoys me, and this is especially with people that you first meet, is when they start talking to you about the weather. I mean, I know what the weather's like, I can see it, I can check it myself, we don't need to talk about it. I just don't see how that is really relevant to a conversation that I would have with a person I just met. I, I don't understand.

2 Oh, I have to say, the thing that really annoys me more than anything else, and it might be because I'm getting a little bit older now, is when you get one of these young people on a bus with headphones in, and it's turned up too loud. I mean it drives me mad. If you're gonna have headphones, it's for your own personal use – we don't all want to hear it on the rest of the bus, thank you very much. Turn it down!

3 It really bugs me when people are late when you arrange to meet them and then they're just 10 minutes late or 15 minutes late and quite often they text to say 'just, just running a bit late'. And, presumably, before phones people just got there on time, but I don't see what difference it makes. And, you know, I've normally rushed to get there, 'cos I hate being late. And then, time after time, a so-called friend just leaves me stranded. I, I, oh, it annoys me so much!

4 So two days ago I met with my friends and we're all sitting in a coffee shop and they all start taking out their phones and checking their emails and checking to see who called them and texting back. And, literally, I sat there for 15 minutes just watching them text on their phones and email on their phones. And it's infuriating – you might as well just not meet with your friends; just text them instead.

5 At the risk of sounding like a grumpy old woman, which I am, um, I've, I really have a problem when I see people snogging in public. I, I just, I don't know, I actually have a physical reaction to it, um, it really bothers me. And I have been known to actually object. And there's a part of me that thinks, 'Oh my God you're just so, you know, stuffy and, and repressed!' But I just, I just think it's really inappropriate when, when people are, uh, kissing in, in public and, and kind of being really intimate I, I just, I can't bear it – really can't bear it.

UNIT 5 RECORDING 2

I = Interviewer   R = Rosemary

I: Rosemary, what are the most common situations where people have problems in communicating?

R: Well, probably one of the main situations where people have problems communicating is where they're unsure of who they're talking to. So, for instance, going to a party, and it's a room full of strangers, people you've never ever met before; that generally, for most people, will prove to be a little bit of a difficult situation. Um, I suppose the second area is where people are unsure of what they're talking about, so the content worries them for whatever reason. And the third area is where we're in a situation of speaking to an audience who we perceive are very different to us, so they are different in terms of their age, their experience or their status.

I: So that's quite general, so why don't we ... can we think of a specific example, maybe that party again?

R: Oh, let's suppose you're, um, introduced to someone – again, a total stranger, you've never met them before – and you don't know them, um, you are introduced to them and you, from the introduction, you gather that they are actually quite an important person, they've got high status, they're very experienced, they're much older than you and all of a sudden, you think, 'My goodness, why would they possibly want to listen to me?' And we feel totally lacking in confidence.

I: Um, in that situation, what are, what are the most common mistakes they're going to make?

R: Probably one of the most common mistakes will be they would want to speak too much, they'd say too much. Er, all this information would come out of their mouths, er, but what they really should be doing in that situation is asking some questions to get the other person talking to them; not too many questions because if we ask too many questions, it sounds like an interrogation, but getting the balance right between giving some information, but also asking for information as well through questioning. Probably one of the other things they would do tied into that would, they wouldn't, they wouldn't pause enough. They wouldn't, um, stop to allow the other person to reflect on what they've said and to give them time to think about what they're going to say next and to reflect on what's being said to them. So that would be something we need to be careful of and to always remember that when we do pause when we communicate, it will seem a lot, seem quite a length of time to us, but it won't to the person we're speaking to.

I: And what about eye contact?

R: Well, if we don't look at someone, they immediately think that they can't trust us or we're not telling the truth, so eye contact is very important. We've got to make sure we get it right. If we give too much, they could

Audio script

perceive that we, er, we rather like them a little bit too much or maybe we're being a little aggressive towards them. So, we've got to get the eye contact about right; about three seconds in general is about right before we move away from the face, then come back to the eyes.

I: A situation I often find I have trouble with is when I need to complain about something. What sort of mistakes might I be making?

R: Well, I think it's very common to feel uncomfortable about making a complaint. Probably one of the most common things that people do in that situation is they're tempted to say far too much, so they become very unclear about the nature of the complaint – they, they're not precise enough. And they may well be tempted to speak far too quickly as well because, actually, we want to get to the end of the complaint because we don't particularly like complaining in the first place. We may also fall into the trap of not listening enough to what the other person has said because, actually, we may be becoming, becoming emotional, too, and therefore we listen less actively to what the person's saying to us and they, in turn, may not listen very well to us either, so the whole, um, complaint may become totally out of hand and we may end up completely falling out with one another. So, that's probably why complaints can be very difficult to, to handle.

I: So those are the problems you might encounter when you're complaining. How do you make a successful complaint?

R: Well, the first thing to do is to think and plan how you're going to voice your concerns. So, don't go straight into it – you've really got to think and consider what's going to, what needs to be said. Make sure the sentences are short. Take out any language which could be seen as being emotional and irritating to the other party. And then wait and be prepared to get a response from the other person whom you've made the complaint to – and really listen, actively, to what they are saying and summarise or test your understanding of what they've said to make sure you totally understand their point of view.

I: And when you summarise something, how, how do you do that effectively?

R: Well, if you think of summarising as being simply restating, in a more compact form, what the other person has said to you, so that you've included all the key things and, um, make sure that you've understood exactly what they're saying to you. So, restating in a compact form what's been said to us.

I: How do you summarise why good communication is so important?

R: Because in whatever situation we're in, we always have to deal with people and we have to communicate with people. And if we're going to get the best out of people and build relationships successfully, whether it be at work or in a social situation, we need to have good communication skills and we mustn't think that good communication skills are something that we all naturally have; it's something that we all need to work on to make sure that we build good relationships.

UNIT 5 RECORDING 3

A A: Karen, hi. Are you in the middle of something?
B: Sort of.
A: Well, shall I come back later?
B: No, no, it's all right. What can I do for you?
A: Sorry to disturb you. I'm having a lot of trouble with my computer. Every time I try to print something, I just get an error message.
B: Have you tried just turning it off and starting again?
A: Yes, well, it just seems to keep on happening. I thought if you had a minute, you might come and look at it for me – you did say if there was anything ...
B: And you've tried restarting it.
A: Yeah, I've done that. Same thing – it just keeps freezing when I try to print.
B: OK well, I've just got to finish this, if you'll just bear with me for a minute ...
A: Right.
B: OK, just let me send this off and I'll be right with you.
A: Thanks ... sorry to be a nuisance.
B: No, that's all right.

B A: Neil?
B: Hmm?
A: Do you fancy a walk?
B: What, you want to go for a walk? Now?

A: No, I thought you might. You know, a bit of exercise ... do you good.
B: No, not particularly. I'm OK here, thanks.
A: Right.
B: What made you say that?
A: Nothing, no reason. Neil?
B: Yeah?
A: Can I ask a really, really big favour?
B: Depends what it is.
A: You know the dry cleaner's down the road?
B: Mm.
A: You know it shuts at 8:00, doesn't it?
B: Ah! You want me to pick up your dry-cleaning.
A: It's just a couple of things. Oh, go on, I'd be really grateful.
B: So that's why you asked if I wanted a walk.
A: Well, partly yes, although I did think you looked like you wanted something to do.
B: I see. And is there something preventing you from going?
A: It's just that I wanted to see the end of this programme on the telly – I'm really into it now.
B: Oh, are you?
A: Oh, go on. I'll make you a cup of tea when you get back.
B: Oh, all right then.
A: Here's the ticket – there's two coats, a skirt ...

C A: Hi, how are you doing?
B: Fine, thank you.
A: May I disturb you for one moment? We have a small problem here and I wonder if you might be able to help me.
B: What's the problem, exactly?
A: As you'll have seen, the flight is very full this morning, so there are no spare seats anywhere.
B: Yeah?
A: We have a family with three small children. Unfortunately, they're sitting separately and, obviously, they would prefer to sit together.
B: Yes. And you want me to move.
A: Would that be at all possible?
B: Well, I'm very comfortable here, actually. I did ask for an aisle seat.
A: Well, we can move you to an aisle seat if you prefer. We would very much appreciate it if you could help us here.
B: Well, I don't see why I should. I mean, I did ask for an aisle seat. Why don't you ask someone else?

D A: ... and as I said, there's absolutely no way we can ... Excuse me a moment. James! Yeah, yeah, I can hear you, yes, just about. Right. Well, I'm, I'm just having dinner. Right. Listen, I'd better ring you back – is that OK? Right. Sorry about that. I'll just give him a ring back ...
B: Excuse me, sir.
A: Yes?
B: I must ask you not to use your mobile phone in the restaurant. Perhaps you could make your call outside if you don't mind.
A: Oh, I didn't realise.
B: It is the policy of the restaurant. Some diners complain that it's disturbing for them.
A: Fair enough. If you say so.
B: Thank you, sir. Enjoy the rest of your meal.

UNIT 6 RECORDING 1

1 I think the prices, the price to go to college is just ridiculous. Um, I was lucky enough that my parents helped me out and that I got a loan, which I'll have to pay for the rest of my life. But, um, like one of my best friends, she is an amazing student and she wanted to go to art school, but she can't because the fees are too high, and I think that putting a limit on people because of, for education, because of money is, is completely unfair.

2 Yeah, the thing I just think is wrong 'cos it is, uh, this amount of exams that they have to study for, kids when they're so young, I mean, you know, kids are kids – kids have to play. They go to school and they work at school, presumably, and they come out and at half past three, four, they're still expected to work, and it's all, you know, to get these exams, to get in some league table and competition, competition.
I just think it's bad for a child. I mean, even, in my opinion, a, a kind of early teenager – 12, 13 – they need their time to experiment and play and, you know, enjoy life a bit.

3 Yeah, I think my issue with, um, schooling for, uh, young children, um, in this country is the fact that they have to go to school when they're so young, when they're four and a half which is, is really a baby, and I, I think there's something really wrong about that. Um, I certainly noticed when my daughter went to school at the age of four and a half that her behaviour changed quite radically, not for the best. Um, and also, uh, I think they need to be at home to develop their own sense of identity for as long as possible.

4 You don't have to be a genius to know that if you don't invest in the younger generation, then problems are gonna come around later on, when they get big. And class sizes is very important because if you have too many children in a class at the same time, the teacher has an impossible task of trying to contain them – because there's simply too many of them. If you had smaller class sizes, the children would learn a lot more.

UNIT 6 RECORDING 2

1 **Gina:** I actually went to theatre school, um, from about the age of ten, and, for people who don't know, you, you basically are at, um, a school like anybody else, except for during the day you'll do your academic classes, um, and then you'll switch to a vocational class. So you may do an English class and then do singing and then come back after lunch and do ballet and then finish off with French, for example.

So that's how it works. Um, I didn't board there and I was there till I was 14. And I would say the, the best things about it is that you have an amazing time. If you love everything about, you know, theatre and, and acting and showbiz, then you have the time of your life, and I absolutely did.

Um, there's very little bullying because bullying usually happens when people don't see eye to eye, and we all had the same, um, sort of goals. And, um, other positives were that you become incredibly mature very quickly. You're, you're earning money for what you do, so your friends at normal schools are doing what normal kids tend to do and you'll be working professionally instead of doing a show, you'll, you'll be getting paid for yours. And um, and I generally found that was a really good thing, it makes you grow up. On the other hand, you could criticise it, um, for being perhaps too, um, worldly wise in making you too grown up, um, too quickly, perhaps.

I know that some people felt that they lost a bit of their childhood and, you know, worrying about work and getting auditions, there's plenty of time for that, so that was one thing. And I think also that some children were there that didn't really want to be there – their parents wanted them to be there – and that's kind of awful, uh, if that was the case. And I also think that, um, you can argue that in some of these schools your education suffers a little bit because, really, everybody's far more interested in the singing and the drama and the dancing than they are doing their English and maths and stuff. So I think that about sums it up.

2 **Steve:** So, yeah, my education was quite unusual, um, compared to other people, perhaps because I went to boarding school, um, and, um, I actually went to boarding school from the age of eight. Um, it was a very traditional school. And so there were lots of rules and regulations and traditions, um, and, um, we had, sort of a very old-fashioned uniform. Um, there was a lot of, um, it was, um, a very, very busy schedule – uh, we had almost no free time at all.

There, there were classes all through the day, um, and some afternoons there was sport or there was music. And at the weekends we also had things like, well, there was, we had classes in the Saturday morning, on Saturday morning, uh, usually sport in the afternoon. And then on Sunday we used to have, to have the, uh, church service, and then there'd be more music.

So probably the only bit of free time, uh, long bit of free time that we ever got was on a Sunday afternoon. Um, but I, I enjoyed it, my time there – I mean, I look back on it very fondly. I made lots of, um, very good friends there and I think it helped me, certainly, to, um, to become very focused on, on, uh, goals and, and that sort of thing and to deal with busy, busy, uh, schedules. So, um, overall, I, I have very fond memories.

UNIT 6 RECORDING 3

1 **Eva:** So I went to a, uh, bilingual school growing up, um, a French-American school, actually. And, um I, when I came to the school I was five years old and I, I didn't know how to speak French at all. Um, my parents aren't French, and, um, I'm fluent in French today, thanks to the school. So in that respect, I think bilingual education is fantastic because children learn languages so much more easily, um, when they're, you know, when they're young. And it, it was wonderful because we had subjects in English and in French, um, so there was a lot of work but, but I feel like a very, I had a very well rounded education as a child. Um, also, a lot of my friends were from different countries – it was quite an international school. So I feel like today I have all these friends, from all over the world, which is fantastic. Um, the minus side to it was that my parents are actually not French. So I was, I felt a little bit – given, given that I was the only Polish person there, uh, I'm from a Polish-American background but other than that, um, I'm, I'm really grateful that I got to experience, uh, such an education.

2 **Lester:** So, um, I went to several quite different ordinary schools, and I didn't fit in very well at any of them. And so when I was eleven, my parents decided to try educating me at home instead, and I actually really thrived on it. They taught me some subjects and they set the overall pattern, but an awful lot of it was self-directed.

And, um, I never actually went back to school as such. I went on to, um, some night classes and a sixth form college to get some qualifications, eventually. But, um, what I really learnt on my own, I mean, it was great being able to dive into the subjects that really interested me and not having to just do them to the official level.

But what I really learnt was how to, how to learn, how to make myself teach myself, and that's actually been incredibly valuable; um, as I work in a technology job, which is changing all the time, I'm actually still using that ability, long after all the actual subject matter, it doesn't matter that much.

Um, so for me, I think it's great, but I did meet some people through it who were a bit aimless, I think. Um, as for things that could have been a bit better, I have plenty of friends cos I've been to various different schools, but I didn't really meet people outside my circle of friends. So when I went to university, things were adjusting to a much bigger, more complicated social environment and starting to go out, and things was actually really hard.

You got into it, but it cost me a year of being a bit disoriented. Um, but all in all, it was really good for me, but it is very different to what anyone else I've ever met's been through.

UNIT 6 RECORDING 4

1 I need to talk to you. Don't rush off!
2 You're walking far too fast for me. Can't you slow down?
3 I'm not waiting any longer. I'm sick of hanging around!
4 Can you put your hands up, please? Don't shout out!
5 We need to get moving, guys. Eat up!
6 Those two seem to be getting on well. Look, they're chatting away!
7 Have you finished with that? Can you put it back?
8 OK everyone, get out your pens. Write this down.

UNIT 6 RECORDING 5

There are times in life when it comes in handy to know a little bit about what to do in an emergency. Say the guy in front of you collapses. What do you do? First of all, you need to check him over. If he isn't breathing, is unresponsive or is breathing like this, it's time to do something. First priority: call an ambulance. The sooner you call, the sooner they can be there with the specialist equipment that could save his life. Then it's time to do some emergency resuscitation. Don't attempt mouth-to-mouth resuscitation unless you are properly trained – no need for kissing! Just go for hands only, or CPR. To do this, you need to put the heel of your hand on the centre of his breastbone – yep, right where a pendant necklace would hang.

Then you need to clasp your hands together like this and press straight down to a depth of about four to six centimetres. Now work hard and fast – use your full body weight and aim to press down about twice a second. Don't worry that you might hurt him – a cracked rib is nothing much to worry about.

And whatever you do, don't stop – keep going until the ambulance arrives! If you want to know more about coming in handy in an emergency, then visit our website at w-w-w, dot, national heart campaign, dot ...

Audio script

UNIT 7 RECORDING 1

1 Well, this lady looks quite extravagant, um, in a fun way, I think, and in an unconventional way. Um, there's also something quite provocative, actually, about the way she's, she's looking, um, she's looking out at the camera, I think. I think she should wear a little bit less make-up and a little bit less jewellery. Um, but other than that, I think it's, it's, it's quite fun, what she's wearing.

2 To be honest with you, I really love this kind of, you know, modern architecture, um, I mean, I like some of the old stuff as well. But, but for me, something, if you look at that, I mean, it's just so sleek, isn't it? It's just like, just arrived from outer space – just love the design, the way there's a curve on one side and a, you know, minimal flat kind of wall on the other side. Just think, it's just one, I think that'll be there, you know, for future generations, and they're gonna absolutely love these kind of buildings.

3 Yes, I'm looking at a picture of a very attractive, uh, woman, wearing a really, really frumpy suit, which does nothing for her whatsoever. Um, the colour doesn't suit her, sort of sky blue, her jacket is a sort of boxy shape, which has no shapes – you can't really see her figure. And she's wearing white stilettos, which, well, well, you know, I was always raised to, to, to believe that white stilettos were a bit tacky, really. So, um, I think she's going for something sophisticated, but I don't actually think, um, it works in this instance. Um, so I think she would look better in something entirely different; in fact, it makes her look older than she probably is.

4 Well, I love him, but this picture is not the best that I've seen of him – it's not, um, not the usual clean-cut image that I expect. In fact, he looks rather scruffy in it, which, yeah, it doesn't work for me at all – I'm not into messy looks, I like something a bit more refined and sophisticated and elegant.

5 Well, it's abstract, uh, it's an oil painting, heavy use of oils with broad brash, uh, brush strokes. It's, uh, not to my taste, to say the least, um, but it would probably fetch an exorbitant amount of money. But it is, uh, very garish and, um, looks like the work of a five-year-old.

6 I absolutely love this design. I think it's a real classic, um, and it's so fantastic to see them come back in a way, especially as they're often digital radios, but they look just like the ones, the vintage ones that my, uh, my grandma used to have when I was little, I remember. So yeah, I'm a real fan – I think it really, really works.

7 Oh, I see, I don't like this, um, this fashion for grown women, and this lady looks to be, you know, maybe 30-something, wearing the top of a five-year-old with a hideous kitten on the front of it. Yeah, I just think it's a sort of twee childish look which, um I, I think is best left for the children, really.

UNIT 7 RECORDING 3

I = Interviewer   T = Tony

I: What were the weirdest fashions in history?

T: Some of the greatest excesses in the history of fashion – and I think most people would agree – took place in the European courts of the 18th century. First of all, there were the women's dresses. The panniers at the side of these dresses, which were kind of wire cages, built underneath the skirt, meant that one of these court ladies would take up the space of maybe three men and would have had to walk sideways through most doors! The aristocrats who lived in these courts, who were, of course, only a tiny elite in society, they saw their clothes as a way of displaying their wealth. They dressed in a lavish way to show off their economic status and, of course, their clothes showed that they didn't have to work or do anything practical. And then there were the vast powdered wigs worn by both men and women; though I do think some of the stories told about them are, in fact exaggerated – I don't know, for example, if many people really had mice living in their wigs or if people really slept in a seated position because of their wigs, but the story of a wig with a model ship built into it is certainly a true one – that really did happen! What is rather strange is that when Americans and Europeans of this period travelled to Japan, they found the fashion amongst wealthy Japanese men for wearing their ponytail stuck to the top of their head Samurai-style, very strange; they wrote about it in their diaries. It didn't seem to occur to them that their own preference for enormously tall wigs must have looked pretty weird, too!

I: Which was the most uncomfortable or harmful fashion in history?

T: There are a lot of contenders for this title, mostly affecting women, of course, since one recurrent feature of fashion throughout history is the way it has made women physically weaker – even disabled in extreme cases, we could say – in order perhaps to make men feel stronger and more powerful. In America and Europe I think we would have to point to the corset, worn by women for so many centuries – these frequently restricted breathing, broke ribs and even caused miscarriages – they really could be very dangerous garments! There was also the rather strange fashion of about 100 years ago of wearing 'hobble skirts'. These skirts mimicked the styles worn by Japanese Geishas and they were so tight round the ankles that women could only walk with the tiniest steps. They apparently wore belts round their ankles to keep their steps short enough! And, of course, there are similar examples in many cultures – the neck rings worn by Padaung tribeswomen from childhood, intended to lengthen their necks, which can also deform their shoulders, and, of course, the tradition of binding the feet of female children to keep them small and 'dainty', which survived in China until the beginning of the 20th century. And I guess many of the super-high-heeled shoes that we see on catwalks today fall into this category. The history of fashion is full of incredibly uncomfortable, impractical garments, in actual fact!

I: What was the biggest moment of change in fashion history?

T: I think I would point to two moments in modern history, really. Perhaps the most important one – for women in many countries, at least – was at the end of the First World War. During the war many women had been working in factories or driving carts and so forth, and they needed to wear more functional, less decorative clothes to reflect their new lifestyle. So the corsets were thrown away, skirt lengths went up from the ankles to just below the knee and long hair, which could get caught in factory machinery and so on, was cut short. Women's fashion essentially transformed from what it had been for centuries to what it is today. The other key moment I think was the 60s and the hippy movement. Up until that time people had seen clothes as a reflection of their place in society, so a labourer would wear a different type of hat from a man who worked in an office, for example. But from the hippy era onwards people began to see clothes much more as a way of expressing who they were – a way of expressing their individuality by growing their hair, wearing bright colours or whatever they felt like, and that is something that has remained with us to a greater or lesser extent, I think.

I: In your opinion, what are the worst fashions of recent times?

T: Oh, I'm spoilt for choice here – I can think of so many! In recent years I would probably pick out hanging pants – you know, that charming fashion for young men, or mostly young men, to wear their jeans so low that you can see their undergarments. I mean, how is that going to look in 20 years' time, really? Another trend I hate is wearing big glasses frames without any lenses in them – very pretentious, in my view. What else? Meggings, 'leggings for men'; that is not a good look in my book. Oh, and another thing I have seen on the catwalks recently which I really don't like is the fashion for wearing mega-high heels with ankle socks. Again, I don't think we'll look back in ten years' time and think, 'Wow, was that cool!' But really, there are so many examples that I could go on and on!

I: How long does it take on average for a fashion to be recycled and why do some fashions keep coming back?

T: It's generally reckoned that fashions make a comeback roughly every 20 years – they are usually at their most 'outdated' about 12 to 15 years after they were originally 'in'. As to why, I don't know if I can answer that question! I would like to say that it is usually the most elegant and classical styles that get recycled – like those of the 50s and early 60s, and we definitely do see those styles coming back again and again, but some of the ugliest fashions also make a comeback; platform shoes, for example, which seem to come back into fashion time and again, or jumpsuits, or shoulder pads! I think the truth is if you wait long enough, every fashion will come round again, so maybe we'll be seeing those low hanging pants again one day – ha!

UNIT 7 RECORDING 4

1 Am I pleased that we left!

2 I felt really sorry for Charlie when I saw him yesterday.

3 This flat is a mess. I do think you have a responsibility to help with

the housework.

4   I'm absolutely exhausted! I really need to get some sleep!

5   I'm sorry, but the way Gina behaves does annoy me.

6   I know you think I don't like your cooking, but I do like it.

7   I was definitely relieved when the day was over!

UNIT 7 RECORDING 5

1   Can you identify this common ... effect? That's right, it's wind. But have you ever wondered how ...

2   **A:** Is it OK if I use your photocopier? I just need one copy.
    B: ... free. It's over there, just by the coffee machine.

3   Henri obviously isn't happy with that decision. He hasn't said anything, but he's giving the referee a very dirty ... .

4   *Die Hard 10.* See it now at a cinema near you. Original ... track available from all good record stores.

5   Well, this to me is the problem of modern-day politicians. They don't have real policies. Instead, they just give us ... bites. To me, they're treating the public like fools. I mean, what do they ...

6   It's going to be the party of the year! It'll be fantastic! We've hired 20 Elton John ... alikes to serve the drinks, and that's not all. We've also got about ...

7   Now, I know you're in love, but that's no reason to marry the girl when you've only known her for a few weeks. ... before you leap – that's what they say.

8   *It's a Wonderful Life*, starring James Stewart, is still one of the most popular ... good movies of all time and is often shown around Christmas time.

9   Why not give us a call here on 94.5 FM Chat Radio and we're giving you the chance to ... off about any subject you feel strongly about. 88300 is the number and our first caller is on the line ...

10 Well, just look at that – an Olympic gold medal at the age of just 18 – and she looks absolutely delighted, doesn't she? She must ... on top of the world as she waves to the crowd ...

11 I think it's very important that all the employees in this company ... up to me. I am their boss, after all, and I think I deserve their respect.

12 **A:** ... and we're discussing today's news, that the Prime Minister has resigned. Charles Lowe, what's your view on this?
    B: Well, to be honest, I have mixed ... about it. Obviously, I'm very sad on the one hand, but on the other hand, I think this is ...

UNIT 7 RECORDING 6

1   Write down the name of a famous person who has a very good lookalike.

2   Write yes if you think most politicians in your country speak in sound bites and no if you think that is unfair.

3   Write down anything that would help to make you feel on top of the world.

4   Write down the name of someone you really look up to.

5   Write yes if you have a tendency to sound off about things you don't like and no if you usually keep quiet.

6   Write down the name of a film soundtrack you really like.

7   Write down the name of a famous person you have very mixed feelings about.

8   Write good if you think you are good at giving people dirty looks and not good if you're not.

UNIT 7 RECORDING 7

1   I love hip-hop music, I think it's such a cool form of music to dance to, just to listen to on your own, um, the beat alone is enough but if, if you listen to the lyrics, they're so, sometimes they can be so poetic and people criticise it for having swear words, but so many, so many rappers and rap groups don't even use swear words. And I think they're verbal geniuses, and, um, also just really enjoyable to listen to.

2   Now thing is right, is that you pay a lot of money to go and watch football, right? And we're looking at one of the best leagues in the world – these players are paid a fortune, we pay money to go and watch 'em, and then you get some idiot referee, comes along, doesn't know what offside is! Give goals to teams that haven't scored! And sometimes it goes over the line by at least two or three yards! And 'cos it's at a big club they don't give the goal! It's disgusting. I mean, I think they've bribed half of them, to be honest. You know they say it's all, no

corruption in, in the English game – I think it's a load of old nonsense!

3   There's one thing that really gets on my nerves – it's this sort of worship of the monarchy and royalty in this country. I fail to understand why there aren't, you know, riots on the streets when you see the amount of money and privilege and assets that these people have. And it seems very odd to me that it's the poorest people, very often, who are the ones that idolise them the most. There's something fundamentally immoral about, you know, people living in this amount of wealth and privilege when there are people who can't afford to heat their homes, who can't afford a home, even. Um, and it makes me absolutely furious, it really does.

4   Last week I was reminded of how much I absolutely love theatre. When it is good, there is nothing like it. And fortunately, last week I saw two productions that just took my breath away – they were absolutely spectacular. It's a type of magic because it's in that room, in that auditorium for only those people who are there; that's what separates it from film and television, is it's like its own well-kept secret. And it's just magic.

5   There's something I can't stand that everyone else seems to love these days, and it's social media. I don't know what it is – I feel a bit left behind and I feel a bit grumpy, and it's not a very nice feeling, but I cannot be doing with people telling me that they've just had this fantastic egg for breakfast or they, they've been shopping and they've just found this nice T-shirt and they want to share that with all their friends on, on Facebook. I think there's, there's a way of using it, these things so that you can keep in touch with friends, but don't tell me about some rubbish that's just happened to you just because you've got nothing else to do – honestly.

UNIT 7 RECORDING 8

1   Welcome to my review channel. My name's Greg and don't forget to click on the thumbs up icon if you like my video reviews. Today I'm going to be reviewing the new E series 9000 from Fabtran. I've had it for about a week now and I just want to tell you a few things about it and give you my opinion. Now, amazingly enough, you don't need to use a remote to operate this – you just need to wave your hand and use gestures to change the channel, the volume and that kind of thing. It's a great feature, but to be perfectly honest, I don't use it. I mean, imagine if someone walked into the room while I was waving at my TV; they'd think I was crazy! So I just use the normal remote and I'm glad to say that they include one of those with the package. And here it is – just looks like a normal remote, really. Lots of buttons that you'll never use. Anyway, let's talk about the quality of the image and the sound. Those are the really important things, right? I'm going to turn it on and, all being well, it's going to work. There! Now, to tell the truth, the sound quality is not the best in the world, but it's not the worst either and, actually, I think that given the price, it's fine. The image quality, however, is fantastic. The colours are vibrant and, quite frankly, it's got one of the best pictures I've ever seen, certainly at this price point.
    If you look on the back, you can see the connections. There are four HDMI connections, two USB connections, two ...

2   Hi, guys. My name's Monica and I just wanted to show you my new Red Circles that I bought online. They arrived today in the post and thank goodness I kept the receipt because they are going straight back for a refund! I really don't like them. There are a couple of reasons. Firstly, much to my surprise, the pockets are tiny! I mean, they're so shallow that I can't even fit my fingers in them, let alone my keys and my phone, so that's really disappointing. And I wouldn't want to put my hands in the pockets anyway because they'd get covered in blue dye. Yes, the worst thing about these is that the colour in the denim comes off really easily. They call it raw denim – apparently, it's quite trendy, but I really don't like it and it's a good job I didn't sit down on my white sofa because it would now be a blue sofa!
    As you can see, they've got buttons rather than a zip at the front, which I'm not very keen on, and to make matters worse, one of the buttons fell off while I was trying them on for the first time. Funnily enough, my friend bought exactly the same pair of jeans and one of her buttons fell off, too. To my utter astonishment, however, she likes her jeans and doesn't seem to care that the dye comes off. Well, she's not going to sit on my sofa, that's all I can say!

Audio script

UNIT 8 RECORDING 1

1 My sister really drives me mad because she won't just have, you know, a normal conversation about something if we just disagree; she'll just go off into a corner and sulk, like a four-year-old and it'll last for ages – she can go on like this, she can not talk to me, she won't pick up the phone – it drives me mad! I'd rather just, you know, come out with it, say what the problem is and move on. You can't have a normal argument and get over it like most people. She doesn't get over it, it goes on and on and on; sometimes for months she'll be quiet and not say anything.

2 I share a dorm room with, um, my friend Laura and she's, she's really, she's really a lot of fun and she's really funny and we always have a good laugh about stuff happening at school. The only problem is that she never stops talking. I mean, like, I love, I love talking as well, but after a long day of classes and then I also have a part-time job, I sometimes just want to come into the dorm room and, and relax and, or do work or just chill out on my own, listen to music or something and she's just always there, and she always wants to tell me everything she's done in the day, um, which I'm glad to hear sometimes, but not all the time, just every single thing she's done that day every single, you know, thing she ate. It's just like I don't need to know every single detail going on in her life. Um, and I, I hate to say this but I, I just really wish she would shut up sometimes – just at least for a few minutes so I can think.

3 The worst thing about Tony, my ex-flatmate was his moods. Uh, he just would swing from one extreme to the other, so for one day he'd be full of jokes and laughs and conversations and I'd think, 'Ah, it's fantastic living with Tony,' and then literally the next day I'd come home and he'd just, he'd be monosyllabic or, or not even speak to me and he'd have a face like thunder. Um, and I felt like maybe I'd done something wrong, have I offended him, have I, you know, is my room too messy or something? And I just, ah, I couldn't be doing with it, you never knew where you stood with him.

4 A thing that really annoys me about my boyfriend is that he's incredibly opinionated and, um, takes the moral high ground on most things. Um, he has been described by people as a bit of a know-it-all. Um, he's got better latterly at sort of pretending to listen and take on board, um, other people's opinions. But you just know that deep down that he believes that he is the, the word of authority. And, um, I find that intensely annoying, actually.

5 One massive problem with my ex-husband was that he was tidy, but, I mean, to the point of fanatically tidy. You know, he would pick up, um, anything, if it had been lying on the floor for two seconds, there'd be a big 'Oh!' and a tut, and then it would be folded with military precision and then put in the correct place instantly, so I just couldn't leave anything, not even for five minutes. If I was going into the shower, left a towel on the floor, everything was then just 'Oh!', sighing and groaning about it, and then putting it away, but putting it away within two seconds and 'It has to go back in the right place, it cannot go in the wrong place, it must go in this place, which is specifically for the white towels!' Uh, drove me crazy!

UNIT 8 RECORDING 2

C = Catherine   P = Peter   L = Liz

C: Peter, did you use to be in the army?
P: Yes, in my time, you, you had to do national service when you were 18 years, and it was compulsory, so you had no choice.
C: So, how did you find it?
P: Well, I remember at the time I was really looking forward to it. It was an opportunity to go abroad and, er, live in other countries, and it was quite a shock when I got in.
L: What, what were you looking forward to? I can't imagine anything worse than being in the army!
P: Well, it was, I don't know, it was exciting, it was that boy thing – and shooting a rifle, and going abroad ... Yes, I remember I was really looking forward to it. The first thing they put in my hand was an iron and they showed us how to iron a shirt, which wasn't what I wanted to join the army for because I'd never ironed a shirt in my life. And then the next thing they did was they, they showed us how to sew a button on a shirt and how to darn a hole in a sock. I think it was about six weeks before I was even allowed to get my hands on a rifle at all.
C: Yeah, what about you, Liz? When did you leave home?

L: Oh, I ... well, I went to boarding school when I was 11. Um, I'd had a wonderfully free life growing up in the country in Australia and suddenly, at the age of 11, my parents decided that they wanted me to go to a school in the city. What about you?
C: Um, well, I started doing some au-pairing when I was 18. Um, I'd done French A level, so my French was relatively good, but still, you know, speaking, conversation and living in the French language for a month was very daunting.
L: And was it different to how you imagined it was going to be?
C: Um, I can't remember now what I'd imagined, but, I mean, we had some fantastic times – the weather was gorgeous every single day and we'd go down to the beach every day. Um, the kids were a good age, so they could go off and play, Um, but it wasn't all kind of playing on the beach, yeah, the parents really wanted them to learn English whilst I was there, so one of my roles was to teach them English, which for an eight-year-old and a ten-year-old on their summer holiday was not what they wanted to do at all, so we had quite a lot of battles, trying to get them to sit down at that dining room table, um, and do their work.
L: But what was it like, what was it like actually just living in a, you know, a place that you hadn't been to before, with a family that you weren't, that you didn't know, and living under somebody else's rules?
C: It – difficult. Being an au pair you're told what to do. You're there, you're getting paid, you're living in their house and you have to abide by their rules. I don't like being told what to do and to be told to go and put on the milk, to sweep the floors, to put the washing out – I find quite hard work, but after a couple of weeks you get to know the routine, so you start doing those kind of things yourself without having to be told. Um, but I did have moments when I just kind of stormed up to my room and shut the door, cos at 18 I was still quite young, I was still quite inexperienced and I found it quite difficult to deal with that.
L: Well, I suppose that's something that you had to do as well, didn't you? Live under, under the rules of the army at 18 – that must've been ...
P: Yes, that's right, yes. The, the discipline was very, very hard, but, um, there's one, another story that I remember about being in the army because, um, suddenly, we found ourselves in a long hut with about 30 beds with a short space between each bed and from all walks of life – we came from everywhere – and the man opposite me, he was a huge man and he was one of these people that you avoided eye contact with because, um, if you so much as glanced at him, he looked as if he was ready to, to attack you. And he had this thick, Elvis Presley-style hairstyle, and, um, on the second day we were marched to the barber shop to have our hair cut and they just cut the whole lot off, and I remember him standing outside, afterwards, and he was, he looked like an overgrown schoolboy, and he was crying – there was tears running down his cheek – and he was quiet for about two days and then after that you couldn't have met a nicer person. He did everything, he joined in everything and he was, he was really completely different.
C: So it was just his hair gave him an ego.
L: Perhaps that was his way of coping in an alien environment.
P: Could be, yeah.
C: How did you feel about having your head shaved, then? I mean, did you ...
P: Well, they didn't actually shave it; they just they gave us what was known in those days as 'a short back and sides'.
C: But did you feel like you lost your individuality?
P: Um, yeah, because that was the whole idea – to make, to make you work as, as one unit so that if they, if they shouted 'Jump!', then 30 men jumped at the same time because that was the whole objective, to, um, to discipline people and to make you an effective force.
L: How did that affect you? How do you feel about it now, looking back?
P: Um, well, at the time it, it was a bit scary, but looking back now, I think it was, it was a good time.
L: Mm ... how boarding school affected me. Well, I said earlier it made me a more independent person and at the time, at the time I hated it. I hated the rules, I hated the regulations, but it did, it did, as I said, give me independence, but it also made me a quite conscientious person because I got used to studying and I think as a result of that, I developed into a very different person, at the end of the day, than I would have done had I stayed in Australia – you know, living my free life in the countryside. So I suppose, looking back, looking back, I'm very grateful that my parents made that decision to send me away, but, certainly, I didn't feel that when I was 11.

UNIT 8 RECORDING 3

1 I'll just take your coat for you.
2 I was so annoyed, I just tore up the letter and walked out.
3 I'm just looking, thank you.
4 The weather was just perfect for my birthday party.
5 These shoes are just what I need.
6 I'll just be a few minutes and then we can go.
7 Look! I've just found that receipt you were looking for.
8 Lunch is just a sandwich. I hope that's OK.
9 Would you mind just holding this for me, please?
10 I've got just enough money to pay!

UNIT 8 RECORDING 4

1 Annie loves her new job. I think it's given her a sense of security at last.
2 He's got this big fear of rejection. I think that's why he won't apply for promotion.
3 You know Hannah – she's always had a love of adventure.
4 Don't take any notice of me. You know I've got a tendency to worry about the slightest thing.
5 I get so fed up of Al! Why does he feel a constant need to show off?
6 I think my mother always felt an enormous desire to please other people.
7 For someone so talented, Ben's got an amazing lack of ambition!
8 One thing you can say about Martin – he's got a great sense of fun!
9 Sorry if I keep asking you the same thing again and again – I've just got this need for reassurance.
10 You can't keep secrets from Alex – she's got this strange ability to read your mind.
11 I'm so glad I've done all that filing. It's given me a weird sense of achievement.
12 It's no good talking to Andy – he's got a complete inability to see other people's point of view.

UNIT 9 RECORDING 1

P = Presenter   B = Benta   K = Kevin

P: ... and no doubt we'll be hearing more about that in the future. Now, while most of us are increasingly feeling like we're drowning in a sea of data, there are some people who can't get enough of it, particularly as it applies to their own lives. Our reporter, Benta McDonald, went to meet some of the people who are living by numbers.

B: How much time do I spend on Facebook? Does coffee really help me to concentrate? Where did I go and what did I do on Sunday five weeks ago? Most of us rely on gut instinct or vague memories to answer questions like these, but there is a growing band of people who are not content to guess. They want cold, hard data and they wouldn't dream of making a decision without it; and modern technology is making it easier and easier for them to collect and analyse huge quantities of data, particularly with the help of that small personal computer called a mobile phone. Sometimes called 'the Quantified Self movement', sometimes called 'self-tracking', this trend is rapidly changing what we know and how we live and it's coming to all of us very soon, according to self-tracking addict Kevin Briar.

K: Measuring stuff isn't new, you know. We're used to measuring our height, our weight, our temperature when we're sick and stuff like that, but the self-tracking movement is taking it all to a whole new level. And it's not just about health and fitness – that's old-school stuff now, you know. Serious self-trackers are tracking more and more complex stuff like their sleep patterns, how much time they spend daydreaming, how their mood changes over time, what affects their brainwave patterns – you know, that sort of thing. And more and more people are doing it, you know. It's becoming mainstream.

B: So what do you track and how do you track it?

K: Well, for example, I have a special fork that tracks how many bites I've taken.

B: How many bites?

K: Yeah, like 80 is supposed to be the optimum amount to feel full, so my fork tells me if I've had more than 80 bites in a day. And it tells me how long it takes me to eat my meal and it sends all that information straight to my computer so that I can see on a graph if I'm eating too fast or too much.

B: Wow! What else?

K: Well, I wear a tiny camera everywhere I go, which takes a photo every 30 seconds and then stores the photos in the cloud, so anytime I want to I can look up a date, say 15th July last year, and actually see what I was doing, where I went, what I ate, who I talked to – that sort of thing. And then I can cross-reference it to my mood database and see how I felt. And over time, I get a picture of what makes me happy and what makes my life better, and I can put that knowledge into action. Knowledge is power, you know, and knowledge comes from information.

B: And Kevin is a relative lightweight compared to some others in the Quantified Self movement. Lucy Granger, for example, keeps a popular blog where she shares data on over 50 different aspects of her life that she tracks, including caffeine intake, sleep patterns and time spent on social media. She even keeps a database of all the thoughts and ideas that she has, each one dated and tagged so that she knows not only what she was doing five years ago, but also what she was thinking about. But the real question is, perhaps, with all this data and analysis, when do you have time to actually live?

UNIT 9 RECORDING 2

P = Presenter   C = Charlotte   R = Roger

P: Following on from Benta McDonald's report, we have two guests in the studio to debate the merits of the Quantified Self movement. Roger Acton, a journalist, blogger, author and committed self-tracker, and Charlotte Marling, artist, winner of the Turner Prize and vociferous anti-self-tracker! Charlotte, why are you so against tracking? Isn't it true that the more we know about ourselves, the better?

C: Yes, of course it is, but you have to learn useful things about yourself. The trouble with self-tracking is that you learn nothing useful about yourself and you waste a lot of time. I mean, apart from the money spent on buying tracking devices and the time spent collecting the data, you then have to spend hours looking at the data in order to learn anything. And what do you learn? That you've spent three hours daydreaming or you've had 90 mouthfuls of food. How does that help?

R: I think it helps a lot, actually. If I find out that I'm eating 90 mouthfuls of food, then, probably, I'm overeating – and that's not healthy. And if I'm spending three hours a day daydreaming, then I'm not being very efficient, so I need to change.

C: That's exactly the problem, you see. People like Roger believe that everything can be reduced to numbers. It's just a typical male obsession with data, like collecting information on football teams.

R: Actually, a lot of self-trackers are female.

C: The point is ...

R: And I don't like football!

C: The point is, if I spend all my time collecting and analysing data, then when am I supposed to actually live? You can't measure the important things, like how sunshine makes you feel or how important your friends are.

R: Self-tracking doesn't stop you living. It helps you to live better. I'll give you an example: through self-tracking, I discovered that I'm mentally at my best in the afternoon between two and five, so I make sure that I do all my boring paperwork in the morning and keep the afternoon clear for important work. That's made me much more efficient. It's made me a better person.

C: What would make you a better person is to spend more time with your friends and family, and not with your spreadsheets and databases!

P: Do you spend too much time tracking and not enough time enjoying life, Roger?

R: No, not at all. Self-tracking is a social movement. There are Quantified Self meetings in over 100 cities all over the world. People come together to talk, to share experiences.

C: They come together to compare spreadsheets, you mean!

R: No, Charlotte, you're wrong. The trouble with you is that you're afraid of what you might learn.

C: I am not!

R: You're afraid that you may learn how unhappy or unhealthy or inefficient you are. You're afraid of the truth. Why not try self-tracking, Charlotte? Why not give it a go?

C: Because it's a waste of time and money ...

P: That's all we've got time for, I'm afraid.

C: ... and I don't need numbers to tell me how I feel!

P: Thank you, thank you. I'm sure we'll be coming back to this debate in the future, but in the meantime, it's time for ...

Audio script

UNIT 9 RECORDING 4

1 My invention is something that I often imagine because, like a lot of people, I quite often mislay everyday objects and I spend a lot of time hunting for them, especially when I'm just about to leave the house, which, of course, often makes me late. It could be my keys or my wallet or my bag or my shoes or my phone, except there's one difference with my phone because I can call it and find it – because it rings! So, my invention would be a small device, about the size of a button, say, which you could attach to those everyday objects that you often lose and which would be linked to your phone, so that you could call them too if you lost them. You could call your keys or call your shoes and they would ring and you would be able to find them in seconds, instead of spending hours searching for them.

2 In an age when society has so many problems with obesity and stress, I think the idea of having a play area for adults makes perfect sense. It would be much more convenient and fun than going to the gym. There would be climbing walls and adult-sized swings and slides, all of which would be really good for building up muscles, using up calories and getting rid of stress. And you could have trampolines, which again are fantastic exercise and really good fun. I think it would appeal to people of all ages, from teenagers to pensioners, men and women. And more importantly, people wouldn't have to make a special decision to go there, and change into special clothes like they have to do when they go to the gym. They could just use it whenever they felt like it, just for five or ten minutes, as they were passing. It would be a great way of socialising, too – much healthier than meeting people for a meal or film and much more fun, too. I think they would soon become hugely popular and spring up in parks everywhere.

3 This is a really simple idea, but I think it would make public transport much more user-friendly and offer a greatly improved service. Time and time again it happens that you see your bus and start running for it, but just as you get there, the doors close and it pulls away. But I'm sure that most drivers would wait for you if they knew you were only a few seconds away. How many times have you wished you could just communicate with the driver and let him know how close you are? So, basically, the idea would be that for a certain fee, you could buy a special bus pass and there would be a chip built in that would connect with the bus and maybe beep or make a light flash or whatever and let the bus driver know that you were running along the road and only a few seconds away, so that he could wait for you. You would never have the frustration of missing your bus in the morning and being late for work or college ever again! I really think this could make a lot of money for bus companies, and make passengers' lives a lot easier!

4 My invention is very simple and very practical, but I think there could be a real market for it. It would be an app that made use of the camera on your phone to photograph and take the exact measurement of things. Its main use would be when you go shopping. If you are buying a new cupboard, for example, you could take a photograph of the space where you want to put it, with its measurements, then when you get to the shop, you could take a photograph of the cupboard and you would know straightaway whether or not it would fit. Or if you were shopping for clothes, you wouldn't need to spend hours trying on different sizes – because, let's face it, sizes vary dramatically from shop to shop – you could just photograph the garment, then compare it with your measurements, which you would keep stored on the app and then just try on the garments that were the right size, saving yourself a lot of time. As I say, I think there's potentially a real market for this – I believe it could catch on in the same way sat navs have. If you think about it, it's potentially just as useful.

5 Whenever polls are done to find out what everyday behaviour people find most annoying, tailgating on motorways – people driving too close to the back of your car in the fast lane – is one of the most common issues. It is nearly always done by people who are breaking the speed limit and it's very dangerous: accidents are much more likely to be fatal if the two vehicles are close together and it's also very distracting and stressful for the person being tailgated. But the problem is that there's no way of communicating with the tailgater to tell him – and it usually is a him! – to back off. You can't flash your lights at him or anything like that. So my invention would be very simple: it would be a sign that lights up on the back of the car and says 'keep your distance', with maybe a sad face that changes to a smiley face when they go back to the correct distance. It would make motorways much safer places and really reduce the stress for most people who just want to drive in a safe way and stick to the speed limit.

UNIT 9 RECORDING 5

1 A: Hello, Software Support. Have you got a service code?
B: Yes, it's CLX8D9Y.
A: OK, is that Ms Raynes?
B: That's right.
A: How can I help you?
B: Well, I'm having some problems with the laptop I bought from your company.
A: What kind of problems are you having?
B: I've only had it a couple of days, but it won't connect to the internet.
A: Can you describe the problem to me?
B: Yeah, well, some of the time it's OK, but most of the time the computer just can't find my wireless router, but when it does and I type in the password, it throws up an error message.
A: And is your router plugged in and turned on all the time?
B: Yes, it is. We've got two other computers in the house and they're both connected the whole time, no problem.
A: Hm … Are you having any other problems with the computer?
B: Well, it's running very slowly and, occasionally, the screen freezes and I have to reboot.
A: When does it freeze?
B: For example, if I try to cut and paste something.
A: OK, have you run the system scan?
B: No, I haven't. How do I do that?
A: I'll talk you through it, but first I just need to check: have you backed up all your files to an external hard disk?
B: Yes, I have.
A: OK, is your computer on now and are you next to it?
B: Yes.
A: Then let's start by closing down any programs that are open.
B: OK, I'll do that now.

2 C: Hi, can I help you?
D: Yes, I'm having some problems with my new phone and I wondered if you could help me.
C: Have you got your receipt?
D: I didn't print out a hard copy, but I've got the confirmation email here. If you scroll down to the bottom you can see it.
C: OK, that's fine. If you tell me what the problem is, then I'll see what I can do.
D: Well, the phone can't seem to find a signal.
C: It can't find a mobile signal?
D: That's right. So I can't make or receive calls. It's pretty useless as a phone, really.
C: Have you done anything to the phone – you know, dropped it or installed any illegal software or anything?
D: No, I haven't. When I first got the phone, I had to update the operating system and then it asked me to set up an account and create a new password, which I did, but now it just doesn't work, basically.
C: Does the phone crash sometimes?
D: It's crashed a couple of times.
C: Have you reset the phone?
D: How do you do that?
C: You turn it off and remove the battery. That usually solves the problem.
D: I haven't tried that. Shall I give it a go now?
C: Sure, do that and see if it helps …

3 E: That's £2.95 altogether, please.
F: I've only got a twenty, I'm afraid.
E: That's fine. I'm sorry, the drawer's jammed. I can't open it. I'll have to call my manager. Mr Walsh!
G: Yes, Lucy.
E: The cash till seems to have broken again. I think the drawer's jammed this time.
G: OK, let me have a look at it. There's a latch under the drawer and if you release the latch, then … it should open!
E: Great, thanks. What do I do now? The screen is blank – nothing's happening.
G: I'm so sorry, madam – this till is very temperamental.

F: That's OK.
G: Lucy, press 'Clear'. Is anything happening?
E: Nothing. It's dead as a dodo!
G: Hold down 'Clear' and press 'Delete'. It's a process of trial and error sometimes.
E: Still nothing.
G: OK, turn it off and turn it on again.
E: That's better.
G: You'll have to scan everything again.
E: OK. Sorry, madam, could I rescan the items in your bag?
F: Sure. Here you are.

UNIT 10 RECORDING 1

This is the true story of an undercover police officer who fell in love with the people he was supposed to be spying on. Names and some details have been changed to protect the identity of those involved.

Jon K grew up on the outskirts of Leeds. The son of a well-respected transport police officer, he followed his father's example and joined the police force at the age of 21. 'You'll never be rich,' his father told him, 'but you'll be proud of what you've done.' Jon quickly impressed his superior officers and he began working as an undercover officer, helping to arrest drug dealers. He got married and had two children, but his taste for adventure meant that he was an unconventional father. He also loved going to punk rock concerts and he was an expert climber, which meant that he was frequently away on climbing trips all over Europe. Because he was good at his job, Jon was asked to join a new police unit, part of whose role was to spy on environmental groups. He was given training and a new identity. He grew his hair long, got his ears pierced and had several tattoos done. He learned to be vegan and when he was ready, started to infiltrate the activists. It wasn't easy to be accepted at first, but Jon's experience as a climber proved very useful as the group frequently climbed towers and tall buildings in order to hang protest banners. Slowly, the other protestors came to know and trust Jon. They nicknamed him 'Johnny Cash' because, unlike many of them, Jon always seemed to have as much money as he needed. For his part, Jon was sympathetic to the environmental movement and what it was trying to achieve. Many of its members were people much like him and he justified his job by telling himself that he wasn't harming the protestors by spying on them; quite the opposite, in fact. By providing the police with intelligence on their activities, he was helping to protect them. He felt that if the police knew what the activists were planning, they could make sure no one got hurt. It wasn't long, however, before Jon began to question this view and wonder which side was right.

UNIT 10 RECORDING 2

In Edinburgh in 2004, Jon joined thousands of other activists at a protest. To protect his identity, local police were not told that an undercover agent was present. As the protestors pushed forward, Jon, who was at the front, found himself under attack. He was hit by a police baton. One of his fellow protestors jumped in to protect him and was also hit. Battered and bruised, Jon left the protest in a state of confusion. The intelligence he was providing was supposed to prevent violence happening, but instead, he had been attacked by his police colleagues and protected by the people he was spying on. It wasn't easy to understand.

It was also becoming increasingly difficult for Jon to reconcile his two lives. Every few weeks he returned home to see his wife and children, but he was a different man from the one his wife had known. He grew vegetables in the garden, refused to eat meat and, eventually, he and his wife became estranged. They stayed together for the children, but their marriage was effectively over. Around this time, Jon also fell in love with a woman in the movement. They became inseparable and spent as much time together as possible. Being in love, Jon found it difficult to lie to her about his true identity. Despite this, his career was going well and his senior officers were pleased with the intelligence he was giving them. The final straw, however, came in 2009, when Jon was asked to secretly record a group who were planning to shut down an oil refinery. Jon was torn because many of the protestors were his friends and he knew that his evidence might send some of them to jail. Reluctantly, he agreed. On the day that the activists planned to shut down the refinery, the police burst into the hall where the group were staying and arrested everyone – over 100 people. They eventually charged just 19 of them and, to his amazement, Jon was one of them. When he asked his senior officers why he was being charged, they said that it was out of their hands. Jon began to suspect he was being set up. He knew that he couldn't go to court and be charged because his identity was false and he didn't really exist – he would be found out. He also knew that if the police dropped the charges against him, his friends in the movement would become suspicious. For the first time, Jon had no idea what he should do.

UNIT 10 RECORDING 3

One week before Jon was due to go to court, all charges against him were dropped. He had hoped that the charges against the other 18 would also be dropped, but this didn't happen and Jon was now under suspicion from both sides. The police worried that he was too deeply involved with the activists and the activists worried that he was linked with the police. Everything quickly fell apart for Jon. He was told by his superior officers that his mission was ending and that he had to get out as soon as he could. When he asked what his next job would be, he was told that there was no work for him in the police force. Having spent many years undercover, he had no relevant skills for the modern workplace and he was no longer trusted by his fellow officers. Jon resigned. His father's words, that he would be proud of what he had done, seemed to ring hollow in his ears. Eventually, he decided that he had no option but to return to his life as an eco-activist. However, his girlfriend found his passport in his real name and the truth about his identity quickly came out. She was heartbroken and his friends in the protest movement turned against him. With all his bridges burned and with no one to help him, he fled to Canada and contemplated ending it all. One day, however, an old friend from the protest movement got in touch and offered him a chance for redemption. He asked Jon if he would return to the UK and help defend six of those who had been arrested trying to close down the oil refinery. Jon said yes and as a result of his help, charges against the six were dropped and the convictions of 15 other activists were overturned. The fallout from the case made headlines around the world. The government ordered an independent inquiry into the spying operation and Jon's ex-girlfriend sued the police for the distress they had caused her in allowing and encouraging one of their officers to form a relationship with her. Soon after, Jon himself decided to sue the police for failing to protect him from falling in love with the people he was sent to spy on.

UNIT 10 RECORDING 5

A A: Right, so I'm going to start with skills and abilities that I have. And you may not know this about me, but I am a qualified nail technician, so I can put on false nails and I can also do manicures and pedicures and all of that. That's my first one. And my second one is that I am an accomplished baker – I've won prizes for my cakes. I do cupcakes, I do all sorts of baking, that's my second one.
And my third one is that I'm an extremely fast touch typer, and I learnt at school and I kept it up, for secretarial work.
And my next skill and ability that I have is I can make jewellery – I make a lot of my own jewellery and I can string beads onto necklaces and so on.
And I, um, I also learnt accountancy and book-keeping and passed an exam in that. And – how many have I done? One, two, three, four, five. And my final skill and ability that I have is I can train dogs and I've trained quite a few – not just my own, but my friends'.
Um, so there you go that's, that's all my skills. Which ones are lies?
B: Oh my goodness, um …
A: You can have some questions.
B: Right, so, with the book-keeping, what exam did you say you took for that?
A: I sat a GCSE in accounts.
B: I see, OK.
A: OK, right, question two.
C: Um, these dogs, what were you actually training them to do?
A: They can, well, I can teach them to sit, walk, heel, and they can fetch and they can lie down. And if they're, like, retrievers, they're very, very good at stuff like that, so I'm very good at retrievers.
C: That's your speciality.
A: Specifically.
C: Right.
B: It … can I just ask you, if you were going to sit and do my nails what would you, what would be the first thing that you would do?
A: Right, well, it would depend if you wanted false nails or you wanted just a manicure.
B: No, I quite like some, can you do acrylic?

A: Yeah, no, I can't. I can do fibre glass.

B: Oh, fibre glass.

A: Yeah, so we'd start by buffing the nails.

B: Yes, right.

A: That would be the first thing I'd do.

B: Yeah.

A: And then you use a resin, which is like a glue.

B: Mm ...

C: So, you say you're an accomplished baker.

A: Yeah.

C: And did you train for this and if so, which college did you go to?

A: Well, in truth, I didn't train for it formally, but my mother was a supreme baker and she won loads of competitions, so she trained me up.

C: I see.

A: For about a year. OK, that's four questions – you've only got one question left. Who is going to ask me something?

C: I was wondering about the touch typing, what, do you know how many words you do per minute?

C: Forty-five words per minute?

A: Yeah, that's your lot. Any ideas?

C: So what do you think, guys?

D: Mm ... tricky, she was pretty convincing about nails after Sarah, wasn't she?

C: And also convincing about the, uh, typing.

D: Yeah.

C: There was no hesitation.

D: No. With dogs I was less convinced – a little wishy-washy. What do you think?

B: I agree with that and I thought the, um, the making jewellery was slightly wishy-washy.

D: Yeah.

C: Do you think?

D: And the baking. She's far too thin to be an accomplished baker.

C: Um, no, so we reckon dogs isn't likely, do we think that?

A: Are you going for that?

D: Um, I don't know.

C: I think so, no? Jewellery then?

B: I, I didn't, I didn't buy the jewellery.

D: I didn't buy the jewellery, so that's ...

C: OK, jewellery. That's it.

D: Jewellery was one thing. The dogs, I was, I wasn't convinced that she's, she's a dog trainer.

B: I would say book-keeping.

C: Maybe.

D: What and is the other lie?

B: Um ...

C: OK, jewellery, dogs and book-keeping.

D: Yeah I, I'm happy to go with that.

B: Um ...

A: OK, shall I tell you how many you've got right?

B: Um ...

C: Uh huh.

B: Yeah.

C: You got two right.

D: Aha. Not bad.

C: Oh. What are they?

A: There's still a lie there. So I didn't train dogs, I don't know how to do that at all. And I don't make jewellery.

B: No, OK, so ...

A: But I did take a GCSE in accounting.

B: No, it's the nails then.

C: No, the nails she was ...

A: No.

D: No, she, she ... no.

A: No, cos it takes more than an hour to do that.

D: Does it?

B: Uh huh.

D: Oh.

C: Oh.

D: Sounded pretty convincing to me.

A: I've only got one left, go for one.

D: What were the other things?

A: You've got baking, touch typist, nail technician.

D: Mm ...

C: I'd go for nails if you think it's ... you know more than me.

D: She sounded pretty convincing to me, but if you're sure.

A: Is that what you're going for? I am a trained nail technician, but I haven't won awards for baking cakes or anything.

B: Oh ...

D: Yeah, you see? Yeah, yeah.

A: I didn't train.

B A: OK, so I'm gonna tell you what I did last weekend. Um, my wife and I went up to Newcastle for a, for a twenty-four-hour visit, so it was pretty, pretty quick, but we got on the train at about 9 o'clock and, uh, had a very good journey up there. And, uh, we went to stay in this hotel and, um, we got chatting to the receptionist and she said it was a bit of quiet night, so she upgraded us to the honeymoon suite, which was frankly gorgeous.
Um, we went out to, um, have a look at Tynemouth festival, just outside Newcastle – there's this fantastic musical festival going on. Um, the bands were pretty good, but, really, what I liked most was the ice cream on sale – they had this little authentic old-fashioned ice cream seller. Um, so their ice creams were £1, which, frankly, you don't see very often these days.
Um, that evening we had a huge meal, a really lovely, lovely meal in a restaurant. Um, and, uh, and then got the train home the next day. The trouble with the train home was that, typically, there were delays, there were some, uh, I don't know, problems with the signalling or something, and we ended up having a, a four-hour journey back to London, so a bit of a shame at the end there. Any ideas?

B: OK, so ...

A: I thought I was gonna settle myself.

B: Yeah, well, we'll see about that.

A: OK.

B: Um, so what were your top three bands at the music festival?

A: Um, well, believe it or not, there was a band called Aswad, uh, which you may have, uh, may remember are quite old. Um, the other band I really liked were the, um, they were called The Calling, I believe, but they're a local, local band – kind of a funk outfit – they, they were pretty good. Um, I can't really remember the other names of the, the bands, but they, there were some very good ones. There was a, a kind of, a sort of Caribbean-sounding band which I, which I really liked.

B: Great, OK. Um, what about the name of the restaurant?

A: The name of the restaurant was called The Bahullish and it was a sort of, it was very dark, very trendy, but, um, I'm, people are there telling us that, that's where all the footballers go to eat, so we felt quite, um, quite posh, but it was a very, very nice meal.

B: OK, um, and, uh, how would you describe the, uh, the bathroom in the honeymoon suite?

A: Opulent – um, there were sort of gold taps and it wasn't so much of a bath – it was more like a Jacuzzi, it was, uh, it was absolutely gorgeous! I could very much get used to that.

B: And, uh, how long was your journey to Newcastle?

A: Up there, two hours twenty minutes. To come back, four hours.

B: OK, hmm ... Um, I don't, I don't believe you went to this music festival.

A: Rumbled. Yeah, that's, we were actually on the outside of it only and, um, but someone, yes, no, yes, I knew I was, I was stuck there when you asked me names of the bands.

B: OK, yeah.

A: Good work, good work.

B: Yeah, and then, um, I don't believe you were upgraded to that honeymoon suite.

A: Ah, again, rumbled – I can't believe it!

B: Happened again. Uh, and you mentioned that ice cream I, I just, it didn't sound convincing when you were talking about it.

A: That's a clean sweep – you got me. It's a fair cop, I'm a terrible liar. I'm obviously a very honest person, what can I say?

B: I thought, I thought it was really subtle, but I'm really happy that I won. Wow, that's, uh ...

A: Gutted.

B: Yeah.